WITHDRAWN

Person and Natural Law

Catholic Thought from Lublin

Andrew N. Woznicki
General Editor

Vol. 7

PETER LANG
New York • San Francisco • Bern • Baltimore
Frankfurt am Main • Berlin • Wien • Paris

M.A. Krąpiec, O.P.

Person and Natural Law

Translated by Maria Szymańska

CARL A. RUDISILL LIBRARY
LENOIR-RHYNE COLLEGE
HICKORY, NC 28603

PETER LANG
New York • San Francisco • Bern • Baltimore
Frankfurt am Main • Berlin • Wien • Paris

Library of Congress Cataloging-in-Publication Data

Krąpiec, Mieczysław Albert.
  [Człowiek i prawo naturalne. English]
  Person and natural law / M.A. Krąpiec ; translated by Maria Szymańska.
    p. cm. — (Catholic thought from Lublin ; vol. 7)
  Translation of: Człowiek i prawo naturalne.
  1. Natural law.   2. Persons (Law)—Philosophy.   I. Title.   II. Series.
K450.K6813   1993   340'.112—dc20   91-46414
ISBN 0-8204-1843-9   CIP
ISSN 1051-693X

K
450
.K6813
1993

may 1994

The paper in this book meets the guidelines for permanence and
durability of the Committee on Production Guidelines for
Book Longevity of the Council on Library Resources.

© Peter Lang Publishing, Inc., New York 1993

All rights reserved.
Reprint or reproduction, even partially, in all forms such as microfilm,
xerography, microfiche, microcard, offset strictly prohibited.

Printed in the United States of America.

DEDICATION

The basic understanding of reality and the human being compose the essence of philosophical comments. The understanding may be realistic or unreal, because it could be *a priori* or unrestricted. In the latter case it will become not a philosophy but an ideology and myth. The Lublin School of Philosophy, continuing the problems of classical philosophy, proposes solutions of the time immemorial problems by using the specific for modern philosophic methods of rendering free from contradiction altogether with historical reflection and looking back into the sources of classical philosophy.

I deeply appreciate the assistance of Peter Lang Publishing, Ltd., in publishing the English translation of this important treatise on philosophical understanding of the natural law. That law understood not unequivocally but analogically, perfects the rationale of human nature bound with the realization of human good which must be recognized by each individual as his or her own real, personal good. That recognition and rational choice of good is the act of each human being as a personal being. Accordingly because it seemed proper to show the connection between the law and a personal being in his or her reasonable and free will, therefore personal activity, I changed the title of my treatise from its Polish version *Human Being and Natural Law* into the English title of this book, *Person and Natural Law*. The law concerns the human being not in the biological aspect but in the aspect of rational and free will, and thus personal activity.

Peter Lang Publishing, Inc., in publishing the philosophical series of the Lublin School of Philosophy, contributes to universalization and understanding of the basics of Christian culture of which the European and Western civilizations are composed. I would like to add that professor Karol Wojtyła, today Pope John Paul II, was a cofounder of the school.

Person and Natural Law is a continuation of an another treatise published by me under the title *I—Man; An Outline of Philosophical Anthropology*, Mariel Publication, New Britain, Connecticut. That treatise analyzed the fact of being a human being and of human activity, as well as personal and social aspects, and the fulfillment of a human being in death as the final personal experience.

I wish to thank Maria Szymańska for her translation of the work into English and especially Sister Prudence Allen, Religious Sisters of Mercy of

Alma, Department of Philosophy, Concordia University, Montreal, for consultation about philosophical terminology and expressions. The same gratitude I have to professor Andrew Woznicki, University of San Francisco, San Francisco, who is the initiator and Editor of the English edition of the series of Catholic Thought from Lublin and takes care of the publications and has expended a great amount of work in preparation, coordination and publication of those disquisitions translated into English. To these mentioned and to all who have in any way assisted in the preparation of this work I express my hearty thanks.

I hope that this work will find its kindly readers studying the problems of natural law and I dedicate this treatise to them.

Editorial Acknowledgments

The General Editor of this series wishes to thank all who helped him in the preparation of the manuscript for publication. Especially to Clara Cooper who made her linguistic expertise so generously available, and to Andrzej Salski for his assistance in the final editing and the preparation of the camera ready copy of this book.

CONTENTS

INTRODUCTION

The set of problems concerning natural law and its role in human life can be presented in a twofold way: either descriptively (phenomenologically, as it were), or strictly philosophically, that is, with necessary explanations.* The first way has far-reaching advantages, since it allows us to take a closer look at the phenomenon of natural law in various cultural circumstances and to seek, on this basis, common moments that are particular to this phenomenon. This way makes it possible for us to become more familiar with various formulations of the problem against a wide background of doctrines which deal with the customs and cultural conditions of human life. Moreover, it shows us the changeable and unchangeable moments of natural law itself and of the way in which it occurs, as well as its binding power.[1]

We can, however, manifest the phenomenon of natural law in a different way which is more in keeping with classical philosophy, namely, in the context of a total vision of the world. Natural law is then a fragment of this whole, and its understanding "hinges upon" how we cognize the basic and essential framework of the "whole." The understanding of the whole becomes the basis for our understanding of this fragment; the fragment makes sense within the context of the whole, which in turn is not merely the horizon for our view but makes meaningful both the very fact of this law and its fundamental nature. Law is not one and the same thing in the monistic as in the pluralistic vision of the world, in the personal as in the individual structure of the human being, or in the affirmation of real morality as in that of a mere commonplace custom.

We can therefore attempt, perhaps as a thankless task, to demonstrate the problem of natural law in a systematic philosophical context. It is true that we notice in modern human reality a tendency to avoid all those systems which, in the process of becoming coherent systems, would enslave the human being, condemning him or her to the consequences of these systems. On the other hand, however, we also see that honest and proper philosophical knowledge does become a system when it takes a specific perspective for its investigations and is consistent and logical; and that it remains a mere collection of information

---

* Editorial note: The Polish word "człowiek" is herein translated as human being, person, mankind, individual, man and woman, and man or woman, depending on the context. The decision to so translate it follows the guidelines of the American Philosophical Association for inclusive language.

when instead it is based on inconsistent thought and has no consistently sustained perspective for its philosophical explanation.

The difficulty lies in choosing a system which can explain and justify, in constant contact with reality, only the ultimate criteria of truth (as a relation of agreement with reality), and which will not constrain thought and cognition and, thereby, the person. It can, therefore, only be a system of thought which is not *a priori* but real, which has the capacity for constant self-correction (in contact with things) and is, at the same time, capable of absorbing every realistic philosophical thought. Such a postulate, when directed at a philosophical system, is more an appeal to the philosopher (the one who really "sees" the problem, and while analyzing it, justifies it) than an appeal to an abstract, prefabricated system, which prevails on the strength of its logical consistency.

The exposition of the problem of natural law within the context of the fundamental framework of a system also has the following value: by indicating the furthest implications of the analyzed fact of a person's legal and ultimate "being-bound" by law (without resorting to another type of cognition), it explains the important fact of the foundations of morality and the socio-legal order.[2]
Thus, it is worth making an attempt to show both the fact of natural law and its nature, in the context of the ultimate justifications of reality (which will be explained), and to provide the reader by that means with a view of reality in the area of the basis of human conduct, and an ultimate justification of precisely such conduct, which is nothing other than providing him or her with a competent (or incompetent) realization of "natural law," as understood in a philosophical way.

There have been periods in the history of Western European culture in which it seemed that natural law constituted an incontrovertible foundation, evident to almost everyone, of the legal and moral order of human activity.[3]
However, closer interpretations of the understanding of law, and of natural law in particular, caused an instability of the very concept of natural law as well as of its role in the moral and social domain. This does not, of course, mean that the social domain is amoral. The XIXth Century and the first decades of the XXth Century constitute a period of negation of natural law to its furthest extent. This was, of course, linked with the climate of thought at that time, particularly philosophical thought, based fundamentally (in currents of thought negating natural law) on empirical nominalism.[4] The elements of extreme empiricism, narrowing the real contents of cognition exclusively to empirical data, which data were interpreted exclusively in terms of *empiria* (sense data), became the basis for various theories of scientific cognition, (I have in mind here Kant's and Comte's theories of science),[5] and for various philosophical systems, as well as for theories of law based on them. However, at that time, too, concepts of natural law did not disappear, since on the one hand they were fought against,[6] and on the other, in theories of positive law, reference was made to more fundamental principles which were to somehow lay the foundations for positive

law, although some opponents of natural law (Bergbohm) regarded the very idea of natural law as contrary to the idea of law.[7] The Historicism and Positivism of the XIXth Century, so negative in relation to natural law, did not, however, constitute the period in which the negation of natural law occurred for the first time, since in Western European philosophical thought, the latter constituted a continuous secondary stream of philosophical thought. It is sufficient to point to the Skeptics (Pyrrho), the Sophists (Protagoras) and the Cyrenaics (Aristippus) in ancient times, the Encyclopedists in modern times, and the Positivists of the XIXth Century, to become aware of the fact that the concept of natural law has often been attacked, while at the same time, always being present in human thought. Basically, objections to natural law came from the starting point of cognition, thus restricting the foundations of what is valuable cognition for the person.[8]

Yet even the most radical negations of the very concept of natural law did not weaken its essential meaning, which is particularly apparent at critical moments in the life of the individual person or of the whole of humanity.[9] It can then be seen conclusively that all positive formulations of law are insufficient in relation to the vital problem of how to make decisions which break with a positive law. That is why the Nuremberg Trials were also the spontaneous recognition of the basic and fundamental understanding of the binding power of law, known to everyone, and why the sentences passed by the International Tribunal condemned the people who had carried out the law of their State to the letter. Although the line taken by the Defense, in relation to Hitler's criminals, went in the direction of showing the legal nature of their conduct, nevertheless the death sentences for war crimes (which lay in the interests of Hitler's State) were a vocal acknowledgement of humanity's supranational conscience obedient to a supranational natural law, which law forbids the doing of evil, even in the name of the interests of the State or the passing interests of governments like that of the Hitler State, which was waging war.

The human being always remains a human being, one who is capable of interpreting and understanding the natural arrangement of things, of what is the human good and evil, done by one individual in relation to another. It is precisely this capacity to understand good and evil, as well as the realization (in one's behavior) of the discerned good, that is of necessity linked with the very understanding of the presence of natural law within an individual and among people.

Here it is not a question of a special cognitive discipline, artificially isolated from the totality of human scientific cognition, it is not a question of understanding definitions of law of one kind or another or the meaning of positive law, but of a fundamental intellectual understanding of the reality of the world, and the reality of a person immersed in the world and co-existing with other people. What we are concerned with is a fundamental understanding of the fact of law as a particular reality, which really occurs among people, binding them together with special relationships which are stigmatized as d u t y .[10] What, then, is the foundation of that law? On account of what does it have its binding power? How does it reveal itself in the person? Can it be reduced to mere norms of conduct? What is the dependence of law, as the fact binding people together, on law-norm, which shows concretely the manner and nature of this connection? In what real contexts does law occur as an interpersonal relation, conceived as *debitum* (a duty relation)?

The understanding of all these matters, which are necessarily connected with each other, goes far beyond the understanding of legal definitions, beyond the direct social-legal context, for it is an understanding of reality apprehended in one aspect, law, insofar as it appears to us not as a result of interpreting a legal norm or a decree—in a word, positive law. In relation to that, it is something fundamentally prior, for it is reality itself, apprehended in a narrow way, it is true, but in a real way, in analogical, philosophical cognition. In a word, we are interested in reality itself, and not in some abstract understanding of it, or in some meaning of it appearing in our consciousness. That is why we will not be concerned with specifying the "meaning" (definition) of law as given only in consciousness, nor of showing the passage from awareness to reality. All that is the consequence of the cognitive attitude, assumed in an *a priori* way, which appeared, for instance, in the philosophy of the subject (and therefore in this domain) from the beginning of the history of the school of natural law in the XVIIth Century. If we recall these points of departure in a historical survey, it will be only for the purpose of seeing how much this trend departed from the cognition of reality, thus becoming the analysis of the idea of person, nation or state, understood in one way or another.

The cognitive interpretation of reality "as existing" (that is, a law which really exists and binds us), is possible only in a special type of cognition, which we do not encounter in the area of science (or particular sciences) but rather in pre-scientific cognition and philosophy, for the scientific cognition of various particular sciences makes use of some types of universalizing cognition. The fundamental structural elements of this cognition are concepts (the apprehended meanings of general expressions), with the reservation that in the area of the sciences we meet with the tendency to transform conceptual qualitative cognition to quantitative language, which it is easiest to clothe in mathematical garb and to express in mathematical language, and which informs in the strictest and most univocal way about the content contained.[11]

And although initially, as Aristotle pointed out, we can interpret in universalizing language, that which is just and right, in a real person-thing arrangement (that is, the famous: *sensibile per se est intelligibile per accidens),* so, in empirical data, we discern with our intellect contents that are not evident to the senses, precisely "abstract" contents—and the cognition of the foundations of law takes place not by means of merely abstractive processes but by means of more complicated processes of transcendental, strictly analogical, cognition.[12] For if I want to find out why I should do good, then I immediately discern that the understanding of "good" is not univocal but, precisely, analogical, for there really exist beings who are not desirable on account of one of their moments, but on account of moments that frequently exclude one another yet nevertheless do not really negate the good existing in them but affirm it more strongly. We must realize that "being" really exists (an existing content, concretely determinate, and which actually exists), which gives rise to desire, on account of the fact that it "is," that it is "real." In such a type of cognition the affirmation of existence (expressed in an existential judgement) is linked with an even more precise interpretation (often becoming more precise through the course of centuries) of the real content. In the area of morality the affirmation of good is always an affirmation of a concrete good, which basically, as good in itself and for itself, realizes itself only in a personal being which is the object in itself and for itself. And it is only in the person that real good in itself and for itself becomes at the same time realized as an end.[13]

Thinking ahead, in our reflections, to the analyses which we will carry out in the course of our work, we can already state that the affirmation of that good which constitutes the ultimate foundation of the natural order of conduct, and thereby also of natural law, is not the affirmation of this good beyond the person, but in the person and for the person. This good of the personal being is the foundation of any legal connection and any interpersonal relationship of duty; and it is not a selected, useful or pleasurable good of mine, but the good which is identified with the "I" as a being-subject, which can become the basis for demanding the right behavior from another person. That good which is identified with a subjective being, and apprehended in judgemental and analogical cognition, is the ultimate instance of appeal and justification in the order of natural moral conduct.

That is why, in the course of the centuries, the difficulties so often encountered in the problem of natural law were so insurmountable that scientists were unable to become aware of the specific nature of transcendental and analogical cognition. Hence, the problem of natural law was constantly kept alive, not only in the area of philosophical thought, but also in human prescientific common-sense cognition, and at the same time, this problem was constantly being called into question, to a greater or lesser extent, depending on the acuteness of the epistemological problems of the time. Its presence in real human cognitive experiences testifies to its real nature and importance. Is it not true that the whole order of human behavior, as the order of realizing a good, is at the same time the order of natural law understood in the proper sense?

On the other hand, it would be both naive and erroneous to seek a kind of natural law which somehow, *modo syllogistico,* by means of natural or (what is worse) formal deduction, would transform itself into positive law, for no transcendental cognition transforms itself into thinking of the universalizing type, since the latter, being fundamentally an abstract cognition, becomes a cognition that is of itself "unreal" but real only by virtue of the human process of thinking. Hence there is not, and there cannot be, any univocal connection of the passage of thought from natural law to positive law. This does not at all mean that positive law is not in accordance with natural law, for then it ceases to be law in its essential sense: it means that positive law can be justified not directly but only concretely, by showing its connections with natural law.

When it is a question of natural law as the foundation of the rational order of human behavior, we must at the outset draw attention to its fundamental dissimilarity from positive law, called, in the philosophical tradition, law constituted by human beings; for if positive law is expressed in a definite norm containing a specific univocally understood content, or at least one that is supposed to be understood univocally, in the legislator's intention, then natural law does not have such a univocally formulated content.[14] That is why it would be of no avail to seek any legal contents understood even in the most general way (but always univocally), contents really expressing a real content, to be the norm of human conduct. It is not surprising that in the philosophical stream of thought connected with Kant, following the master's example, philosophers renounced the search for a univocal real content of a supreme legal norm, for it is not possible! On the contrary, in the most varied cultures and States there did exist supreme legal norms that were mutually contradictory. There is probably no norm of legal conduct which would not be negated theoretically (and in practice) in various conditions of human life.[15] Thus, in this stream of (Kantian) thought, only one f o r m a l imperative was accepted, and the content of the commandment had to be, of necessity, c h a n g e a b l e.[16] Thus, a strange conceptual construct appeared: one "natural law of changeable content."

Nevertheless, it is at the same time the only possible solution in the area of the universalizing manner of cognition, for, if the only source of content is empiricism, conceived as the negation, at the same time, of the distinctness of the intellect,[17] then necessity and generality can appear only *a priori,* as a subjective category. The general form of commands can and must be devoid of content and merely purely formal. What is really general was expressed by Kant in his categorical imperative: act in such a way that the maxim of your conduct can become a generally valid maxim of conduct.[18] The changeable nature of the content of this maxim is a concession to realism and realistic cultural conditions, in which the most varied contents of the commands and norms of human conduct appear.

How differently, however, does the matter appear in the case of analogical and transcendentalizing cognition. All our attention is directed towards the really existing contents of conduct that are proportionately the same, that is, on really analogical contents. If, as will be shown in the process of this work, the analogical norm of natural law can be expressed merely by the words "do good" and "good should be done," then the real content of good is (just as the content of being) analogically one real content, and not a formal rule of activity. The discerning of real good is always connected with the function of reason, concretely showing w h a t is a good and h o w it is a good in the concrete conditions of human activity.

We are not, however, in a domain of situation ethics and moral relativism, since the most objective factor in the human being is normally functioning reason, which draws all the contents of its cognition from things. In the order of moral activity (a context of human activity which is also objective) is the world of persons, within which the moral field of activity is to be found. In such a state of affairs, the real good is identified with the good of persons as beings in themselves and for themselves: beings-ends.[19] Finally, "good" understood in this way eliminates, or ought to eliminate, the confusion of the substantial, essential, personal order, with a merely accidental order, the latter constituting the basis of situation ethics. Above all, human beings must be prepared by social education (men and women also organize themselves cognitively in society) to properly discern fundamental, essential, and personal contents, that is, the good p e r s e, in affirmation and in their choices.

Natural law, appearing in this way, is fundamentally the expression of the objectivism and realism of the basis of moral order. In any other arrangement, if we were to take anything other than good understood analogically as the supreme rule of human conduct (good in its prime sense, which is personal being, being the only subject of law in its fundamental sense), we would run the risk of moral situationalism, of absolute relativism, even if we were to consider as the supreme rule the ultimate end apprehended in the sense given to it by Catholic theology or the rules of an organization, etc. For then we would deprive a human being of a personal act of decision in which there is a vision of good and at the same time a personal choice in the context of the whole of reality. It is through an act of decision with regard to a real good, which is personally seen and chosen, that a personal being affirms himself or herself in relation to other persons (and ultimately in relation to the transcendent T h o u of God) as a person (understood in the prime sense).[20] When taking as the supreme rule of conduct anything other than the perceived and affirmed analogical good of the person as the subject of law and its commensurable object, we lose our objective and real ground and at the same time we absolutize a relativism in which the personal being becomes merely the means to another, superior, end, which is connected, to be sure, with a chosen norm of conduct other than a personal good.

The matter, therefore, is not trivial, since it concerns the very objective and real foundations of human conduct. We cannot make the charge of subjectivism in relation to the affirmation of a good, as if the perceived and affirmed good were to be totally left to the goodwill of the affirming person and to the strength of intellectual cognition, for, as we know, not all people are people of goodwill and not all of them perfectly "know" what is a good and in what sense it is a good! On the other hand, there would not be any other higher instance showing "real" good, unless it had been affirmed by an acting subject! Each good would have to go through the filter of human practical reason, which is known as the conscience. Unfortunately, objections of this kind could, in some cases, be real, but there is no guide for human conduct that is more objective and at the same time more real than the reason, which of its nature is directed towards the interpretation of the real contents of things, directed at the object, and which, of itself, does not possess any cognitive contents beside those which are the contents of reality itself. Thus, the denial of trust in reason is the denial of trust in the human being as a person, and this is tantamount to regarding man and woman as incapable of moral decisions. That is why, remaining close to practical reason directing human conduct, we perceive that precisely this reason is inseparably connected with the apprehension of the good which the person, in choosing, realizes in his or her human conduct, thereby realizing the highest, analogical precepts of natural law, which law already makes its appearance in the very mechanism of rational conduct.

If we examine this "mechanism" of human conduct more closely and analyze it more precisely, (which has already been done many times in the area of the theory of ethics, and which, on Polish ground, Cardinal Karol Wojtyła did with unusual perspicacity in his work *Osoba i czyn*),[21] then we will perceive above all the personal and nonpersonal (as if natural, determined, given for the purpose of experience) aspect of human experiences, which has been well expressed in Latin: *actus humanus* and *actus hominis* (human act and the act of a human individual). We can, following in Cardinal Wojtyła's footsteps, express this as follows: "what the person does" and "what takes place" in him or her, with the reservation that we would extend the semantic aspect of what "happens" in the human being from the perspective of passions *(pati)* to the perspective of causality as well (but not to specifically personal causality, which derives from the intellectual-volitive order).[22]

As we consider, therefore, the personal aspect of human activity, we perceive that it makes the assumption of human a w a r e n e s s , which expresses itself by the presence (i m m a n e n c e) of the "I" in "my" acts. This awareness of the self, in the acts which it radiates, is nothing other than self-knowledge, originating from cognition and derived from it. By cognition we understand here the contact with being, expressing itself by a perspectival u n d e r s t a n d i n g of being. The cognitive contact with reality liberates awareness and self-knowledge, in which the acting subject actively enters the world, cognizing it consciously and, under the influence of cognition, chooses that which is apprehended as a concrete good suitable, in specific circumstances, for practical affirmation. Thus, the whole mechanism of human behavior is not blind but directed by cognition, in the context of self-knowledge and also by choosing a known good, which becomes recognized as a practical end, truly desired, and thereby causing rational (in the psychic sense) auto-determination. The rational factors of the cognition of reality, its perspectival understanding, self-knowledge, affirmation, as well as the successive acts of desire and concrete want (choice) of being which appear as the object of desire (and therefore as a good)—this is the fundamental route taken by human conduct. This is the path of the r a t i o n a l   c h o i c e   o f   t h e g o o d , which appears in cognition as a *hic et nunc* good for me. The achievement of this good liberates the human mechanism for the realization of a rational choice, made in the matrix of acts that are specifically personal (for they are acts of the intellect and will), but not to the exclusion of the materiality of human nature which accompanies them.[23]

If, therefore, the mechanism of human conduct can be reduced fundamentally to auto-determination by the practical judgement of the reason, in the activity realizing a known and desired good, then we can say that in fact each conscious human act can be reduced to the realization of a cognized good, even though this cognition may sometimes be erroneous, warped, etc. Of course, we are here considering the good in the analogical sense, as the object of human desire; for not every good, as a precise object of human desire that causes rational auto-determination, is a real personal good, a good in the moral positive sense. However, the matter of the moral reality of this good at this moment, when considering the very mechanism of human conduct, is secondary and belongs to another domain, for example to the domain of assessments (on value judgments), and not to the description of the very fact of activity. The short description presented here, and the analyses of human conduct extensively carried out elsewhere, show one thing only, a rational choice, and the realization of good through human conduct.

All this reveals the natural law in the person, which can be reduced to the conscious supreme norm "do good." Precisely this is the "revelation" of human natural law. We are generally made aware of this natural norm, which appears in the very mechanism of human conduct, directly or is presupposed, both by particular people reflecting on the sense of their conduct and by many philosophical systems giving out theories of human activity.

Of course, the law directing conscious activity (a law revealed in the analysis of human nature and human conduct), requires not only the very statement of the fact that it exists, but its being placed in the context of the most important non-contradictable elements of reality, that are: the world itself, and the human being present in the world. Only a philosophical apprehension of the whole of reality, and of man and woman immersed in it, is capable, not only of shedding light upon, but also of justifying, the human natural law "do good" in a necessary way. A superficial apprehension of this precept, originating from the nature of things (from the structure of reality and of the human being as such) can, on the one hand, be ridiculed as the "breaking down of open doors" and the justification of what is in itself and through itself evident (which is, in fact, to a large extent true and is the content of a common-sense apprehension of the basis of morality). On the other hand, it can be distorted, if one considers only one factor of reality, one aspect of it, which, when absolutized, can become unusually serious, as for instance the absolutizing of the command "obedience should be given to authority," which is undoubtedly true in the totality of the rational social order. Thus, systematic justifications are necessary in order to better show and justify, as well as to deepen, the apprehension of the supreme precept of natural law "do good."

One of the oldest sciences, already formed in ancient times, was the science of law, known initially as *iurisprudentia* (jurisprudence). It limited itself at first to knowledge of legislated law and was, in fact, *iuris peritia*. Slowly, however, the need for a deeper understanding of law, its essence, bases, extent, etc., began to develop. Thus, the philosophy of law arose, which at first, in Cicero, was confused with the general apprehension of law:

> *non ergo a praetoris edicto, ut plerique nunc, neque a duodecim tabulis, ut superiores, sed penitus ex intima philosophia hauriendam iuris disciplinam putas.*

> (The science of law should be drawn not from the decree of the praetor, as many people do today, nor from the twelve tablets, as older people do, but from the very heart of philosophy.)

Cicero's postulate that a deeper knowledge of law should be connected with philosophy is, in principle, always fulfilled. Philosophy itself, however, has gone through, and is going through, the most varied developmental meanders. There were, in the past, many concepts of philosophy: from macrophilosophy, which attempted to explain all being, to microphilosophy, which limits itself to the human being, in fact, they explained all data in human thought or only some scientifically valuable types of human thinking. They ranged from the kind of philosophy which attempts to rationally e x p l a i n the world in an ultimate way, through philosophical trends illuminating the facts of consciousness, to types of philosophy which express us, ourselves, as "having been melted into" the web of the world's history.

Together with the development of philosophy, and varied ways of conceiving philosophy itself, there began to appear, at the same time, modifications in the understanding of the traditional concept of science, conceived as justified responses to the question "DIA TI" (thanks to what) is something?—and there even appeared new concepts of science, like Immanuel Kant's or Auguste Comte's. These concepts developed, overlapped and were conditioned by each other, and as a result they had repercussions on various understandings of what law is, and particularly on what are its foundations.

There began to arise, therefore, in the course of history, the most varied theories of law, which usually dealt with the analysis and systematization of fundamental ideas occurring in the more specific sciences concerning law, of which not one could give a satisfactory explanation of the very fact and essence of law. Fundamental concepts include responses to the questions: What is law? What are its bases or "roots"? What is its scope? What is its future?—and so forth. Responses to such questions are connected with the analysis of a whole series of matters, like the institution of society, the state, the problem of natural law, custom, common good, and so forth.

The domain of cognition, organized by means of different methods, dealing with precisely these problems, had various names: "the encyclopedia of law," "the introduction to jurisprudence," "the law of nature," "the general science of law," "the theory of the state and law," "the theory of law," and "the philosophy of law."

The last names gained wider usage and application in university studies. The theory of law, in attempting to respond to questions of a specific nature, can, however, abstract from clearly philosophical, and thus ultimate solutions, and can limit itself exclusively either to an "encyclopedic" presentation of current concepts or to a purely phenomenological description, or else to the psychology or even sociology of law. That is why some authors, for example E. Jarra, believed that several methods appeared in jurisprudence, such as the dogmatic, historical, sociological, critical, psychological, and even philosophical method.

However, the strict application of each of these methods would create separate scientific disciplines. That is why, if we leave aside, quite consciously, the encyclopedia, and the psychology, sociology and phenomenology of law, and attempt to give ultimate responses to the questions posed above, we will find ourselves in the area of the philosophy of law.

The general understanding of the philosophy of law presupposes an understanding of philosophy as such, which is purely theoretical cognition, in the light of first principles, of being as existing (which is primarily given to us in sensory-intellectual empiricism), with the object of discovering the ultimate factors which make non-contra-dictable the very fact of its real existence.

Philosophy thus understood is, above all, metaphysics as the cognition of being in its analogical generality; and metaphysics thus conceived has its ever increasing particularizations, in which the philosophy of law should also be sought. It presupposes a general knowledge of philosophical anthropology and moral philosophy (sometimes called ethics), of which it is an integral part—the foundation. In this sense the philosophy of law is a cognitive discipline that is distinct from the whole of jurisprudence; it is a strictly philosophical discipline.

If we draw attention to the fact that scientific cognition is fundamentally a theoretical cognition, one that has as its aim the correspondence of our cognition with reality, that is, the attainment of truth (as opposed to practical cognition, constituting the domain of morality and "poetic," that is productive, cognition, for example, constituting the domain of general creativity)—then it has as its goal the discovery, in an appropriately specified aspect, of the "necessary" connections of the investigated world or fragments of it. We can cognize the world either by means of spontaneously formed universal concepts, which the particular sciences employ, or through analogical transcendental concepts, which philosophy employs.

When we draw attention to the fact that Aristotle had already distinguished three degrees of abstraction in theoretical cognition, that is, three general ways of constructing concepts proper to a given type of cognition and their methodical employment, then, with this in mind, we will also discern today methodological distinctions which are still important. The first degree of abstraction can correspond to our real sciences, and the "third degree of objective abstraction" would deal with the domain of philosophical cognition.

In the real sciences we perceive a fundamental division into sciences employing a quantitative language, which was formed in the study of nature (strictly speaking, in the sciences of physics and chemistry), and a qualitative language, by means of which we investigate above all the products of the human mind. This language is used by the arts, whose object is either the human being as such or the spiritual products derived from it. These products can be connected with man or woman as an individual or with a social group. Precisely jurisprudence belongs to the domain of the real arts, employing a qualitative and appropriate (historical-exegetical) cognitive method.

Philosophy, on the other hand, examines the phenomenon of law in yet another way, by means of a specific method of cognition previously elaborated in the area of metaphysics. By applying this method to the fragment of reality which is of interest to the philosophy of law, we examine the ultimate basis of the existence and nature of law, which can be discovered by means of philosophical analysis. The philosophy of law poses the same questions to law as metaphysics poses to being (being as existing) in general. Thus, it examines what law is, how it develops. In order to be able to respond to these questions, we must take into account, though in various degrees, the following problems: a general understanding of the human being, a philosophical analysis of the very fact of law, as well as the problem of natural law and its developmental "dialectic."

Each of these problems will have questions and answers providing more detail, which will be discussed in appropriate chapters.

It appears that in order to better understand the totality of these problems we must discuss in Chapter I the fundamental concepts which come into play in the area of the philosophy of law. Thus, we must analyze the very idea of law, of legal norms and their ontic nature. This will allow us to become aware of the specific nature of the philosophy of law, which will be deepened by a historical illustration of the understanding of this problem.

This philosophical specificity needs to be referred to in a fundamental context: a view of the real world and a deepened view of the human being. This will become the subject of Chapters II and III.

A deepened understanding of reality, in which the fact of law occurs, makes it possible to consider fundamental reflections on natural law. These reflections do not remain suspended "in air," but gain their full conceptual base in the philosophical analyses made so far, conditioning, as far as possible, an adequate understanding of the problems presented in this way. The planned exposition of the philosophical concept of law will not necessarily include a whole series of problems which are connected more with the socio-political and economic sciences, as for instance the theory of the state, the theory of economic and political morality.

The concept of natural law presented here, as can be seen from the concept for this book and the problem itself, is connected with a philosophical understanding of the human individual as a subsistent concrete being, since all social products, such as the family, the State, the Church, presuppose an adequate understanding of the human being. Depending on whether the ontic independence of man and woman is affirmed or negated, the role of society in the concept of legal order is stressed or not. It therefore seemed a particularly important matter to connect the concept of natural law with the philosophical understanding of the human being as a subsistent being. The ontic nature of the human being determines the very understanding of the nature of legal order. Depending on an appropriately understood or conjectured concept of the human being, various modifications appeared in the understanding of law itself, and particularly in the concept of natural law. Thus, metaphysical and anthropological problems will provide a basis for becoming aware of the very fact of law, its nature and its individual and social functions. The outlined concept of natural law will show the connection of law thus conceived with morality and also the binding power of positive law and its inter-human functions. A particularly interesting case of the radiation of natural law is its connection with positive law, a connection which cannot be apprehended as the emanation or else the developmental dialectic of natural law itself.

In relation to contemporary interpretations of the theory of law, or the theory of the state and law, the concept presented here is intended to be strictly philosophical, drawing on a specific thought-stream of philosophy, namely metaphysics, and philosophical anthropology which is organically linked with metaphysics. The evident presentation of the context of the problematic of natural law appears necessary in order to avoid unnecessary misunderstandings and disappointments, and above all in order to have a deeper understanding of the problem itself. Of course, for many people who restrict, for whatever reason, (and there are other reasons besides merely rational ones), the value of scientific cognition to merely empirical language, the reflections presented here, and their language, will be completely absurd. We can, however, override such a point of view. For many people who accept the value of philosophical investigations according to an *a priori* specific model of philosophizing, the very fact of employing terms which refer to the Transcendent One (God, eternal law and so forth) will be the basis for including the reflections presented below in the domain of theology or belief, and not rational cognition.

The author, however, takes the position (which he attempted to justify extensively in the work: *Z teorii i metodologii metafizyki* (On the Theory and Methodology of Metaphysics, written together with S. Kamiński), that metaphysics in its classical stream, (when one adopts a method of cognition which is in keeping with it), is knowledge that is inter-subjectively meaningful, verifiable in a particular way and socially important. And the philosophy of law, conceived as the particularization of metaphysics thus delineated,[24] is also an expression of rational cognition, subject to the same methodological rules as general metaphysics. It is, then, a rational cognition, important for life, for it concerns the basis of the social conduct of the person and ultimately explains it, thus not having recourse to other domains of rational cognition. It does not claim (as in Petrażycki's theory) to play the part of legislative politics, but attempts to ultimately explain the very fact of law, its interpretation, its extent, binding power, and so forth. A cognitive task conceived in this way, in the context of the concept of philosophy presented here, is to this day lacking in philosophical writings. That is why the author has decided to fundamentally stress the very concept of the "analogical law" of the human being, and basically to limit both the literature and reports on the problems connected with related or disputable interpretations to that indispensable minimum which needed to be taken into account for the modern reader.

NOTES

INTRODUCTION

[1] Lévi-Strauss in his work *Natural Right and History*, Chicago and London, 1953, showed how natural law was understood historically, starting with the assumption that "modern sociology rejects natural law for two different though closely connected reasons: it rejects it in the name of history and in the name of the difference between facts and values" (p. 11). His work, therefore, shows and analyzes the understanding and occurrence of natural law against a historical background, particularly of philosophical thought. Similarly, though from another aspect, P. Delhaye presents the permanence of natural law against a historical background in his *Permanence du Droit naturel* (The Permanence of Natural Law), Louvain, 1964. Just as the occurrence of what is called "natural law" is shown against a historical background, so too it could be shown against an ethnological background. However, such an operation, in my opinion, would be rather artificial, since an author analyzing texts would already have assembled them according to a conscious (or still subconscious) principle. Thus, taking advantage of the historical heritage and of phenomenological and descriptive analyses (of the rank of *Phenomenology of Natural Law*, Pittsburgh, 1967, W.A. Luipena), we must from the start become aware of the ordinative philosophical thought which will allow us to show and make non-contradictory the fact of moral order.

[2] The problem of natural law, as will be constantly expressed, is fundamentally linked with moral order and only secondarily and not directly with the socio–legal order. That is why the inverse, or any assessments of the concept of natural law from the sociological position (as for instance made to a certain extent by K. Opałek and J. Wróblewski in *Współczesna teoria i socjologia prawa w Stanach Zjednoczonych Ameryki Północnej* (Contemporary Theory and Sociology of Law in the United States of America), Warsaw, 1963, are probably a mistake. Moreover, we see there (p. 98) an epistemological positivism as well as the remains of Kantism. This does not mean that many criticisms directed at contemporary interpretations of natural law are incorrect, although the methodological comments of the authors on pages 26 and 27 are strange, on account of the role of "world-view" in methodology.

[3] Here we can point to ancient, medieval and modern times. It is true that there were different formulations of natural law; however, the conviction about its binding nature (the fact of natural law) was accepted.

[4] Already from the time of Descartes, philosophical systems were based not on an analysis of being, but of cognition—to be more precise, thinking. Empirical nominalism, on the other hand, formulated by D. Hume became the foundation of XIXth Century concepts of science.

[5] Science-forming questions were, for Kant: What are the *a priori* necessary conditions of valid (given to us in sensory empiricism) cognition?—for Comte, on the other hand, the question: How? Both the first and the second question assumed the standpoint that the only source of information is empiria (sense data), yet conceived in such a way that the

content and scope of valuable information coincides with empiricism. The possibility of interpreting necessary contents, inaccessible to the senses, in empirical data, was negated.

[6] G. Manser, *Das Naturrecht in thomistischer Beleuchtung* (Natural Law in the Light of Thomistic Thought), Freiburg in d. Schweiz, Switzerland, 1944, pp. 14–23, shows the opponents of natural law in a fierce conflict with this concept.

[7] Manser presents (ibid., p. 18) three possible relations of natural and positive law: a) natural law fills the lacunae in positive law; b) positive law is only a supplement of natural law; c) natural law is the norm and foundation of positive law. All three variants are negated.

[8] Restrictive cognitive foundations always struck a blow at the cognitive operations of the mind and this is extremely interesting from the psychological point of view. Superficial rationalism attacked the wide field of activity of the mind, attempting to reduce the type of valuable cognition to only some, narrow, cognitive concepts.

[9] Cf. the case of Antigone; similarly, the acts of decision of many people in Hitler's prisons and camps.

[10] This will become the object of more detailed analyses when establishing the "fact" of truth. Duty *(debitum)* has a wider interpretation here than the part it plays in the problem of justice. Indeed, in the domain of justice, *debitum* possesses its most important meaning. Above the order of justice, however, there is the order of equity, where duty corrects that which, on the basis of justice, could have had harmful consequences for a real person.

[11] The tendency towards mathematization occurring in modern science, though it has without doubt its important moments, facilitating the development of science, is, however, connected with the very difficult matter of converting qualitative language to quantitative language. Unfortunately, there is a great deal of selectivity here which does not always focus on what is necessary.

[12] On the subject of this type of cognition cf. S. Kamiński, and M.A. Krąpiec, *Z teorii i metodologii metafizyki* (On the Theory and Methodology of Metaphysics), Lublin, 1962; Z. Zdybicka, *Partycypacja bytu* (The Participation of Being), Lublin, 1972, pages 95–149, the last one containing deep analyses. Another important problem is linked with the transcendental method of cognition, a problem that is the object of a special deep monograph of G. Kalinowski, *Le Problème de la vérité en morale et en droit* (The Problem of Truth in Morality and in Law), Lyon, 1967. It is a question here of the problem of truth in normative consideration. Kalinowski, having presented the problem in a historical light in part I, proceeds to a meritorious response in part II of his monograph. The general line of his thinking appears both correct and open to discovery, particularly in moments in which he indicates the analogy of transcendental cognition. Unfortunately, however, as it appears, he connected the problem of truth insufficiently with the judgemental-transcendental type of cognition itself, which both in pre-scientific and philosophical cognition is fundamentally the bearer of truth, since the transcendentalizing type of cognition is based on existential judgements, and these judgements fundamentally affirm existence (*iudicium respicit esse*—judgement intends existence, as Thomas wrote in the commentary *In Boeth. De Trinit.*, 5. 3).

[13] In the tradition of Classical philosophy the following were distinguished: a) *bonum utile*—the useful good, as the means to an end; b) *bonum delectabile*—the pleasurable good, as that which takes into account the very function of desire; c) *bonum honestum*—the "honest" good, which is a good in itself and for itself. Only the person as a being in itself and for itself fulfills the conditions of the "honest" good as good in the supreme sense, and thereby, of the good as being an end in itself.

[14] On the whole, authors dealing with the problem of natural law are aware of the equivocity of this expression; they discern this ambiguity, however, in different concepts of natural law (cf. Opałek, Wróblewski, as above, p. 25ff.). The failure to understand the analogy of natural law, which originates from the analogy of being, is generally at the basis of misunderstandings in this area.

[15] This is the classical objection to natural law, for even the commandment "thou shalt not kill" was, in specific historical and cultural contexts, not only disregarded by law or tradition, but even contested. If, therefore, such a fundamental commandment was treated with sometimes a theoretical justification, then, it was concluded, natural law is without content.

[16] In this way, too, the Kantian (Neo-Kantian) concept of natural law of a changeable content appeared. Cf. on this subject: M. Szyszkowska, *Neokantyzm. Filozofia społeczna wraz z filozofia prawa natury o zmiennej treści* (Neo-Kantism. Social Philosophy and Philosophy of Natural Law of a Changeable Content), Warsaw, 1970; *Dociekania nad prawem natury, czyli o potrzebach człowieka* (Investigations on the Law of Nature, that is, on Man's Needs), Warsaw, 1972; *U źródeł współczesnej filozofii prawa i filozofii człowieka* (At the Sources of Contemporary Philosophy of Law and the Philosophy of Man), Warsaw, 1972.

[17] This was precisely I. Kant's standpoint.

[18] I. Kant, *A Foundation of the Metaphysics of Morals:* "The categorical imperative is, then, only one and it goes as follows: act only according to the maxim which you can at the same time want to become a universal law. ... Since the universality of the law according to which results occur constitutes that which we actually call nature in the most general sense (on account of form), that is, the being of a thing, insofar as it is defined according to universal laws; thus, the general imperative of duty could also go as follows: act as if the maxim of your conduct by your will were to become a general law of nature."

[19] How strangely (in the same work, from real inspiration, not by *a priori* means) and how correctly did Kant express this: "Act in such a way as to use humanity, both in your person and in the person of everyone else, always at the same time as an end, never only as a means."

[20] Abstract norms, though they sometimes seem noble, as for example "the ultimate end—God," are, however, in separation from the good of another person, also liable to situationalism and relativism in the realm of morality.

[21] Karol Wojtyła, Osoba i czyn (Person and Act), Cracow 1969. This work shows personal being on the basis of moral decisions.

[22] Ibid., p. 67ff.

[23] This problem was extensively analyzed by St. Thomas Aquinas—in the whole 1a2ae part of his *Summa Theologiae.*

[24] Cf. my work *Metaphysics,* Peter Lang Publications, Inc., New York, 1991.

Chapter I

LAW IN GENERAL

A. THE THEORETICAL ASPECT

1. LAW AS A FACT

In general, we encounter the fact—the existence—of law everywhere where there is some kind of activity. There are "laws of nature," which a person discovers and cognizes as a certain objective "order of things," for example, an objective ordering of the activity of beings in the world of nature to equally objective ends, which in an internal (immanent) or external (transcendent) way explain the nature and mode of existence of these beings. Law is conceived here as a certain regularity of the occurrence (or non-occurrence) of a specific ontic state of activity in specific circumstances. This correctness, concerning beings in act—in activity, expresses the objective ordering of this activity to a proportional object; it expresses the connection of activity with an end.[1] Lawright is always the law-right of something (or someone) to something (or someone). The law of nature, that is, the law of activity of a being determined by its physical-biological nature, is the law-right to realize this nature—to be such and such a being—in relation to other beings of a specific nature.★

The discovery of "nature"—PHYSIS—in ancient Greece, though probably posterior to the concept of "law,"[2] was immediately taken up in order to explain law in itself, which had a basis both for be-ing *(agere sequitur esse)* and for regular, permanent, determined and necessary activity, precisely in the structure of being—substance and not in custom, nor in the tradition of the elders.[3]

On the other hand, the most varied activity, and particularly regular and necessary activity, is always an objectified activity, an activity in relation

---

★ Editorial note: The use of the expression "law-right" comes from the Latin *jus* meaning "right," and *lex* meaning "law" which need to be joined together in a kind of conjunct in order to emphasize the two foundations of the legal field.

to something, or to someone. Activity itself, therefore, which connects the acting subject with the object, already comprises the relationship of being "among." This does not mean that activity itself is a relation, but it means that any activity (particularly natural activity) causes a relationship between the subject and the object.

Thus, if in natural activity we find a relation between the acting subject and the object of activity (and natural and regular activity itself reveals this "law" as a permanent relation, characteristic for the acting subject), then we can, in the most general sense, give the name "law" to "being on account of..." or in other words, "being-relation" having its subject in the acting being, determined as to its nature (essence) and, on account of the activity of this being, directed towards a certain object (end)—"telos." If this direction of activity is in accordance with the nature of a being which acts[4] as well as of a being that is an object of activity, we then say a being acts "correctly"—i n a c c o r d a n c e w i t h l a w.

If the matter is presented in this general way, and if it is a question of natural law in the world of nature, then how, in turn, is this law realized where the human being is concerned, who, on account of his or her rational nature, is the author of its activity, capable of conscious and free acts of decision, auto-determination, the choice of an end "telos" and, thereby, of a moral nature of activity?

The fact of law in the conditions of human existence, even when viewed so superficially, appears to have a completely different nature, in proportion to the "distinctness" of the human being in relation to products of nature and also to the ends of human activity in relation to the natural ends of the activity observed in nature. This is so, to such an extent, that the authors of various more or less philosophical theories of law (its basis and genesis) often deviated very far from the concept connecting human law with "natural law," and sometimes did not even draw on such a concept at all. The common point of departure of these theories, often differing fundamentally by the results of their investigations, was not so much an analysis of the subject of law as an aspect of human activity but rather, as a psychological phenomenon, for example the feeling of a psychic "connection," or expressed in yet another way, "the feeling of duty" (especially in the Kantian theory of morality), for which more or less adequate and satisfactory justifications were sought. Particularly the sense of duty, "debitum iuris" was analyzed, and attempts were made to find an empirically attainable basis for this debitum.

In this respect, among others E. Jarra writes on this subject:

> Society is the common life of people, conditioned intellectually by their possession of a psychic capacity to make judgements about the usefulness or harmfulness of actions for the existence and development of a particular bond. According to the accepted expression—society presents the whole of organized relations, that is, relations based on more or less stable links giving this society

the nature of order and permanence, distinguishing it from a transient phenomenon. These links are precisely norms.... The sense of order that is decisive for the concept of norm is at the same time the basis of organization, that is, of society; norms are psychic links welding social organization.[5]

Jarra refers to Aristotle's saying, in conjunction with this, that "law is order."[6]

Reflections of this kind, having as their subject above all the psychic subjective state—"the legal psyche," are, however correct they may be in many details, generally speaking insufficient for the explanation of the totality of the problem of law. This is because they concern only the relation of the legal person, and this only as the relation apprehended in the categories of probabilistic knowledge, that is the psychological motives for the acceptance of a particular norm. They cannot, then, lay claim to the role of being the most general explanations that are, at the same time, real and necessary. Also, they do not completely explain what law is, in the conditions of human existence.

2. THE UNDERSTANDING OF LAW

Any reference made to the dynamic structure of reality indicates a general and unspecified understanding of law, implying also a very general understanding of relationships.

When, however, we draw attention to the various meanings of the term "law-right" *(prawo)*, the matter becomes more complicated, since this term occurs with many meanings, both in colloquial and in scientific language. Let us consider the most important of them. Thus, when I claim that "I have a right to an apartment," I state a r e l a t i o n of mine t o a t h i n g ; when I say that "I have a right to go for a walk" or "to rest," I stress a real potency to do something. Another time, when speaking of Canon Law or Civil Law, Criminal or Administrative Law, I have in mind a set of rules or norms. I can, moreover, speak of studying law, and then I label the study of law by such terms.

An initial understanding of the term "law-right" *(prawo)* indicates, therefore: a) the relation of the person to the being which is at his or her disposition, or which is within reach of his or her disposition; b) the moral potency of doing or possessing something; c) a set of norms or legal rules; d) the science of law. The last two ways of understanding law are derived from a more basic understanding, and that is why we should pay closer attention to the first two meanings, that is, of law-right as a relation, and as moral potency. They are generally called subjective law-right *(i u s s u b i e c t i v u m)* in opposition to the objective law of norms and science *(i u s o b i e c t i v u m)*.

Theoreticians of law are above all interested in subjective law-right, understood in general as the moral potency of doing something or possessing something. In this respect expressions are very divergent from each other and unspecific.[7] This imprecision and divergence derives, fundamentally, from a confusion between the ontic and the psychic orders. In fact, "subjective law-right," when apprehended as the moral potency of doing or possessing something, is without purpose, for, what can the meaning of moral potency—*facultas moralis*—be? It is a term connected with a very wide area of real human possibilities, which go considerably beyond the domain of law, since they concern all that I c a n do myself, emanate from myself or experience in myself, independently of any subordination of myself to another person. Thus, I have the "moral potency" of doing or of experiencing unhampered thinking, desiring, breathing, etc., as factors of my nature. In such a state of affairs, moral potency denotes a presently acting being or one that can act at the present moment. Thus, the expression "moral potency" does not denote any special power or organ, nor any moral order connected with the norm which distinguishes between good and evil with regard to another person.

Moreover, let us draw attention to the fact that in the colloquial sense, later confirmed by an analysis of law, wherever law-right appears there appears also duty, an obligation of the other as the correlate of law, whereas there is no such obligation of the other where we are dealing with the concept "subjective law" (as "moral potency of doing something or of possessing something").[8]

Thus, we do not define subjective law by means of metonymical, purposeless expressions, for, every time I have a right to something, I am the subject of a r e l a t i o n, by virtue of which something is due to me. When I claim, for instance, that I have a right to go for a walk, I presuppose and foresee at the same time such a mode of conduct from others, that they will neither forbid me to do this activity nor prevent or hamper it. Thus, by virtue of this r e l a t i o n, of which I am the subject, my activity is permissible (insofar as it makes allowance for other people) since, as my good (realized by means of a walk), it does not lessen or restrict the good of other people. And therefore, this "moral potency" *(facultas moralis)* often occurring in expressions of "subjective law," is a special aspect of the relation between myself (as the subject of the relation) and other people, to whom my activity or my desisting from activity are of particular concern. Consequently, when we give the name "moral potency" to this relation, we use a vague and metonymical expression to denote incorrectly the nature of those activities which come under the meaning of "law," for law-right concerns particularly one very fundamental aspect of my activity or non-activity, namely, another person who will not be in some way curtailed in his good through my activity (non-activity). Law-right, therefore, guarantees an interpersonal good, that is, the good of the acting person and of others whom this activity concerns. The permissibility, due, duty—*d e b i t u m*—of the deed in the legal sense comes from the side of the other person.[9] If this moment *d e b i t u m* does not occur, then the legal order does not occur, although perhaps the human order of moral activity would normally occur.

The question of the relation of law to morality is, however, subject to special considerations, which will be kept in mind during the analysis of natural law. Irrespective of later considerations on this subject, we must begin by emphasizing the specific character of the interpersonal, legal relation that *debitum* is—"duty," "due" or "due-duty." In Polish we do not have an expression that renders the content of the Latin *debitum,* and that is why we must express it by the combined term "due-duty," for what i s   d u e   t o   one person, as the correlate of the legal relation, the other person s h o u l d do at the same time. One legal relation connecting two persons as corrlates is characterized by "due-duty" as that moment which distinguishes the morally just-legal order from another dimension of morality. Of course, there still remains another question: can there be a morality that is not connected with other persons?[10]

3. THE ONTIC NATURE OF LAW-RIGHT AS A RELATION

Since we initially defined the being of law-right in a most general way by pointing to the category of relation and therefore to the kind of "being on account of," we must now analyze more closely the specific nature of the relation, so that we may thereby cognize the ontic nature of law-right. We must therefore examine: 1) the subject and object of this relation, and its limits of reference; 2) its basis, for example its reason for being, that is, the objective reason for its coming into existence; 3) its specific nature. These three moments characterize each relational being, from the philosophical point of view.[11]

According to the metaphysical theory of relations, there exist two fundamental types of "being on account of..."—known as relational being: necessary relations, by which independently existing being is constituted, and non-necessary relations, which "are added to" being that has already been constituted by necessary relations. Necessary relations constitute the inner composition of being, from elements which are not entitled to independent existence and which, nevertheless, cannot exist without an inner ordering to a correlate that also lacks independent existence. An example of this type of necessary relation is the inner bond in the human organism, which is made up of integral parts such as the head, the hands, etc. These could not exist without being ordered in a necessary way to the rest of the human body.

Other, equally necessary, relations obtain between the elements which constitute being in the ontic sense, such as matter and form, essence and existence. (Moreover, we distinguish in metaphysics a special type of necessary relations, namely "transcendental relations," which are realized in a particular way in each contingent being, and which order being to the reason for its coming into existence, commensurably.) Necessary relations, and (from the ontic-existential aspect, in a particular way) transcendental relations, form the basis of the metaphysical explanation of nature and the real, concrete existence of beings, in the light of ultimate non-contradictable reasons.

Thus, every being is ultimately explainable and comprehensible on the basis of necessary relations, which are ultimately transcendental. Yet there exist beings which, though in reality discernible by the senses, are not constituted only through necessary relations; what is more, these relations could not reveal themselves, could not come into existence, in the form of an ontic concrete being ("this particular being" of a defined nature-content), if it were not for a series of different non-necessary relations (categorial ones), which, in a sense, "build themselves onto" necessary relations and actualize ontic potentialities.

Non-necessary, categorial relations, whose content is "to be among..." or "to be for..." or "to be on account of," etc.—*(cuius totum esse est ad aliud se habere)*, together form being as a concrete object, one that is defined in content and determined: an individual.[12] These relations modify the be-ing of a thing in a more or less permanent way, depending on the nature of the subject with which they deal and the foundation on which they are based. The categorial relation can be more or less directly connected with a being, just as any other property of a thing, which is connected more or less closely with the structure of a given being. The relation, which constitutes a human being as man or woman, has a different ontic nature from relational being, such as "being a student," "being a monk," and a different ontic nature from "being similar" or being "tall," etc. Each of these different types of relations determines the nature of human being differently. Insofar as the lack of physical attributes of sex, or depriving the human being of them, is defined as a blemish made on nature, as something "unnatural," the fact of "not being a student" or "not being a monk," and all the more of "not being similar" or "not being tall," is not usually called something "unnatural," and these characteristics are commonly defined as a c c i d e n t a l. What is more, being in relation is universally recognized as the weakest type of being, since a categorial relation is totally exhausted in the very ordering, the very reference to the correlate, and can be called a way of being "between."

Consequently, there forms before our eyes an ontically stronger and weaker set of relations found in the world of contingent things:

1° necessary relations, which constitute the very being of being, becoming realized everywhere where we are dealing with contingent real being, for example among the relation of existence to a concrete essence commensurable to itself; they are transcendental relations, occurring in the same places as contingent being; they do not exhaust themselves in a mutual ordering of essence to existence but also embrace all forms of external causality;

2° necessary real relations, but not transcendental ones, that exist when various ontic constituents or elements become ordered to one another. In such a state of affairs each changeable being constitutes a "bundle of relations" that are necessary, insofar as it is at one and the same time composed of various parts;

3° real non-necessary relations, built onto existing being and arising as a result of the most varied existing beings becoming ordered to one another; they are categorial relations, which entwine each being with limitless bonds.

In the light of these general comments we must, therefore, consider:

a) what type of relation is law-right?

b) between whom (or what) does law-right occur?

c) what is its reason for being, that is, why does law-right occur rather than not, and why is it "binding"?

Ad a) Does law-right enter the structure of the human person as such? Does "to be a person" mean "to be in a necessary way determined by law-right"? Since we have previously ascertained that law-right is the "regulator" of human activity, and since we defined this activity, which is specific to rational nature, as conscious and free, then, from these established facts (obtained through an analysis of rational nature as revealed in personal acts), we can conclude merely that human activity, insofar as it has as its goal the good proper to its nature, is in agreement with law-right. We cannot, however, conclude from this that for man or woman to exist as a person, there must occur a relation of law-right which will constitute him or her. It is a human being, a person, who is the reason for the being of law-right as a relation, and not the other way around.

Another matter is that, just as a person's existence can ultimately be justified with reference to the Absolute, so also the existence of law-right, of which man or woman is the subject, has an analogical, ultimate justification in the area of metaphysics. It is important to note that where the definition of the nature of law-right as a relation is concerned, in the light of what has been said, law-right is not a necessary relation, that is, one constituting the individual's being in the formal, causal-effective or final sense. The human being does not exist only as a "legal personality," in a sense which exhausts his or her nature, either thanks to law-right or for law-right, although precisely such implications seem to be suggested by the theories which place law-right above the human being.

Law-right is, then, a categorial relation, whose subject lies in the human person, in whose activity it is usually realized and concretized.

It is, nevertheless, true that the "being a subject of law-right," proceeding from the fact of "being in relation to others" modifies the human person to a very considerable degree. If a human being happens to act against the law-right, to act "illegally," then in a certain way he or she does harm to his or her own nature, the individual becomes in a certain sense "less of a human being," especially because this conduct against nature, that is, illegal action, concerns human cognitive-volitive acts, acts that are *sensu stricto* personal.

The categorial relation of law-right, which binds persons, is co-natural to them, it flows directly from their nature, that is, it has its direct justification in human nature, in necessary relations (which constitute the human person). Law-right is a categorial relation based on necessary relations, as will be seen later.

Ad b) Since (in human conditions) law-right has some being which has its subject in rational nature, and since the action of this nature is particularly manifested in acts of reason and free will, then the primacy, proper object and aim of acts of cognition, love and free will is also "personal being." Law-right, therefore, defines the relations of one person to another on account of the natural way the human individual is directed towards another human being. From the nature of personal being there "follows" this relation to other persons, a "being towards a person" as to a proportional end: good.[13] We have already mentioned that the human person is a "being in itself"—a good "for itself"—insofar as it is at the same time directed towards a proportional personal correlate, insofar as it is a "being for another," a good "for another." Hence, also, from the subjective side, this fact reveals itself in the form of a "psychic connection" and d u t y in relation to another person who appears (or other persons who appear) in the human consciousness. It is a psychological expression of cognizing and experiencing law as an interpersonal relation. Of course, this *debitum* (duty) is not merely a psychic category but a real relation to another person.

Since the person is a "bearer" of law in the sense that, in the conditions of human existence, law-right appears whenever human rational nature acts (that is, conscious and free human rational nature), then we cannot fundamentally give the name law-right to the relation between person and thing (all the more so between things) unless we use it in the secondary and metaphorical sense. When we speak of a man's or a woman's right to material goods of some kind—things—we always have in mind the right of this particular person with regard to another person, who also "has a right" or else "does not have a right" to possessing or using these goods. The determinant—rule—of lawful or lawless conduct, also with regard to things, is always the good of the person in relation to another person. Law-right "takes place" between persons, who f o r p e r s o n a l e n d s dispose of material goods, as well as those indirect goods which are defined as "spiritual culture." It does not "take place" in isolated arrangements, nor does it occur in things, since a thing cannot become a subject of law-right. Only a person with regard to a person can "claim rights," "assert rights"; on the basis that, by virtue of human nature, he or she is related to another person and acts particularly in the domain of specifically personal acts

"on account of" another person, this activity or non-activity of one person i s
d u e t o another person by virtue of law. This o b j e c t i v e d u e has its
subjective expression in the human psyche in the form of a feeling of psychic
commitment and also in the experience of duty in relation to another person.
This feeling proceeds from an intellectual interpretation of the objective state of
things, a state of the mutual ordering of individuals to one another on account
of their activity and free acceptance of this state in the name of a common end:
good. This cognition, as well as the acceptance of the fact of personal duty—the
acceptance of a law as a rule—takes place within the person, in the act of
"practical reason" known as the conscience. Hence, the feeling of being bound
by law-right has a fundamentally moral nature.[14]

Ad c) The basis of the coming into existence of the relation of law-
right—"being among" human persons—is then the fact of making a relation
between one individual and another, that is, the activity of people, their
interaction and cooperation; and all this is ultimately aimed towards common
good. Law-right, therefore, is concerned with the activity or non-activity of
human persons, who in carrying out their activities realize a common good.[15]
The nature of this good, as well as the nature of subjects—human persons—is
the real basis of the b i n d i n g p o w e r, [16] that is, of the obligatoriness of
law-right. Law-right is really valid insofar as it obliges, insofar as it is in
accordance with the nature of the person and perceived common good. The
person acting rationally and in accordance with his or her rational nature, on
account of the personal good perceived in the act of practical cognition, the
personal good which is at the same time the common good of the whole of
society, acts in accordance with the law-right.

If we emphasize the moment of d u e — *debitum* in law-right, then we shall
see that the activity or non-activity of some persons in relation to others is
mutually due to them on account of their proportional ordering to common good
as an end. Every human being as a potentialized[17] personal being, is internally
ordered towards the actualizing and perfecting of his spiritual potentialities,
particularly intellectual and volitive ones. The person lives precisely in order to
develop his or her rich potentials of intellect and will, and bring them to
maximum perfection *(optimum potentiae)*. The perfecting of cognition in
whatever domain, the perfecting of the faculty of the will, makes not only the
person better and improves his or her work, but at the same time enriches other
persons, namely human society. These are quite obvious matters.

That is why, if each person is ordered to perfecting the self, that is, to
actualizing personal potentialities, then it is his or her due—a "right"—not to be
prevented by the other person from precisely this realization of good; he or she
has a right and it is his or her due that the other person should begin to act, or
stop acting, if this prevents him or her from carrying out personal good.

If, in human conditions, the actualizing of the potential of personal being and spiritual perfection requires a great deal of expenditure of material resources, then material resources should be conceived only as means, that is, indirect ends, and not the ultimate end that is common good. These material resources are also "due" to each person perfecting the self (developing the self) and that is why the social proportional distribution of these resources is necessary in order to make it possible for all people to realize their personal good to the greatest extent. Hence, human activity, both in relation to others and in relation to the world of matter, is not something indifferent for the other person; on the contrary, it always directly or indirectly takes into account the other person.

Ultimately, therefore, law-right should be conceived as a real r e l a t i o n
b e t w e e n a c t i n g p e r s o n s , w h o s e a c t i v i t y (or non-activity) i s
m u t u a l l y d u e t o t h e m o n a c c o u n t o f t h e p r o p o r t i o n a l l y
c o m m o n o r d e r i n g o f t h e s e p e r s o n s t o t h e c o m m o n g o o d a s
t h e e n d o f p e r s o n a l a c t i v i t y .

As we have mentioned many times, this common good ultimately, from the aspect of the object, good, where there exists a hierarchy and essential ordering, is identified with the Absolute, that is, the supreme Good, to whom all goods are ontically ordered as goods and to whom, through the realization of the potential of his or her nature, each human person has the right and a duty to tend or strive towards.[18]

Such a concept of law-right is a finalistic concept. Within its framework, human being—the good of human nature and a person's right to this good—has a dynamic perspective: this good appears not as an object, which the individual is to obtain, or once and for all attain, but as an existential fullness of being, conceived in the sense of the highest personal activity directed at others and together with others, as well as "through others" ("through"—in the figurative sense, of course) to the ultimate "inexhaustible" fullness, that is, to the Absolute, in which each existential fact, each existence, obtains its ultimate justification. Thus apprehended, end-good from the subjective side, at the same time constitutes the happiness of the person.[19]

It is worth noting that the term "happiness," which St. Thomas employed, drawing on the Peripatetic tradition, takes on a meaning different from that in Aristotle in the light of Thomas' existential metaphysics. The subjective happiness of the human person is not the formal aim of his of her activity, but constitutes an inseparable "property" of personal acts, in which "being for another" is revealed. And therefore a person is "happy in himself" or "happy in herself" to the extent that he or she "exists for another person," in the ultimate instance—"for" the Absolute as a person, that is, the transcendent T h o u . In this perspective of personal happiness, anything which is not a personal being is merely a means to activity, and not the end of activity. The satisfaction of biological or psychic drives is a moment that is ordered to the whole of personal life.

Thus, the proportional ordering of all people to a common good fundamentally conceived in a subjective way (but not excluding an objective and ontic understanding of the common good) constitutes the ultimate basis and reason for the coming into existence of the very fact of law-right as an interpersonal real relation and is the basis of real obligations which we owe another person. And the apprehension of law-right as a real interpersonal relation is the ultimate apprehension of the very f a c t   o f   t h i s   k i n d   o f   l a w — the fact that law-right really exists among people.

4. LAW — AN ANALYSIS OF LEGAL NORMS

As we have previously analyzed the very phenomenon of law or, to be more precise, the existential fact of law and its bases, we should now examine the content of law (the essential side of law), its "objective" aspect, for it has been agreed that the very "fact of law" is contained in the category of the ontic relation linking people as proportionally ordered in the same way to a common good. Now we shall analyze more precisely the content of this relation, that is, the fact of law, not so much from the aspect of its existence as from the aspect of its essence—content. Here we are concerned with responding to the question: how, in the social order, is the essential nature of law-relation determined, that is, what is the intellectual content—conceived in the most general way—of law, being in its being a relation?[20]

The ontically-existential nature (fact) of rights in Latin is called *"ius,"* which in Polish is sometimes called *"prawo podmiotowe"* (subjective law) or *"uprawnienie"* (entitlement) or *"prawo do czegoś"* (the right to something).[21] The contentual aspect of law, on the other hand, known in Latin as *"lex,"* has sometimes been translated into Polish as *"prawo obiektywne"* (objective law), *"prawo jako norma"* (law as a norm), or—under the influence of legal terminology used in Russian—*"zakon,"* that is, "order."

A differentiation between subjective law, that is, law conceived as "an entitlement to do something" and objective law, that is "law-norm" is made on account of the rather different function of what is most generally defined as "law." Both expressions, however, concern (ought to concern) the same being (meaning something different), insofar as we apprehend this being from the ontically-existential *(ius)* aspect or from the contentual aspect of law *(lex)*. For law, as a relation existing between human persons on account of the proportionally common ordering to good (as a result of which certain actions or refraining from them from the side of persons with regard to other persons are mutually strictly due to them), has a determinate nature, if it is generally known what actions (concretely—to what extent, when, etc.) should be carried out and also how we can eventually demand such actions. Determination for law as *ius* is given by law as a norm—*lex. Ius,* however, and *lex* are two aspects of the same object, where once we emphasize the very fact as due and another time the content of this fact. In a word, law as a relation takes on a determined content when it is revealed as *lex,* as a legal norm. Since the real contentual aspect of law always presupposes the presence of the existential fact itself, the whole question, for example of natural law, has passed into literature not as *ius naturae,* but precisely as *lex naturae.* The philosophy of law in general fundamentally analyzes law not from its existential aspect, that is, from the side of its ontic nature—*ius,* but from the side of its content as *lex.* This exclusive character of one-sided treatment has become the cause of a whole series of misunderstandings.

Law has two inseparable aspects: an existential one, that is, the fact of law, and an essential one, of the analogical content of law. What is more, it is not hard to notice the primacy of the existential aspect of law and its transcendence over the contentual, objective aspect, for a legal norm will never fully render all that is contained in an interpersonal legal relation, developing "in a live way" in a concrete human social situation. Generally, a legal norm defines in a partial and aspective way, and thereby to a certain extent petrifies that which appears initially as a fact in a legal relation (law—"an entitlement to do"). The reason, together with norms interpreted by it and aspectively formulated rules, is something secondary and dependent (in its interpreted content) from the very arrangement of natural relations that exist between persons. But precisely because law-norm has been rendered more univocal, it has become a convenient point of departure for making conjectures on the very theory of law, although this in the primary sense means interpersonal relations in the aspect of indebtedness—*debitum.*

The expression *lex* was explained etymologically in ancient and medieval history.[22] Scholars pondered over the etymological source of this expression. Thus, Isidor, in his book of etymology testifies to the tradition that the expression *"lex"* comes from the word *"legere"* (to read), since the oldest laws in Roman tradition were declared in writing, so that everyone could read them and reach a conclusion about their rightness. St. Augustine drew attention to the relationship between the expression *"lex"* and *"eligere"* (to choose), since laws are to be made with deliberation by a legislator and he or she is precisely "to choose" what is best. Thomas Aquinas declares himself for the source-word *"ligare"* (to bind), since laws are the "bonds" both of society and of human conduct. The question of etymology, however, is not important in this matter. Here we are fundamentally concerned with establishing that aspect of law which concerns the content character (in the analogical sense) of law: what law is as a concrete norm of conduct.

In this matter the articles and considerations made by St. Thomas in *Summa Theologiae* 1a2ae q. 90a 1–4 are worthy of note. Having completed his analyses, Thomas Aquinas gives a definition of law-norm, which has become a classical definition in certain *milieux;* it goes like this: *"lex est quaedam rationis*

*ordinatio ad bonum commune, ab eo qui curam
communitatis habet, promulgata"* (we shall call law-norm some
ordinance of the reason which is promulgated on account of common good by
the one who is entrusted with the care of society).

This expression includes, therefore, the following essential elements of law
as a norm:

  a) the ordinance of reason;

  b) the regard for common good;

  c) the one to whom care of the society belongs;

  d) promulgation.

This type of expression in the history of Aristotelian doctrine became an
example of definition by the enumeration of the "four causes," where the formal
cause would be expressed by the part of the expression "ordinance of reason,"
strictly speaking, the very expression "ordinance," since the expression "of
reason" would express the function of the material cause. The final cause would
be expressed by the following part of the expression: "on account of common
good"; the efficient cause "by the one to whom care of society belongs"; while
the last part of the expression, "promulgated," would express the indispensable
condition of the binding nature of law.

Let us take a closer look at the way Thomas Aquinas justifies the particular
terms of the definition which he has formulated.

Ad a) He answers the question: *"utrum lex sit aliquid rationis?"* (is law
something from the domain of reason?) in the following way:

> Law is a particular rule and measure of actions, insofar as it is the reason that
> someone brings himself to refrain from some action, for law is called *lex* in
> Latin from *ligare* (to bind), since it obliges man to some activity. The rule and
> measure of human actions is reason, which is their first source, as can already
> be concluded from analyses previously carried out. The task of reason is to
> order things to some end, which is the first factor really justifying activity itself,
> according to Aristotle. In every order, the measure and rule of a given order is
> that which is the first justifying factor (the source) as for example unity in the
> order of numbers and the first movement in the order of the most varied
> movements. That is why we must agree that law is something that belongs to
> the domain of reason.

In his responses, he makes his reasoning more complete by indicating, in response to the first objection, that the concept of rule and measure can be apprehended either from the aspect of the person regulating and measuring, and in precisely this sense law is a measure and something from the reason, or from the aspect of that which is regulated and measured. Measure conceived in this way is contained in legal subjects, expressing a particular inclination towards something. In such a sense we can also speak of law, not however in an essential but in a participative sense.

In response to the third objection he draws attention to the fact that the problem of will occurs in an analysis of law conceived in an essential sense. Will itself, however, is also regulated and measured by the reason, since the will is precisely a rational desire. Non-rational will would be lawlessness, if it were to impose a norm of conduct not based on the reason.

The historical basis for St. Thomas' justifications is Aristotle's statement that law is order (harmony): *HO GAR NOMOS TAXIS.* Harmony and order can be apprehended actively and passively. Law is the active aspect of social harmony, for it is that which is the reason for order. Reason thus apprehended is the work of the intellect, since only the mind is an ordering factor, that is, one that establishes the relations of one element to another and to all of them together. It is all the more so the work of the reason that the order introduced by law does not merely concern the static aspect of social life, but precisely its dynamic aspect. Law "regulates and measures" human activity. Human activity as human is conscious (rational) activity and free activity (within the limits of human existence); thus, law is something coming both from the reason and the will.

At this point an argument can arise, and in fact has arisen, whether law as law is specifically a work of the reason or rather merely presupposes reason and formally as an order is the work of the will. This argument has taken on (and takes on) greater force in periods of absolute power, because usually the laws passed by absolute rulers did not turn out to be fundamentally a work of the reason but rather of the will of the ruler, in accordance with the ancient legal formula: *quod principi placet, legis habet vigorem* (That which pleases the authorities has the power of law).[23] It is not surprising, then, that eminent theoreticians of law, like Suarez[24] and several of his adherents, fundamentally taking into account positive law and being under the influence of the voluntaristic Scotist doctrine, were of the opinion that law is fundamentally a work of the will, that is, the ruler's order. There were also other medieval thinkers like Gerson and Becanus, who believed that law is a work both of the reason and the will.

In discussing the problem of law, Thomas was fundamentally concerned with law as the basis of social harmony, and particularly with law in the most important sense of the term, that is, natural law, which is interpreted and expressed in a concrete legal norm. That is why he emphasized the factor of reason in law-norm as a formal factor.

Later centuries, under the influence of a discussion with Suarez' school, made the problem even clearer. According to the terminology used in Suarez' law school, law was a work of *imperium*, of a particular kind of command. Scholars, however, drew attention to the fact that the act of *imperium* belongs to the domain of acts from the order of execution and is in itself a complex act, like the nature of each human act, which is manifold and complex, for in each human act we perceive both that which pertains to consciousness and reason (the intellect), and that which dynamizes the arrangement of content pertaining to consciousness when it realizes itself in concrete activity (the will). Moreover, human acts go through the following states: a) the state of intention, b) the state of choosing means to the end, and c) the state of carrying out the intended act, using the means chosen.

This may be illustrated in the following way by a table:

THE ASPECT OF REASON (WILL)	THE VOLITIVE ASPECT (INTELLECT)
a) In the order of intention as the basis of action	
1. A general—analogous grasp of the apprehended good	2. Love of the good as the general desire of personal happiness
3. The intellectual vision of a concrete good	4. The wanting of this good
b) In the order of choice of concrete action— Choice of means to an end	
5. Pondering over the means toward realizing the good	6. The approval or disapproval of the will
7. Practical judgement about a concrete action	a) theoretically practical judgment

b) practically practical
   judgment

8. Free c h o i c e of the will—
   self-determination as the source
   of human action

---

c) In the order of execution of the free decision of the person

---

9. The command of reason
   regarding the performance

   a) *ordinatio*—by concrete direc-
      tion concerning how to do it
   b) *intimatio*—by signalling the
      will to move the motor
      powers
   c) *motio*—motion

10. *fructus*—an intellectual delight
    in attaining the intended act

11. Execution—the movement by
    the will of the motor powers of
    the person

12. Pleasure of a higher order,
    from attaining the end: the
    satisfaction of desire—*quietatio
    appetitus - delectatio*

Now, having in mind the table given above, illustrating the analysis of the complex human act, we can perceive that in the domain of *"imperium"* with which legal norm was always connected, there are concealed three "sub-constituents," of which the first two, ordination and rational transmis sion of the ordination, are indisputably the work of reason, while the third, motion, binds the sphere of the reason with the volitive, purely dynamic order. Law-norm is fundamentally united with the first factor, *ordinatio,* but not in isolation from the ones that follow. Thus, law is fundamentally the work of the controlling reason, to the extent that this is not something isolated, but internally combined with the volitive sphere. Nonetheless, formal law is a work of the commanding reason and not of the commanding will, since the latter is blind without the reason.[25]

Ad b) The second element of St. Thomas' definition is the ordering of law to the "common good," which is interpreted in the form of the question: *utrum lex ordinatur ad bonum commune?* (is law always ordered to common good?).

St. Thomas' justifications proceed in the following way:

> As has always been said, law concerns the very sources (the fundamental reason) of human deeds, and this is because it is their rule and measure. And

just as reason itself is the reason of human acts, so too in the very order of the reason there is something that is the reason in relation to all other acts of the person and that, fundamentally and in the greatest way, is connected with law. And precisely in the order of practical reason, the aim is such a reason of the whole of activity. On the other hand, the ultimate aim of human life is felicity or happiness, as has been mentioned above. That is why law must above all take into account an ordering towards happiness. And keeping in mind also the fact that each part is ordered to its whole as that which is imperfect to that which is perfect, and that each particular human being is merely a part of the perfect society, then by necessity law in the proper sense takes into account an ordering to a common happiness. That is why Aristotle *(Eth. 5)*, giving a definition of law also mentions happiness and the political community. He also says in *Ethics 4* that he calls "just laws those which both cause and keep the happiness of all parts united in the society of the state," since the state is a perfect society, as he says in his *Politics*. In each order, on the other hand, all that is greatest is also the reason of the remaining [elements of a given order] and the remaining elements of order are ordered to their reason, as for example fire, which is the hottest, is also the cause of heat in complex bodies, which are hot to the extent that they participate in fire. That is why law, too, is ordered to the greatest extent to the common good and no other particular command (having in view some particular good) has the f o r c e o f l a w if it is not ordered to the common good. For this reason, too, each law is ordered to the common good.

St. Thomas derives his justifications from the standpoint accepted in the preceding article that law is a work of the reason. Here, however, he specifies more fully the nature of the "rationality" of law, for law is the work of the practical reason, and not the purely theoretical reason. As can be concluded from the table presented above, law as a command of the reason already presupposes the whole practical-practical domain (the sphere of choice) and that is why when dealing with the fact of law we are no longer dealing with a purely theoretical consideration about possibilities, but with a concrete command. The domain of reason thus apprehended is something practical, and thus it is ordered directly to e x e c u t i o n , whereas in the execution of activity something that is absolutely first is the a i m , which is justified by the very fact of the emergence of activity; it is the "reason of being," the reason why activity itself i s r a t h e r t h a n i s n o t , just as there also exists a reason of being why a given activity (which already is) is such as it is. And precisely the reason of being of the coming-into-being of activity itself is called the aim, which "acts" through self-love and removes from passivity the rational appetitive powers of "causing" desire, that is, self-love. Thus, an end is a reason of human activity.

If, therefore, law regulates human activity, then the cause of the coming-into-being of regulated human activity (its reason of being) is an aim, that is, the common good, for common good, according to the considerations made above, is precisely the aim of human activity.

Consequently, law as a command of the practical reason is always, on account of the common good, conceived as a common aim, which, taken objectively in the metaphysical interpretation, is the Absolute, while taken functionally, also from the aspect of the subject, is the actualization of the potency of the potentialized human personality.

The common good as the aim justifying the very fact of law, its coming--into-being rather than its not coming-into-being (its existence as such) is at the basis of grasping the content of law. Any content of law not in accordance with "common good," preventing its realization or freely conditioning its attainment, is merely a pseudo-law and a pseudo-command, which cannot "bind" the human person from within. The human person, by virtue of its structure, is totally ordered precisely to the attainment of the "common good," which, objectively speaking, is the ultimate aim of human life.[26]

Ad c) The third element of law is the passing of law by a competent authority. St. Thomas briefly discusses this problem in the third article: *utrum ratio cuius libet sit factiva legis?* (is anyone's reason law-giving?).

St. Thomas' response is as follows:

> Law in the proper, primary, and fundamental sense takes into account an ordering to a common good. An ordering to a common good can take place either through the whole of society or through someone who is the representative of the whole society. That is why law-making is to be done by either the whole society or by the public person who has charge of the whole, for in every domain, ordering to an aim always belongs to the one for whom the given aim is proper.

In a word, laws may be made either by a competent authority, who is a representative of the society or the whole of society through itself, if that were physically possible.

Of course, in a clear presentation of the answer to the question posed, we have to deal with the analogical interpretation of the "common good," for not every authority passing a law is obliged to have the "common good" (conceived as merely the Absolute) as its aim, but it generally has as its aim the kind of good which is connected with the development and ennobling of the human personality. And the common good apprehended in this way by virtue of the (autonomous) hierarchy of goods is of itself ordered to the Absolute, that is, to the "common good" conceived in its primary sense—as the *analogatum princeps* (prime analogate). Generally, this ordering of the "common good" in its primary sense is defined negatively by the statement that law cannot impose something of which the fulfillment would be evil, as we shall discuss below when the dialectic of natural law is considered.[27]

Ad d) Finally, the fourth element of law is promulgation. To the question: *utrum promulgatio sit de ratione legis?* (does promulgation belong to the essence of law?), St. Thomas responds:

> As has previously been said, law is established for others in the manner of rule and measure. Rule and measure are in fact imposed on something by their very application to what is ruled and measured. For this reason, too, in order to guarantee law with the force having a binding capacity, which is something proper for law, it must be applied to people who should proceed according to a legal rule, acting in accordance with a rule of law. Application of this kind takes place through the fact that law becomes known on the basis of promulgation: that is also why promulgation is necessary for law to possess its binding force.

Of course, promulgation thus conceived is not included in the very essence of law, but it is an indispensable condition of law, without which law cannot formally become a law-norm.

The four causes presented by St. Thomas which constitute law, together with the indispensable condition—promulgation, define the nature of law fundamentally from its essential aspect, that is, law as a norm of conduct. This is a general expression, referring analogically both to particular law and to natural law. This definition, though it apprehends law from the aspect of context, does not, however, abstract from its existential fact, for legal norm concerns the social human being, that is, a man or woman who cannot be thought of in abstraction from the "being of law."

The understanding of law outlined here generally from the existential and essential aspect allows us to avoid one-sided interpretations of this problem and also to bind it more with reality, for in one aspect law, being an interpersonal relation internally characterized by *debitum*—a "due" (in a wider sense—duty), is a real relational being, just as each categorial relation is a real being (although it may be of the weakest form of be-ing). This interpersonal relation, however, in order for it to effectively bind and not cause confusion (and sometimes through confusion, greater social harm) must be concretely specified and determined. Determination comes from the reason concretely controlling how, where and when interpersonal relations characterized by "duty" occur in society. The legal norm (which is here discussed) is to concretely direct the interpersonal relations of "duty."

Both interpersonal relations and legal norms "appeal" to the practical reason of man and woman, who through self determination are to carry out, or refrain from carrying out what is in fact expressed in the legal relation and concretely established in legal norm. Thus, the ultimate, concrete way of realizing law occurs in the person, who through practical cognition (ordered to concrete activity), knowing the relations of duty "fills" them with a legal content determined by norm and determines the self (through the choice of a practical-practical judgement) to "such and such" an activity.

5. THE ONTIC NATURE OF LEGAL NORM

In ancient Greece, in Aristotle, there arose the clearly delineated problem of practical knowledge, which was to direct human moral and civil conduct.[28] Practical cognition, which is of a singular character, distinct from theoretical-informational cognition, as well as creative cognition, is in a sense a normative cognition. Scientists generally agree on this subject. The matter will become more complicated, however, from the moment we attempt to specify more closely the nature of this normative cognition, and thereby, normative knowledge.

A special monograph was devoted to this problem by J. Kalinowski,[29] in which he reaches the conclusion[30] that we can distinguish a threefold sense of the expression "normative science": a) as that which p r o v i d e s the norms of conduct—and precisely this kind of cognition, drawing its origins from Greek antiquity, was developed and extended by scholastic philosophy in medieval times, and in modern times is associated with the names Wundt, Goblot, Lalande, Husserl, and others; b) normative science—insofar as it c o g n i z e s and a n a l y z e s norms, as exemplified in J. Kelsen's and Petrażycki's concept of law; c) finally, in the third sense, normative science—insofar as it provides the bases for norms, with the reservation that these bases are not generally connected with metaphysics, but with the cognition of specialized domains of science, such as sociology (Durkheim) or biology (Baruk, Chauchard, Teilhard de Chardin).

The three meanings of "normative science" distinguished above are proof of the fact, according to Kalinowski, that the unity of normative science can be conceived merely metonymically, but these three trends of solutions are not mutually exclusive; on the contrary, they supplement one another, especially when we draw attention to the different nature of cognition applied in those types of normative science. A basic problem, however, is in what sense practical cognition can p r o v i d e norms for our conduct and, in connection with this, h o w that "n o r m" is apprehended in itself; what is its ontic nature? If a norm is to be obligatory in our conduct, then it must s o m e h o w exist.

If natural law, too, appears to every human being in the form of a n o r m, which analogically formulated in the most general way (as shall be justified later), goes along the lines of "the good is to be done," then a practical judgement formulated in this way, being at the same time a legal norm in the widest sense of the term (or any other legal norms of positive law), possesses some kind of ontic status of its own. Does it merely exist in the mind of the person cognizing or expressing this judgement? Is it merely a purely psychic experience that is different for each person? Is it perhaps something objective, something which for many people reveals itself in the same way in the same cognitive conditions, which is something objective, which somehow exists? And if this norm s o m e h o w exists—then h o w ? What elements or ontic moments does it consist of? And if a legal norm were to be something objective and objectively one, then how: univocally or analogically? Is it something ontically real or merely intentional?

These are the problems which we should analyze and for which we should seek, if possible, rational solutions.

We become involved here, consciously, in a dispute that has quite far-reaching consequences (one of them is precisely the apprehension of legal norms) on the subject of intentional being and its structure, for it may not be irrelevant to recall what R. Ingarden[31] wrote on this subject:

> Despite all theories, so great is the force with which particular p u r e l y i n t e n t i o n a l objects impose themselves on us, for example particular literary works, musical works, objects of the social and state system, p o s i t i v e l a w etc., that in particular cases investigators are not inclined to negate their existence, but usually psychologize them in order to save their existence in this way.

We must, therefore, recall once more the fundamental concepts of intentional being, and on this basis we must stress those moments of this theory which were not very clear and caused certain misunderstandings. Above all, a revelation of the realistic concept of intentional being will allow us to become aware of the real ontic bases of the binding power of a legal norm, which norm appears analogically in the form of a practical judgement about the obligation to realize the good (in this sense the legal norm is the natural law), as well as in the form of a univocally formulated norm of positive law. The very understanding of the structure of intentional being, on the other hand, (here it is connected with the understanding of the ontic status of legal norms) is also vital for the totality of the philosophical system and for key problems of interpretation, such as the nature of human existence, the theory of culture, the concept of the artistic and aesthetic work of art, the concept of legal norms, and even the concept of matter. We can, therefore, say that the concept of intentional being "verifies" philosophical theories in a particular way, at least in the sense that it cannot be coherent with the totality of the philosophical system. And in fact it is connected with one or another attitude towards philosophy and with its fundamental nature: idealistic or realistic. There are two different attitudes in the philosophical interpretation of reality: a) a Platonic one, that is, one taking its point of departure from facts of consciousness; b) an Aristotelian one, analyzing being (although in Aristotle himself the question of what is first, being or cognition, is difficult to establish).

In the Platonic approach to explaining reality we above all have to deal with an ever constant, unchangeable and universal meaning of general expressions. Of course, according to Plato, these "meanings" (a horse as a horse; a human being as a human being etc.), as they are the object of intellectual cognition, will only be valuable when they in themselves as "eternal" will be the "real" object of cognition of the mind. Plato, as an intuitionist (he was not yet acquainted with the concept of abstract conceptual cognition, which was to be formed only later by his disciple, Aristotle) believed that all that constituted the object of valuable noetic cognition was at the same time a real object in itself. The analysis of meaning, therefore, was at the same time the analysis of reality in itself—of that which really is.

When the philosophy of the subject posited, meaning, not in the Platonic *pleroma* as the celestial repository of ideas, but precisely in human consciousness (or consciousness as such, B e w u ß t s e i n   ü b e r h a u p t), analyses of the "facts" of consciousness constitute an essential point of interest to philosophers. It is clear that the philosophy of the subject, from Descartes to our times, enriched its analyses and was able to distinguish in the analyzed "senses" their ideal, real, intentional "states," and even an absolute state,[32] but here, however, we have to deal with a fundamentally Platonic "idealistic" mode of thinking—not cognizing.[33] This is particularly revealed in Husserl's phenomenology, whose point of departure is not the real cognition of reality, but precisely the survey of the content of the idea revealing itself in the consciousness. We have here the case of "noesology" rather than "gnozeology."[34] -

In this type of thinking the real existence of being is deliberately and *a priori* put in brackets; also, by definition, both the existence of the object-being and the existence of one's own being are left out of consideration. Having bracketed existence already in the first act of thinking about the content of the idea, our thought will never come into contact with real existence either. And even if the special arrangement of content will be called intentional or real "existence," this will be merely an "endowment" of quality (an appropriately chosen content) of the "object" of the mind. Of course, intentional "being" conceived in this way will accordingly be the content of the thing constructed by our mind, insofar as it is thought by us and not insofar as it exists "weakly."[35] Semblances of "ontic states" of reflected contents are merely the consequence of the mechanism of human thinking, deriving from the cognition of reality.

For this reason, too, in the positions of the philosophy of the consciousness, we cannot seek ultimate solutions for really existing states, since this existence is, by the nature of things, driven away from there. Let us draw attention, therefore, to another alternative explanation of reality and the act of cognition, as well as that which is essentially derivative from cognition and has been built up on acts of cognition.[36]

A legal norm is a sentence: a) fundamentally concerning that which should be carried out (or not carried out) by human conduct; b) expressing— like each sentence—an appropriate set of contents.

As far as the first problem is concerned, it is usually connected with the matter of the cognition of being and duty, as well as the "passage" from a cognitive assertion of being—that which is—to that which is not yet and which should be realized by the human act. From the times of Kant,[37] this matter has taken on particular meaning, when the possibility of passing from being *(Sein)* to duty *(Sollen)* was negated and when both domains began to be set in sharp opposition to each other.

In the area of universalizing cognition, the kind that was employed by Kant and most philosophers, as well as different sciences, there really is no passage, just as there is no logical passage from possible states to real states: *a posse ad esse non valet illatio.* The matter is different, however, in the area of analogical and transcendental cognition, in which we do not abstract ourselves from affirming the real existence of being, but on the contrary, in judgements we apprehend real contents as existing. The set of contents "under" actual existence can present not only actual, real, static reality, but potential, dynamic reality, equally real as its perceived and affirmed actuality. Precisely this dynamic, potential reality is nothing other than the *"Sollen"* expressed in Kant's language, a state that is to occur. This state of things which is to occur in appropriate conditions is already an intellectually perceived value, which we can express in a normative sentence, also concerning reality in its dynamic aspect, interpreted in transcendental cognition.

The normative sentence, on the other hand, expressing an appropriate set of contents, does not differ in its function of presentation from other sentences, and constitutes a special state of being, which is characteristic of cognitive constructs, known as intentional being.

What is specific in intentional being? To answer in the most general terms, what is particularly characteristic of intentional being is the drawing together of the subject-being and object-content aspects. If in natural products (products of nature) the real content of things takes form "under" the actual existence which constitutes being in reality itself, and at the same time the real content which is being formed is commensurable to its actual existence, then in intentional being we perceive the heterogeneity, the "alien character" of the content in relation to existence, being the existence of the subject itself, to be more precise, "derivative" existence, though really "supported" existence, for it is constantly flowing from the subject.

Let us take a closer look at precisely this problem. Above all, we must draw attention to the fact that all intentional beings are built upon cognitive acts. This basically means that the intentional being is the cognitive act itself,[38] presenting some kind of content apprehended in some aspect, as well as everything that is derived from the act of cognition, that is, the most varied cultural products in the most varied domains of culture.[39] Nevertheless, in order to understand the structure of intentional being deriving from cognition (cultural products), we must first become aware of the intentionality of the act of cognition itself, or, to be more precise, the content of the cognitive act. In the cognitive act we perceive the personal, subjective aspect: the fact that it is m y act. It is I who cognize, I am most certain of this. I am conscious in cognitively experienced contents. I can, therefore, state that the cognized contents are as if "threaded onto" the I. Since "I" emanate these acts from myself, they exist through the "I." In other words, the existence of cognized contents is the existence of the cognizing subject.[40] Without going into greater detail (this is not necessary at the present moment for the cognition of the analyzed problem) about the nature of this subjective existence (of course it is secondary existence, emanated, accidental)[41] we must generally say that it is the real existence of the subject itself. Besides, it is evidently given to me, since I know that it is I who cognize I perfect myself through my cognition since I experience the effort of the process of cognition and I delight in the fact that I have understood something.

The negation of the subjective existence of cognitive contents would be an attempt to negate the immanence of "I" in all that is connected with life. If cognitive contents had some, even if defective, contentual existence "of their own," then there would not exist such a clear immanent "I" in cognitive acts; what is more, there would always be needed a special act of cognition of intentional beings, which, as "created" by me, would exist separated further from me. This, of course, is not true. Above all, we would immediately fall into idealism, since concepts would be a separate world for themselves; a world of ideas, which we must (again, I do not know how) cognize, in order to "reach" the contents themselves, for a new act of cognition would only remove me from the object of cognition (which is my concept) for it would end in the new production of a new intentional being—and so on into infinity. All this is, however, unacceptable, and it is discussed here only because this is precisely the way in which intentional being with its own existence is accepted in Platonism and modern phenomenology, which is, of course, simply equivocation.

The second matter in this domain is the question of cognitive contents. They are likewise visible as "not mine." Cognitive contents are constantly "imposed" from the outside. Just as on the one hand I know that it is I who cognize, that the process of cognition is mine, that it is both emanated by me and existing in me, so on the other hand I also know that I am "not responsible" for the content itself of cognition, for the arrangement of characteristics of the concept obtained in cognition. Content derives wholly from the thing in the manner of a film on which, as on an existing base, the content, being a reflection of things, is fixed. Of course the difference is this: that the imprinted content is "imposed" on light-sensitive (chemical) elements, while in a human being, the content is entirely "carried" on (existing) acts of the intellect. Contents are not arbitrarily constructed, but completely built by the cognized thing. As a result of this, the content being cognized is "alien" in relation to the cognizing subject; it is in a state of constant "attack" from outside by the subject: *est in statu obiectali.*

There comes about, then, a strange ontic construct, unique, constituting precisely the "intentional" order of being, precisely incomplete; "tending towards"; "in the act—of attacking—by..." Contents do not exist *per se* through their arrangement,[42] but they exist through acts of the intellect, which are modified to express the set of contents of a cognized being.

The understanding of such a state of affairs is only possible by accepting an ontic structure in which existence and content (essence) are not the same, but something different. Intentional being is precisely the kind of being in which existence is the real existence of the subject and the content (essence) is alien; it is a content aspectively identical with the content of the thing itself. All that constitutes the content of intentional being is radically foreign in relation to the existing base of this content.

In content (essence) itself, however, the act of existence is not, and cannot, be contained, unless we express ourselves metonymically, that is, equivocally.

When it is a question of the "construction" of intentional content, then in cognition of the universalizing type, this content is potential, and thereby not completely explained; it is aspectively identical with the content of the thing itself (in selectively apprehended moments) and it has a significatory nature, that is, we can examine it in itself, see how it is built, and also as aspectively presenting the identical content of the cognized object. The phenomenologists made many interesting and accurate analyses on this subject, especially R. Ingarden, whose analyses of the way in which content is constructed and of how the content of a real object is represented, are regarded as epoch-making. It is difficult, however, to agree with Ingarden as regards his thesis on intentional "being," since this matter is a continuation of the erroneous Platonic route.

When it is a question of legal norm and its ontic status, then we must distinguish the norm of natural law from the norm of positive law. The first is formulated in analogical, transcendentalizing language, whereas the second in universalizing language.[43] Analogical language, which is an expression of transcendentalizing cognition, presents cognitive contents differently than occurs in universalizing language, since the contents expressed in analogical language are not abstract, that is, potential, but merely "vague," indistinct, though actual apprehensions of real being. This was probably taken into account by theoreticians of analogy in medieval times and the period of the Renaissance, when they claimed that the transcendental-analogical concepts *actu confuse*[44] present the thing, for in transcendental-analogical cognition we are constantly in contact with cognized, concretely existing reality and what takes place is not an abstract presentation of the content of things but rather an affirmation of its existence actualizing a concrete content, which generally presents itself indistinctly to us. When I use the expression "being," "good," etc., then I am concerned with understanding a thing on account of its existence and its concrete desirability, as existing, causing the beginning of the process of decision. Thus, natural law, expressed in the judgement (later justified) "do good," does not present any generally univocal content, which would be a defined intentional being of the type such as a sentence, being the legal norm of positive law, expressed in a judgement constituting the result of universalizing, abstract, univocal cognition. Such a sentence is precisely a typical sign of intentional being having its subject in (and existing through) the mind of the lawgiver, insofar as he or she, having in view the common good, aspectively apprehends an appropriate arrangement of things (or constructs this arrangement of content based on selective conceptual cognition) ordering it to realization in society.

Consequently, the legal norm of positive law is an intentional being (in the order of practical cognition) and as such, just like intentional beings, it is presently, and often has been, the subject of special studies, as Kalinowski writes more extensively and deeply.[45] An essential moment, however, is differentiating between the legal norm of positive law and the norm of natural law, on account of the different nature of human cognition involved in each case. The person, cognizing in various ways, presents (sometimes constructs) the content of the norms of natural law differently from those of positive law. The content of the norm of natural law is constantly imposed upon me in a cognitive contact with really existing being; above all, with being-person. On the other hand, the content of the norm of positive law is made known to me by the promulgation of this law. Promulgation, however, would not be possible if intentional being did not present contents aspectively identical with the content of being.

B. THE HISTORICAL ASPECT

The formulation of Ulpian, a Roman lawyer from the period of the Empire, concerning natural law has become classic, and it has even become in a way sacred, by the following words being placed at the beginning: *D. Iustiniani sacratissimi principis institutiones. Lib. II tit. II Proem. de iure naturali gentium et civili:*

> *IUS NATURALE EST QUOD NATURA OMNIA ANIMALIA DOCUIT: nam ius istud non humani generis proprium, sed omnium animalium (quae in coelo) quae in terra, quae in mari nascuntur, avium quoque commune est. Hinc descendit maris atque feminae coniunctio, quam nos matrimonium appellamus; hinc liberorum procreatio, hinc educatio: vidimus enim caetera animalia, feras etiam, iustius iuris peritia censeri.*

This formulation, however, was already the result of a specific philosophical attitude, for it turns out that we have to deal not so much with a concept of natural law as with various philosophical trends, which call upon "nature,"[46] understood in diverse ways, as the ultimate rational source from which all law derives. And although sometimes two given texts set forth an identically sounding definition of the nature of natural law, the interpretation of this definition nevertheless may be fundamentally different in the work of different authors, depending on the prime concept of the philosophical system, as happens in the case of the same definition in St. Augustine and St. Thomas Aquinas.

In the most general sense, we may find f o u r concepts of natural law (without including the related interpretations of German Idealists) that have been generally accepted up to the XXth century.[47]   One of these concepts—St. Thomas' theory of analogical natural law—will become the subject of special analysis in the final part of this work, since it requires a new explanation, and needs to be confronted both with the theory of general being and personal human being.[48]

The first concept of natural law is the ancient Greek and Roman concept of cosmic-theological law.[49]   The second concept of natural law, a psychological and theological one, drew its origins from Plato's speculations and its formulation from St. Augustine; it found its full expression in the Franciscan medieval age and in the Jesuit Renaissance.[50]

The third concept, the concept of natural law "of the school of natural law," has its epistemological basis in the rationalistic theory of cognition, initiated by Descartes' era.[51]   Its further transformations are the speculations of the German Idealists and also those theories which arose as a result of conflicts between the adherents of natural law and the historical school. For the thinkers inspired by the historical school and by positivism, opposing the concept of natural law, nevertheless often assumed standpoints of those who held the theory of natural law, but under another name. It is also worth noting that some theories propounding sources of law other than natural ones, (as, for example, the theory of social contract, the theory of legal psychologism) in some aspects join the wide stream of theories of natural law.[52]

A short historical survey of the tendency of natural law interpreted in so many different ways will bring into sharper perspective the very problem of the ultimate sources of law and the ultimate bases of their binding nature. These sources appear to be placed either in the r a t i o n a l   or p u r e l y   n a t u r a l aspects of the human being. And precisely the differently formulated and differently apprehended definitions of natural law are probably attempts at seeking the ultimate sources of law and their binding power in the r a t i o n a l sphere of beings.

The survey of concepts outlined here is not a systematic, historical presentation, but merely serves to explain from different aspects the very fact and nature of "natural law." The fact that the matter was elucidated in this way in history does not eliminate the truth of these formulations. It is a question precisely of these, for the variety of formulations is proof not only of the richness of the problem, but in my view also constitutes the proper b a c k g r o u n d for the formulation of the fundamental interpretation of natural law as an analogical law, which every human being (as a personal being) is capable of perceiving intellectually as an objective norm, on which basis he may determine himself towards moral activity. The moral aspect of human conduct, as we shall mention later, necessarily implies a proper understanding of natural law.

1. THE COSMOLOGICAL AND THEOLOGICAL INTERPRETATION OF NATURAL LAW

THE DAYBREAK OF THE GREEK AND ANCIENT WORLD

Greek antiquity, in its concept of natural law, as in other domains, lies at the very roots of Western European culture. Its views concerning natural law, like the whole of philosophy, are connected with rationalistic mythology and the passage from *THESEI THEOI* to *PHYSEI THEOS,* which is a departure from the mythological explanation of the world, but at the same time a pantheisation of the world.[53]

In Ancient Greece[54] there were three terms for expressing the concept of justice: *THEMIS, DIKE, NOMOS*. The first two concepts initially denoted divinities, though *Themis* was an older goddess, a pre-Olympic one; she was regarded as the daughter of Gaia and Uranos, but during the period of the war she took the side of the younger Olympic deities and she became one of them, initially as the nurse-maid and then as the second wife of Zeus, after Hera. Themis was the guardian of order on Mount Olympus, and moreover she was to lay down order for gods and men, even for the cosmos, being vigilant that fate was fulfilled. She would advise the gods, and would indicate to men by oracles in what way they were obliged to act.

The second divinity, the goddess Dike, daughter of Themis and Zeus and sister of Eirene, Eunomy and Tyche, mainly looked after the people who were organized into the *polis*. As time went by, Dike's role became greater and the role of Themis was gradually forgotten. Dike, the guardian of Zeus' law, made laws herself, watched over the execution of these laws and in particular measured out justice for conduct. In relation to Themis, Dike showed a greater interest in the fate of human beings. Themis was probably a reflection of ancient relations based on blood ties and the power of the head of the family. For this reason, too, the laws proclaimed by kings were called "themis" and had a sacral nature. Sacredness is the characteristic feature of royal laws and all those which are regarded as the expression of the deity's will. *Nomos* is a law fundamentally based on the authority of the social union.

In the Athenian society governed by Solon, a fundamental role is played by the divine law *dike*, as well as *nomos*, a law established by man, but one which was supposed to be an incarnation, as it were, of Dike. The role of *dike* as the law of the universe makes its appearance together with theoretical Greek philosophy in the work of Anaximander of Miletus. The whole universe, according to him, is set up according to the rules of mathematical reason; thus, there is "symmetry" and "analogy" in the universe, since different parts of the universe have proportionally equally divided being amongst themselves, being eternally emerging from *APEIRON*—pre-being. Thought—logos is contained and bewitched, as it were, in the order of the universe. And whereas some parts of nature have taken more of the "being" of the universe, they must all, in the face of eternal change and the Great Cosmic Year, give each other back that of which in their "greed" they have taken too much. In this sense *Dike,* being the incarnation of eternal change, is at the same time the incarnation of cosmic justice, making sure that beings draw from or participate in the pre-being of the divine *Apeiron* in a proportionally identical way, *Apeiron* being of himself still not yet self-conscious, but nevertheless always a cosmic logos.

The concept of a logical universe as the highest l a w , giving meaning to the changeable, ever fluid elements of the world which are engaged in ceaseless war with one another, appears in the work of Heraclitus of Ephesus. Law-that which is a self-conscious cosmic deity—can be perceived not in ordinary abstract cognition or empirical cognition, but in the special kind of cognition that we have, for example, when we summon up the courage in our own consciences to make appropriate decisions. Heraclitus called this cognition *PHRONEIN,* that is, a particular kind of sacral cognition; born out of pain, it was a deeper cognition, being a deeper intuition into given, ever changing phenomena. The divine *LOGOS* (law) penetrates everything and is symbolized by an all-consuming fire. Law-logos is at the same time a law of the universe, as well as a law revealing itself in the interior of every person. We must obey this law, for it governs both the person's inner self and governs societies, and finally the whole universe. In the universe and in the human being, there is constantly struggle and inner tension; but in all this we can perceive a higher sense of law, just as we can hear the melody in the vibrations of a lute.

In the history of Greek philosophy Anaxagoras and Empedocles have often been indicated as the two thinkers who stressed the role of law. Anaxagoras viewed law in a s p i r i t that was coextensive with the quantitative mixture of elements *(KRASIS),* a spirit which directs the course of the world, which is the same in the universe as in the human being, for it is undivided.

According to Empedocles, there is one cosmic law embracing animals and people, for the human soul goes through different stages of incarnation, according to the belief of Orphism. This law is not a divine work, but the gods are to stand guard over this law. Good and truth are something universal and they do not have to be learned, and precisely law is the expression both of good and truth.

It is difficult to say anything more precise about the concept of law on the basis of doxographical records, since these records have only been preserved in fragments and they are subject to different interpretations.

Generally speaking, however, ancient Greece and Rome held beliefs about the divine—which guaranteed the "naturalness"—origin of laws.[55] In the *Digests* the view is expressed that all laws are the invention and gifts of the gods. Plato in the *Laws* (I 624) mentions that in Knossos there ruled Minos, who consulted with Zeus every 9 years. Virgil, in the *Aeneid* (VIII 321) writes: *Is [Iovis] genus indocile ac dispersum altis composuit, legesque dedit.* Cicero,[56] on the other hand, writes: *Lex vera atque princeps apta ad jubendum et ad vetandum ratio est recta summi Iovis.* Yet Cicero's belief—as a Stoic—that only the reason of the supreme God is a source of truth, is already the culmination of thoughts on the rationalization of mythology and the ultimate passage from *THESEI THEOI* to *PHYSEI THEOS*. This is, however, strictly linked with philosophy.

Like the Greeks, ancient peoples who had a highly organized society regarded their divine founders also as the first lawgivers. Legends or convictions are known about the directly divine origin of appropriate laws. For instance, in ancient Babylon, in Hammurabi's Code, there is information given at the beginning that this splendid state was founded by the gods themselves and it was they who called Hammurabi to the throne. This man, in turn, received from Marduke (the god of the Royal family, and thereby the god who was supreme in the state from then on) laws, which he announced to the people as "Hammurabi's Code."

In the Old Testament there is also the account about God's intervention on Mount Sinai when the law was being made. In the Book of Exodus (Ch. 20) it is written that from God's mouth comes not only the Decalogue, but also civil and criminal law (Ch. 21), as well as civic, family and moral law (Ch. 22–23).

In ancient Egypt there existed a belief that law was given by the god Thoth himself, whereas according to the beliefs of the Peruvian Incas, laws come from the god Inca. The Hindu Book of Laws, *Manu,* begins with an introductory prayer for laws, addressed to God, from whom all laws come. According to the beliefs of Islam, the Koran, which also contains legal rules, is a work of Mohammed, who acted however under the inspiration of Allah.

The beliefs, myths and convictions conveyed to us from antiquity are connected with the concept of natural law, just as mythology is connected with philosophy, which in the case of Classical Greece, was to a great extent the rationalization of religious beliefs. That is why it is difficult to perceive in these convictions any kind of separate concept of the origin of law, as some theoreticians of law do,[57] when they distinguish a special theory of "divine intervention," for if the theory of "divine intervention" exists somewhere, then it only exists in systems of belief, for example, in the Catholic Church, which recognizes the "law" of the Gospel as the Divine law of Jesus Christ. On the other hand, all early convictions about the intervention of the gods in the founding of towns and states can be regarded as the dawning of the concept of natural law.

Classical Philosophical Views

The views of Plato, Aristotle and the Stoics became the fundamental basis not only for the understanding of the cosmic-theological natural law, but also other interpretations of this problem, especially for tendencies that are still alive in Christian culture; but not limited only to it. The richness of thought of the Classical philosophers is still important, even in today's concepts of law and the state.

a) Plato's standpoint

Plato's concept of law is easy to apprehend when it is a question of the moments which Plato himself taught about truth. When, however, we take into account the influence of the theories of Plato on the later, Christian concept of natural law, then the matter does not appear so simple, since Plato exerted an influence on the concept of natural law, such as became recognized in Christian thought, not through his theory of law, which he conveyed to us in *The Republic, Politics* and *Laws,* but through his theory of ideas.

The conception of law itself in Plato is not especially original; but it is only connected with the concept of man and society and ordered to one of Plato's main thoughts, namely the e d u c a t i o n of humanity.

> The matter is no different when the problem of justice is concerned, which constitutes an introduction to the totality of solutions and from which the further course of the work then develops. What an inexhaustible subject for the theoretician of law, not only in our times, but in Plato's day, an era which first issued a comparative science about the state. But here, too, there is no question of real, legal relations, and an analysis of the problem "what is it that we call justice?" ends with a scientific lecture on the "parts of the soul," for ultimately, Plato's *State* concerns the soul. What we read in it about the state itself and its structure, the "organic concept of the state in which scholars often wanted to discern the proper atom of the Platonic *Politeia,* merely serves as a "magnified reflection" of the human soul and its inner structure. But Plato also approaches the problem of the soul in principle not from a theoretical but from a practical point of view, namely as an educator of souls. ... The essential content of the state is education.[58]

As Plato saw it, the education of a citizen was all the more necessary in that Plato himself was a witness of the slow decay of Athenian society. That is why a universal reform was necessary, which he, Plato, proposes in his work.

> Plato came to the tragic conclusion that law and system of government are also forms, which are valuable as long as there is in the nation a certain moral content which they guard and which they help to survive.[59]

On this basis the problem of law, which Plato fundamentally understood as a legislative act, is neither especially interesting nor worthy of deeper deliberation. It was not on the basis of law but on the basis of the virtue of justice and the mutual relation of three souls to one another, as well as the three states, the reflection of these three souls in the state, that Plato saw the essential moments of justice and concordance with nature.

> He views justice in the state in this—each member of society should fulfill his specific functions in the best way possible. The rulers, the watchmen and the workers have their clearly appointed tasks, and if a man in each of these three states pays heed, as far as he is able, to fulfilling this function, then the state formed from their co-operation will be the most perfect that can be imagined. Each of the three states has a virtue characteristic of itself: governors should be wise, soldiers brave. ... The third virtue, which is sensible self-control (SOPHROSYNE) is not, to tell the truth, connected with the third state to a similar degree, but it does, however, have an exceptional meaning for it. It is the basis for the concord of classes deriving from the fact that those who are naturally worse freely subordinate themselves to the better. All these virtues should characterize both the governors and the governed, but sophrosyne precisely places the highest demands on the state from which it requires obedience. ... Justice is the function of how, to what extent, each social state realizes the virtue proper to it in its conduct and how far it fulfills the tasks which are incumbent upon it.[60]

> To execute justice—is this not the same thing as to establish mutual relations, in accordance with nature, of elements of the soul?[61]

In the concept of natural law, which is later accepted in the Roman circle, particularly the Christian one, a special role is played by the Platonic theory of ideas. Ideas for Plato were a necessary, permanent, general object of human conceptual cognition. On the epistemic route they revealed themselves as the senses of general expressions and the content of definitional cognition. Plato, assuming the standpoint of the absolute value of our intellectual cognition, could regard such a type of cognition as valuable only under the condition that one supposes the real being of the object of intellectual cognition. If intellectual conceptual cognition has the value of truth, then general ideas "are," as "real" objects of precisely this intellectual cognition.

The whole theory of ideas already belongs to Plato's metaphysics. General ideas constitute reality in itself, the ultimate, whereas changeable earthly reality participates only in the unchangeable contents of ideas in themselves. Consequently, all contents of the changeable world have no value of themselves, for they are merely the reflection of true values, which in themselves are contained in the Platonic "world of ideas."[62]

Where are these ideas? Plato did not pose this question. Besides, from the point of view of the theory of knowledge and Platonic teaching, it did not have any value. What is most important is that these ideas "are" the object of our intellectual cognition. We can form myth-stories about them and say that they are the *"pleroma,"* that is, the perfect world—"in the eternity of Nature"—where eternal living souls contemplate these ideas; these matters are not, however, treated too seriously in the Platonic system, and at least they are not as important as the theory of cognition and science, as metaphysics. These matters, like all matters concerning the changeable world, are fundamentally the object of *doxal,* that is, less valuable cognition.

The Platonic concept of ideas later became the model for the concept of *lex aeterna,* as the arrangement of divine ideas. This basically occurred in Augustine, but with the mediation of Plotinus' *Logos.* In the meantime, however, the Stoic concept of natural law appeared, which had a fundamental influence on Roman minds, and also Aristotle's concept.

b) Aristotle's interpretation

In Aristotle we find a differentiation made between natural law and positive law, as well as many deliberations on what is right and what is, at the same time, some higher law. These problems, together with ethical problems, are established in the Stagirite's metaphysics. Aristotle, through his general formulations had a greater influence on the medieval age, for example the defining of law by St. Thomas, rather than through his direct reflections.[63]

Highly important for the understanding of the Aristotelian concept of law and also the later Christian approach to this question are the following moments of Aristotle's philosophy:

1° Being is the object of our intellectual cognition and all that we cognize and explain is ultimately reduced to the concept of being-substance.

2° There exist, together with the concept of being, certain sentences that are "through themselves" evident *(propositiones per se notae),* which are objectively evident, as the first clarifications of being.

3° *"Bonum est quod omnia appetunt"*—the analysis of this expression, as well as the finalistic concept of good have become a factor explaining human conduct, common good and society.

4° The concept of order elaborated in the *Metaphysics* and *Nichomachean Ethics;* order is expressed by unity, particularly analogical unity.

In relation to these fundamental assertions we can perceive in Aristotle formulations of natural law and positive law as secondary to them and occurring against the background of them. Aristotle connects the concept of natural law only with the human being, for having rejected the Platonic cosmic ideas he has no basis for accepting any kind of cosmic law, unless we would wish to recognize eternally existing order in the universe through this law. Order and law have much in common, since law itself, too, is a certain kind of order.

Natural law in the human being manifests itself in tendencies deriving from one form, in this case, the human soul, which is one, and thereby we attribute all natural tendencies ultimately to this same form.

The human soul tends towards that which is good. And the estimate of the reason about what is good constitutes the basis of a just action, just because it is in accordance with nature. Just as in individual life there exist natural tendencies towards good, so in human social life there appear natural tendencies to life in the family, the village and the state.

> For one property of man distinguishing him from other living creatures is the fact that he alone has the capacity to distinguish good from evil, justice from injustice and so on, whereas a community of such beings becomes the basis of the family and the state.[64]

For Aristotle there exists a necessary convergence of interests of the individual and the society and for this reason too there exists a convergence of natural law and laws of political societies which expresses itself in the nurturing of that which is just; if justice were to fail, it would be necessary to have recourse to that which is right and honest. However, justice, as well as rightness and honesty, are perceived by the human reason and desired by a person as a good. To be sure, the understanding of natural justice and natural honesty is the basis of human conduct regulated by law. Aristotle has recourse to the structure of things and of the human being in order to explain the meaning of life under law. From this it follows that man or woman must interpret contents-norms as being a rational being. Of course, this "interpretation" is social and expressed in state law, but above this law there exists an appeal to that which is right—if justice fails.

Here is how the Stagirite formulates the matter for us briefly:

A doubt, on the other hand, arises from the fact that what is honest is just, not in the sense of constituted justice, however, but it is a correction of constituted justice. This comes from the fact that all law is general. We cannot, nevertheless, make a correct judgement about some things in a general way. Thus, where it is necessary to make general statements about something but we cannot do this in a correct way, there the law deals with the majority of cases, being aware of the erroneous nature of such conduct. Nonetheless, however, it acts correctly: the error does not lie here either with the law or with the lawgiver, but in the nature of things, for such is the material that all practical actions operate on. If, then, the law adjudicates upon something in a general way and a case occurs which does not fall under this adjudication, then it is a proper thing, since the lawgiver has omitted something and through a general formulation has made an error, to fill this lacuna, adjudicating as if the lawgiver himself pronounced judgement, as if he were present, and as if he himself made the decision, as if he knew about the given case in advance. That is why honesty is justice, and even something better. And precisely this is the essence of honesty, that it is the correction of law where it fails as a result of a general formulation. ...[65]

Consequently, Aristotle, in explaining authentic human conduct, ultimately resorts to adjudications and to decisions of naturally functioning reason. The Stagirite's hypothesis was to a large extent correctly expressed by Lévi-Strauss:

In each conflict there exists a possibility of correct decision, based on the full consideration of all circumstances, that is, the decision required by a given situation. Natural law depends on precisely such decisions.[66]

Undoubtedly, Aristotle's correct intuitions did not, however, save him from making many grave errors. Not the least is the desire to justify slavery by making reference to nature and almost to natural law, when the Stagirite not only accepts the state of slavery as a fact, but attempts to justify it by an analysis of human natural structures, as it were, which in point of fact are not structures but a specific profile of activity, arising from, and conditioned by, a specific social situation. A sample of such thinking will best show the problem:

For the essence which, thanks to reason, is capable of foreseeing, governs by nature and commands by nature, whereas the one that can only carry out these demands with the help of bodily forces is subject and by nature is servile; hence, the interests of master and slave are convergent. By nature, then, the fate of a woman is different from that of a slave.[67]

c) The Stoic-Roman tradition

The Greek concept of law, as philosophy in general, ends in a particular panlogism—to be more precise, pantheism. Whether the Stoic concept of law had an influence on the Roman concept of law itself is a matter of dispute, or at least the degree of this influence is a matter of dispute. At any rate, the Stoic system probably had an indisputable influence on the spirit of Roman law. According to the Stoics there exists only one absolute being: Nature, a preforce known as ZEUS, universal LAW—*NOMOS*. From this common being all things emerge on the basis of a cause-effect relation. The highest good is happiness, depending on concordance with nature. That is why happiness is, for the human being, in accordance with a rational nature and in general with the reason governing the world. Universal reason is the supreme law, it is the king of divine and human things. Above human law there exists the law of nature and whoever has grasped it does not have to care about positive law. In the work of the Stoics the idea of citizenship embracing the whole world took on the form of a world state *(civitas maxima),* where the distinction between Greek and barbarian is avoided. The idea of a community of gods and people arose. This concept recalled the Christian idea of a community, in which there was no longer to be either Jew or Greek, barbarian or freeman nor again slave.

Together with the Stoics we have already found ourselves to a large extent in the Roman tradition of law, for Roman philosophers and lawyers adopted Stoic thought to a large extent and they developed this thought in the aspect of law.

Independently, however, of Stoic thought and of the influence of Greek thought in general, which began about the year 150 B.C., we encounter a great development of the concept of law in the Roman milieu.

The first codification of the law of the twelve tables dates from about the years 451–450 B.C., that is, long before the influences of the philosophical thought of the Greeks, although we do not exclude here the filtering in of Greek thought from Southern Italy and Sicily. From the year 242 B.C., that is, from the moment the praetorian office was separated into Praetor Urbanus and Praetor Peregrinus, a distinction arose between "Roman law" and *ius gentium.* In the concept of *ius gentium* we can perceive its bases in the form of *ius naturale,* for according to newer opinions of the historians of Roman law, *ius gentium* was a set of rules, either for a colony or for foreigners staying in Rome, based on *ratio naturalis,* or else it was simply a set of legal general laws, the basis of which was legal conscience. From the time of the writers of the republican period, Plautus and Terentius, the delimitation between *lex* and *mores* was known, and the latter was a sign of the practical wisdom of the people. It was simply natural law, insofar as it passed through the filter of the conscience of the people. The Praetor Peregrinus had jurisdiction over precisely these legal questions. Without doubt after the year 150 B.C., the influences of Greek thinkers also came to be felt.

The one who to a large extent received Greek thought also in the concept of law was M. Tullius Cicero, who found himself under the particular influence of the Stoics. The formulations of Cicero concerning the law of nature became classics and also exerted a great influence on the thought of St. Thomas Aquinas. His texts are proof of the consciousness of natural law:

> Nature is a law which takes its rise not from an opinion but from some force rooted in nature, in the same way as there arose religion, respect, charity, justification, truth.[68]

> There is the same reason in these as in the human race, the same truth, and for both there is the same law, which is the command to do what is right and to shun that which is wicked.[69]
> Only those who employ reason live under law.[70]
> Only that which is honest is also good.[71]

> Justice, on the other hand, commands to put everything in order, to help people; to give each his due, and not to disturb those things which are sacred, those which are common property, and those which belong to others.[72]

> Real law is honest reason, in accordance with nature, extending to all men, permanent, eternal, which imposes obligations, forbids deceit, which does not order or forbid honest people to do things in vain, and does not move the dishonest by ordering or forbidding. And this law cannot be abolished, abrogated, nor can any part of it be nullified, nor can it be abrogated in its totality. Neither by the Senate nor by the whole populace can we be liberated from this law. And we need not seek anyone to explain or lecture on this law. Neither is it true that there is one law in Rome, another in Athens, one in the present, another in the future. One eternal and unchangeable law embraces all nations and all ages. And there is one teacher and one ruler of all men, common to all men—God, who made this law, extended it and spread it; and when we shall not be obedient to Him, we shall betray ourselves, we shall disdain human nature, and thereby we shall run the risk of incurring the heaviest punishments, although we might manage to escape from immediate punishments.[73]

> Law is the highest reason rooted in nature; it is law which commands what should be done and forbids us from doing what is contrary to nature. Law is the same reason that expresses itself among people and is confirmed in thinking.[74]

> All this is contained in the law of the XII tables, rightly and according to nature, which is the norm of law.[75]

Cicero's texts cited here clearly testify to the reception of natural law by the Stoics and their quite far-reaching speculation on the subject of natural law. Cicero, probably as a result of Chrysippe, is very close to the formulation *bonum est faciendum, malum vitandum*. Besides, the above texts contain equipollent formulations. Fundamentally, his concept of natural law refers to man's rational nature, since law itself is some kind of basic, honest reason, commanding good and honesty *(ratio recta, praecipiens bona,* that is, *honesta).* Cicero, however, knows the opinions of the Greek philosophers, the Pythagoreans and Empedocles, who extended "law" also to non-rational animals.[76]

Cicero mentions the fundamental inclinations of animal nature, which can be regarded as a particular law of nature and which the human being as an animal also possesses; but the human being as a rational being completely surpasses the animal and only he alone is in the proper sense the subject of law. And the strict concept of law—*lex*—is limited only to human nature.

The above-cited texts of Cicero, who, as we can see, did not concern himself especially with the elaboration of the difference between *ius gentium* and *ius naturale,* became to a great extent the basis for St. Thomas' speculations on the subject of natural law.

Two further Roman lawyers, Gaius, the most prominent representative of the earlier classical period of law (he published his *Institutions* about the year 161) and Ulpian, the main author of the late classical period of law (died 228), were the authors who contributed to the specification of St. Thomas' formulations in the area of law.

Gaius, the author of *Institutions*, provided a textbook for law studies. Quotations from his work entered Iustinian's *Digests* and hence became known in the Middle Ages. It was probably also from this source that St. Thomas got to know Gaius' thought. In Gaius' work we clearly encounter the difference made between *ius naturale* and *ius gentium,* both based on the activity of *ratio naturalis.*

Domitius Ulpian, the chief legal adviser of the emperor Severus, was not a very original compiler. From his time the division of law into *ius naturale, ius gentium* and *ius civile,* borrowed from Gaius, became permanent, since it was incorporated into Iustinian's *Digests,* together with the famous definition of natural law cited at the beginning of this chapter.

With Ulpian ends the fundamental Western Roman legal tradition, from which Thomas Aquinas later drew. St. Augustine is still to be added, but his speculation already has a completely different character, a psychological and theological one. This is the second great concept of natural law, if we treat the cosmological concept of the Stoics rather more extensively, together with their influence on the autonomous legal thinking of the Romans.

2. THE PSYCHOLOGICAL-THEOLOGICAL CONCEPT OF NATURAL LAW

The Platonic concept of ideas left its mark on the Christian thought of St. Augustine. Ideas, according to Plato, were the prototypes of changeable things of this world. The great reformer and continuator of Plato's thought, Plotinus, posited these ideas in the *LOGOS,* that is, in the intellect, as the first hypostasis, emanated from the "ONE"; besides, this thought appeared earlier in Philo, a contemporary of Jesus Christ. It was taken up by St. Augustine and he "posited" ideas, as rational "reasons" of all things, in God's intellect, identifying ideas with the intellect of God, and the intellect with God himself. Nevertheless, in order to more precisely explain what ideas are, in the divine intellect, and to interpret their role in relation to the world, scholars had recourse to Platonic analyses:

> ... for ideas are the principal forms or the permanent and non-transformable reasons of things; they themselves have not been formed and that is why they are eternal and unchangeable and are contained in the divine intellect, and although they have neither any origin nor do they go out of existence, nevertheless it is in accordance with them that all that which can or does come into being or go out of being takes form;[77] ... individual things have been formed from the ideas proper to them.[78]

Of course, all that is in God is at the same time God. Changeable things, however, have their unchangeable ideas, proper to themselves, as Plato taught.

These ideas are the reason for order in the world. Order is for St. Augustine a basic concept, perhaps drawn from Platonic myths or from the Old Testament. "Eternal law," St. Augustine says, "is God's reason or God's will, which commands us to observe natural order and forbids us to interrupt it."[79]   In connection with this, É. Gilson writes:

> If eternal law converges with reason or God's will, it is strictly related to ideas, of which each is essentially an eternal and unmoved law, abiding in God's Wisdom, that is, in God's Word. We already know that God's ideas are God. We must say, then, that since God's law identifies itself with God's reason, then it is identical with God.

According to St. Augustine's expression it is:

> ... the artistry of God, who has created all things and governs everyone. Although all these expressions contain only comparisons, we should take them in the strictest sense. Artistry is the rule throwing light on the thoughts of the creator and determining what his masterpiece will be. When it is a question of God, we must always remember that his art is not some perfection added on to his nature but his nature itself and we should also not forget the fact that his effectiveness expresses itself not in merely ordinary creativity, but in actual creating. Thus, wanting to take into account both aspects of the problem, it is necessary to say that eternal law is God himself, whose reason, just as it formed all things, rules and moves all things,[80] [and] ... in the eternal and unchangeable laws of God, which live in his wisdom.[81]

> It is sufficient not to perceive the strict bond ... linking the concept of law with
> the concept of creative providence, in order to completely make it possible to
> discern the particular character of law, distinguishing Christian law from Plato's
> law.[82]

However, its discernment cannot rule out the common content of Platonic and
Augustinian ideas. God's eternal law, apprehended by St. Augustine, will later
be accepted by St. Thomas and explained more clearly:

> Thus, just as the order of God's wisdom—insofar as everything has been
> created by him—has the nature of an art or an idea or a model, so too the order
> of God's wisdom, insofar as it directs everything to its proper end, has the
> nature of law. In this sense eternal law is nothing other than the order of God's
> wisdom, insofar as it directs all acts and movements.[83]

According to St. Augustine, God "co-created" the natural laws of beings
which he called to being. Just as through their being they analogically participate
in God's very be-ing, so too, by the very fact that the rule of their activity has
been inscribed into their nature and ontic structure, they participate analogically
in God's eternal law.

> Natural law is to eternal law as being is to Being. This principle extends to all
> areas of creatures without any difference."[84]

This thought of St. Augustine was adopted by Christian thinkers, first by
the Fathers of the Church and then by theologians, who saw that this concept
was in fundamental agreement with Revelation: *Signatum est super nos lumen
vultus tui, Domine* (The light of your countenance is marked upon us, O Lord)
Ps. 4, 6; *Praeceptum posuit et non praeterbit* (He gave a commandment and it
will not go by) Ps. 148, 6; *Per me reges regnant et legum conditores iusta
decernunt* (Through me [wisdom] kings rule and princes decree justice)
Proverbs 8, 15. God's eternal law was to some extent inscribed in human hearts
and whenever we seek advice from revealed law or from our consciences, we are
seeking God's advice.

The sublime concept of God's eternal law shows, on closer analysis, rather
different, less sublime aspects. The key to understanding God's eternal law was,
according to St. Augustine, the concept of the idea, adopted by him from
Platonism. Thus, an essential part in the apprehension of the unchangeable and
eternal contents of "God's law" was played by the Platonic interpretation of
ideas. St. Augustine, insofar as it is generally known, did not have particular and
specific understanding of Platonic ideas, apart from the moment that ideas in
God are God himself. When, however, we ask "how are we to understand these
ideas?"—we will obtain the answer that we can probably only understand them
in the Platonic sense, in spite of the fact that Augustine talks of an idea "proper"

for each thing, since each of the ideas is a general content. At precisely this point a great danger arises—the univocal and general understanding of natural law.

According to Plato's concept of the idea, ideas are in themselves a general, unchangeable and necessary content, whose univocal, non-necessary and changeable reflection we find in the world of the objects surrounding us and in ourselves. If, then, the general, necessary and unchangeable content of ideas in God constituted a general, necessary and unchangeable content of eternal law, then this content would necessarily bind all people without exception and in a necessaristic and unchangeable way. Hence, a (State or Church) lawgiver could, on the basis of an eternal law interpreted—in his view—constitute legal rules for men and women, their particular functions and for different social groups, rules which would be "at the same time a natural law" binding all people identically.

Such a law, as understood by the lawgiver, would be an interpretation of God's eternal law, and therefore "natural law," since natural law is considered to be only a participation in God's law. In such a case the danger would arise of drawing up a univocal code of natural law, univocally, necessarily, forever binding all people or some natural groups of people. Such an eventuality, apart from the dangers of a totalitarian nature, is not in accordance with the fundamental principles of metaphysics, according to which all beings are not "univocal"; they are not the univocal realization of some idea, for beings are analogical. And one individual does not differ from another merely accidentally, realizing "the same" nature of species. One person differs from another person ontically—substantially; for each of us is an individual substance, I am a subject—a person, a being for myself; every human being differs individually—essentially from every other human being. It is true that we, in our intellectual-conceptual cognition, are able to apprehend all human individuals in one general concept: "human being"; it is only apparently that the general concept "human being" does not ontically realize itself in a univocal way in particular individuals. Among human individuals as persons there occurs the kind of difference that cannot be overstepped without eliminating the person himself.

That is why natural law, really binding "from within," can bind particular individuals not univocally but merely analogically, in accordance with the structure of being. For this reason, too, in relation to a law that sounds like being univocal, appeals to a higher legal norm, to a "correctness" guarding natural law, are always possible. On account of this, there is no univocal-sounding law which can of itself bind a human being unconditionally "from within" if it is not accepted by his conscience, that is, his objectively acting practical reason. Of course, personal acceptation is not something free, although it refers to the moment of a person's inner freedom.

The problem of Platonic ideas and their univocal "binding" of changeable things, participating in ideas, is an ordinary transfer of the conceptual manner of human cognition to the cognitive content itself. As people we are not capable of cognizing the content of things other than in merely a conceptual-abstract way, that is, in a general way (in a schematized way), but this generality of our conceptual cognition, although it greatly facilitates the cognitive process, is at the same time an expression of our intellectual weakness. Our minds are not capable of directly, essentially and necessarily grasping an individual essence in a concept and that is why it immediately abstracts from individual features, forming a schematized general nature by means of abstraction. Plato's disciple, Aristotle, discerned the role of abstraction in the formation of our concepts. Cognizing a thing, we generally cognize it simultaneously differently from the way the thing exists—and it always exists individually, "concretely." Plato did not know the concept of abstract cognition and he recognized only intuition. At the same time wanting to be a realist and to overcome the cognitive relativism and scepticism of the Sophists, he accepted the fact that what we cognize and how we cognize intellectually all exists *a parte rei*. Otherwise we would have to reject scientific cognition. The concept of ideas as real objects was the result of his naive cognitive realism (extreme realism). Plato extrapolated our human mode of intellectual cognitive cognition to reality itself. Plotinus and St. Augustine transferred "Platonic ideas" to God's intellect, thereby anthropomorphizing the cognition of God as well as anthropomorphizing the concept of eternal law.

St. Thomas Aquinas had to deal with these matters anew in his philosophical workshop and in the question—*de ideis divinis*—he put them in a completely different way, in accordance with his own concept of metaphysics. St. Thomas' theory will be presented in the next chapter. On the one hand drawing on tradition and on the other modifying it fundamentally, this theory can become the basis of the understanding of law.

Augustinian thought lived in an ecclesial environment and particularly gained strength on the basis of the speculations of John Duns Scotus and later of Suarez, who adopted Scotus' metaphysical concepts and supplemented the theory of natural law and the theory of the state. According to Duns Scotus,[85] a particular being, in this case a concrete man, constitutes a kind of "mound" of stratified forms. The last, most important general form was the form of manhood. Beneath it was the "animal" form, further below, the form of the family, the body, substance and being. Precisely these forms, realizing themselves in particular individuals were to become the ontic "reason" of univocal binding by law. And in fact, if we were to accept precisely such a structure of individual being, then the univocity of natural law would gain a solid foundation in the structure of individual being. In such a case, however, personal unity would disappear, the essential ontic unity of the human individual would disappear.

Suarez also accepted the traditional concept of eternal and natural law, with the reservation that he based the structure of the state on natural law, and he based the structure of the Church on divine law. In his conception of the state Suarez made very many new and valid statements.[86]

3. NATURAL LAW ACCORDING TO THE SCHOOL OF NATURAL LAW

In the domain of law, the XVIIth century is particularly marked by a great development of philosophical and legal problems. No doubt the doctrinal context of this phenomenon is Cartesian rationalism. However, Cartesian rationalism itself and the legal rationalism that appeared in the writings of Hugo Grotius were conditioned by the renaissance of Spanish scholasticism and the Spanish school of law, which produced such authors as F. Vittorio and F. Suarez. Particularly the latter, as a Jesuit, through his Order and Jesuit colleges, prepared a rationalistic philosophical background, for Suarez' philosophy was very widespread in the whole of Europe (Descartes was a pupil of the Jesuit College in La Flèche in the years 1604–1612). In precisely this renaissance school of scholastics, particular emphasis was placed on the concept of cognition, at the same time reducing intellectual cognition to the formation of concepts. This can be seen not only in the great publications of the Jesuit school, but also in those of the Dominican school, as for example John of St. Thomas for whom different stages of human cognition are merely different stages and degrees in the formation of appropriate concepts. In Suarez' writing has been originated the terminology to understand *conceptus obiectivus* to indicate the content of a thing insofar as it is known, and *conceptus subiectivus* as a personally formed image of things, thanks to which we cognize the thing and the *conceptus obiectivus* itself.

In this period of Scholasticism (and this tendency dates from the time of Duns Scotus), little is said of the thing itself, of being, but the expressions "concept of being," "concept of a thing," etc. are constantly employed. In the Suarezian school we reach a point at which we are not in fact concerned with the cognition of the thing-being, but with the cognition of the "concept-thing." That which is not contained in a concept of some kind does not exist at all. Well-known in this matter is Suarez' discussion with the Thomists on the subject of the difference between essence and existence. Suarez argues that there cannot be any difference here because, in spite of reflection and effort, a concept of existence as different from that of essence cannot be formed; there are only different states of essence, which are to a greater or lesser degree abstract. In the scholastic school, it was the analysis of the so-called "objective" concept which stood for the thing itself as known, that became the point of departure in the analysis of things.

The same point of departure became to a large extent that of Descartes, for whom the supreme form of truth is subjective evidence, which can be reduced to the possession of a clear and distinct idea. The clear and distinct idea (which had the same function as *conceptus subiectivus* in the stream of renaissance Scholasticism) was a simplification of the Scholastic standpoint, for *conceptus obiectivi* were rejected as unnecessary; for everything that constitutes the content of *conceptus obiectivus* is already given to us in a *conceptus subiectivus.* The analysis of clear and distinct ideas constitutes the point of departure of Cartesian philosophy, and the operation on ideas, forming a "chain of evidence," is the essential feature of Cartesian rationalism, which grew up on a Scholastic base of philosophical thought. However, the real bond of the world of things and nature with God, as the multi-faceted reason of the world of nature, was broken. The cognitive connection contained in the idea of God himself was stressed. God appeared as the ultimate E N G I N E E R of the world, and the world "as a watch" moving according to laws imposed by Him. The thing, however, was not the object of analysis, but the idea of a thing, even the idea of God to the extent (it is understood) that this is given in our consciousness.

Precisely these moments of the analysis of the idea, and particularly the idea of the human being as a social product, an analysis of the idea of society in one aspect or another, also constitute an essential feature of rationalism of the "school of natural law." Although Hugo Grotius wrote his work *De iure belli ac pacis* before Descartes' main works appeared, whom he probably knew, we do however find a similar rationalistic atmosphere in the works of Descartes and Grotius. In the work of other philosophers dealing with natural law, the influence of Cartesian thought is very significant.

Besides the philosophical atmosphere favoring a return to the concept of natural law, humanism and the renaissance also drew on ancient concepts, particularly those of Cicero, the Roman rhetoricians, historians and lawyers (the *modus docendi gallicus* in opposition to the *modus docendi italicus,* in which medieval commentaries and glossaries were employed). These moments especially influenced the foundation of a school of natural law to which the following philosophers, above all, belong: Grotius, Hobbes, Locke, Spinoza, Pufendorf, Thomasius, Wolff, Rousseau, and to a certain extent, Kant. These authors are the Classical representatives of philosophical rationalism in the problem of the theory of law.

Whereas in Suarez natural law is still based on God's eternal law, which is a law by virtue of its essence, while all other manifestations of law (with divine positive law) are merely law "through participation," finding their ultimate explanation in divine law, from the times of Grotius onwards there is another concept of natural law. Here we no longer encounter an appeal to "eternal law" to explain natural law, but the very analysis of the i d e a of human, social nature. In Grotius we read:

> *Ius naturale est dictamen rectae rationis, indicans actui alicui, ex eius convenientia aut discenvenientia cum ipsa natura rationali ac sociali, inesse moralem turpitudinem aut necessitatem moralem.*[87]

(Natural law is a dictate of right reason, which shows that in each activity, depending on its accordance or non-accordance with human rational nature, there lies moral abomination or moral necessity.)

Consequently God, who is the creator of nature, forbids or commands such an activity. In this new definition of the law of nature, God also appears as the one who is the guarantor of law, but an appeal to Him does not take place by virtue of the connection of the participation of the law of nature in God's law, but by virtue of the fact that, according to the opinions accepted at that time, which appeared particularly clearly in Descartes, God is the engineer of the world and the creator of human nature.

"The school of the law of nature" founded by Grotius, operating on the concept of nature, that is, the period in the life of humanity preceding the social state grounded on political agreement *(pactum unionis* and *pactum subiectionis)* claimed, however, that the state of nature is by no manner of means free of the rule of law. On the contrary, according to the adherents of this school, law, to which people are subjected in the state of nature, has a universal and stable power, and therefore it also is binding on the social state found under the rule of the state and of positive law.[88] The law of nature derives not from human will, but is a necessary dictate of the reason and derives from rational nature. The term "law of nature" coined by Grotius can be explained by the fact that its adherents believe that it was possible to construct a total system of the law of nature as a formed codex, binding all nations for all time. This codex was to contain rules which, having their source in unchanging human nature, are called to normalize all inter-human legal relations: private and public, property, family, political relations, both within the state and between states. Of course, this stream of thought even reached the ridiculous in some of its manifestations, when on the basis of "the law of nature," standards of social life were formed.

a) H u g o   G r o t i u s   (1583–1645)[89] published his main work, *De iure belli ac pacis,* in the year 1625. Besides *ius gentium,* he discusses *ius naturale* as the basis for all other laws. This law is a result of the very rational and social nature of the human being and nobody, not even God, can change it. This law is something primordial and binds the individual even when he or she associates, by a social agreement, in social organisms based on the law of nature, whose first and most important manifestations accessible to every rational nature are the following:

1° *promissorum implendorum obligatio*—the keeping of contracts, which came into operation under the motto *pacta sunt servanda;*

2° *alieni abstinentia*—the respecting of other people's property;

3° *damni culpa dati reparatio*—harm done to someone is to be recompensed;

4° *paenae inter homines meritum*—the penalty of the crime, for everyone who is willing to do evil is willing to bear the consequence of his evil conduct.

These first dictates of natural law are the result of *appetitus societatis*, that is, the inner tendency (instinct) towards association among people. Of course, this must yet be supplemented by a special "social arrangement," when people form concrete societies. State societies are eternal, although constitutions may change. The subject of supreme authority is always the people; every ruler (government) is merely an organ called forth by the will of the people to exercise authority.

b) T h o m a s   H o b b e s (1588–1679) was a rationalist in the domain of the theory of the state and of law. His point of departure is the concept of the human being, who is rational but nevertheless directs all conduct by individual desires and passions, for the fundamental tendency of human nature is selfishness. All motives of human activity primarily aim at self-conservation and the acquisition of power over others. This causes the *bellum omnium contra omnes* (war of all against all), *Leviathan,* I, XIII. That is why in the state of pure nature, before individuals come together to form society, the natural state of humanity can be regarded as being that of enmity of one individual against another: *homo hominis lupus.*

The human being, however, even in the state of pure nature, possesses reason and this reason shows that in order to keep alive, it is necessary to seek peace. That is why the first of the commands of the law of nature of a human being as a social being is *pacem esse quaerendam,* (peace should be sought); next, the readiness to give up one's right in order to attain peace, together with the keeping of agreements. A further manifestation of the law of nature is gratefulness for services rendered; universal politeness; the forgiveness of an offence in the face of the repentance of the person who has committed it; the prohibition of excessive revenge; the prohibition of expressions of contempt; the recognition of equality; the impartiality of judges. The general law of nature is designed as the freedom possessed by every person, to use, as he thinks fit, his power towards the conservation of the power of nature, as well as to do what seems most appropriate to attain this end (*Leviathan,* XIV).

The totality of all fundamental laws of nature can be summarized in the principle: "Do not do to another what you do not wish others to do to you."

Guarding the laws of nature is to be the state, which has arisen from a social arrangement, as a necessary evil, but nevertheless one that is to safeguard people from an even greater evil that precisely *bellum omnia contra omnes* would be. The only aim of the state is the keeping of order among people and their defence against other people.

A state which has arisen as a result of the renouncement of sovereign laws by individuals is a state having absolute authority, which arouses respect in the face of the law. It is a law of nature that of two good things the better should be chosen, and of two bad things, the less evil should be chosen. Consequently, a human being who wishes to follow instincts of irrational selfishness should know that he or she can encounter a greater evil from the authority dealing out punishment. But reason bids us to use the universal authority of the state in such a way that it may inspire respect and educate its citizens. In this, the idea of the old Greek Platonic *PAIDEIA* returns.

c) S a m u e l P u f e n d o r f (1632–1694), born in Chemnitz (Karl-Marx-Stadt), published *De iure naturae et gentium* in the year 1672. He was probably the most typical representative of the school of the law of nature. He constructed an almost perfect system, making a sharp division between *ius naturae* and *ius gentium* and he set forth the supremacy of the law of nature for all nations and for all time.

Pufendorf believed that the human being has an *appetitus societatis,* but that it is an egoistical instinct. The human being, who is at the same time infirm and weak, must unconditionally be a social being, both for self-preservation and for the peaceful use of goods he or she possesses, and must be associated with others into a state for his or her own protection. *(De iure nat. et gent.,* III par. 15).

In the concept of the law of nature, which is the basis for every other law, Pufendorf for the first time separated it from religion and morality (he was criticized by Leibniz for this). According to Pufendorf, the law of nature is contained only in the dictates of natural reason. One way to acquire knowledge of the principles of this law is to analyze the concept of nature and of man's tendencies.

The state is a work of convention or consent, and according to Pufendorf, as many as three conventions: a) the pact concerning association into a social organism, b) the pact upon a constitutional system, and c) the pact concerning authority.

d) B a r u c h S p i n o z a (1632–1677) is a classical, almost extreme representative of rationalism of the Cartesian type, and therefore of both its points of departure in philosophizing and its rationalistic method of pursuing philosophy. Proceeding from an analysis of the concept of substance fundamental to Cartesianism, Spinoza *modo geometrico* (in a geometrical manner), as he understood it, reached monistic pantheism, recognizing that there exists only one substance which is God, and everything that can be discerned or analyzed is merely an attribute of God. There is an infinite number of these attributes.

The whole universe, being an external manifestation of the same substance—God—is at the same time a manifestation of life and His truth, and this to the extent of its connection with substance—God. *Ordo aeternus* extends to the whole universe and to man in the state of nature: *quidquid itaque unusquisque, qui sub solo Naturae affectuum impetu, iudicat, id summo Naturae Jure apparere* (whatever anyone, under the influence of nature alone, judges to appear by the highest law of nature). If human nature were equipped in such a way that everyone lived according to the indications of his reason, then these indications would define the law of nature of each and every human being. People, however, are governed by blind lust, which is also a manifestation of nature, and this lust would cause a clash between human aspirations. Consequently, for a safer life, it becomes indispensable to go from a natural state to a social state, which takes place, of course, by means of a social agreement. (*Tr.* p. XVI and IV. 6). Thus, a social agreement is a work of the apprehension and uncertainty of people in freely taking advantage of the law of nature due to them. Moreover, there still is in the human being a drive towards fellowship. Hence, not force and lust define the law of the individual but the will of the people at large, which naturally compensates human beings, to a certain extent, for the individual laws they have lost. In the state that has been formed, freedom is to reign through the merely partial renunciation of individual rights, and laws are to be a help and not an encumbrance to humanity. By emphasizing freedom, Spinoza approaches Rousseau.

e) W i l h e l m   L e i b n i z (1646–1716), in cognizing the principles of the law of nature, passed as if from a metaphysical standpoint to a psychological and, in a sense, empirical standpoint, for he based his considerations on the natural tendencies in human psychic life. Natural inclinations are, as it were, a reflection of God's law in the human heart. This standpoint recalls, on the one hand, St. Paul's thought that God's law has been carved in the heart of the person, and on the other, St. Thomas' saying: *secundum ordinem inclinationum naturalium datur ordo praeceptorum legis naturae* (the order of the precepts of natural law is given in accordance with the order of natural inclinations). Without the discovery of the natural inclinations, Leibniz does not envisage any possibility of reaching the law of nature merely by way of reflection. Thus, the law of nature is not given to us in the form of ready rules, but in the course of history it forms and becomes more perfect through a gradually better awareness of what is already contained in our nature.

The law of nature has, according to Leibniz, three degrees: *ius strictum* (law conceived in the strict sense), *aequitas* (equality), and *pietas* (respect); and their counterparts are the three dictates of law:

1° based on the Aristotelian principle of exchangeable justice (*iustitia commutativa*), the command: *neminem laedere* (do harm to nobody);

2° in relation to *aequitas* there is the command: *suum cuique tribuere* (give back to everyone what is due to him);

3° in relation to *pietas,* embracing human and divine relations, there governs the command: *honeste vivere* (live honestly).

These three commands are the reception of natural law from the Classical era (Ulpian).

f) Thomasius Christian (1655–1728) believed that the state of nature was at the same time a state of peace and war: the free recognition of other people's law but at the same time violence. In order to keep the peace, people unite in societies. Human life, in order to be happy, must realize *honestum* (honesty), *decorum* (propriety), *iustum* (justice), in relation to which virtues good, evil and intermediate acts have been recognized. Evil acts are those which impair external peace; good acts are those which aim at attaining inner peace; intermediate acts are those which do not impair external peace but are not sufficiently intense to assure inner peace.

The fundamental command of *honestum* is: *quod vis ut alii sibi faciant, tu tibi facias* (do for yourself that which you would like others to do for themselves).

The principle of *decorum*: *quod vis ut alii tibi faciant, tu ipsis facias* (do to others what you want others to do to you).

The principle for *iustum* declares: *quod tibi non vis fieri, alteri ne feceris* (do not do to another that which you do not want to be done to yourself).

Legal norms concern only external relations between people, and the inner sphere of life is devoid of morality. The law of nature expounds only the principles of justice, and injustice and in this way it differs both from ethics and from politics.

g) Christian Wolff (1679–1754), a very important precursor of Kant, distinguished, in the area of law, the law of commands *(leges praeceptivae),* of prohibitions *(leges prohibitivae),* and the sphere of entitlement to rights *(leges permissivae).* All laws are a system of authorizations deriving from the moral obligations which are incumbent upon man. To each moral obligation there corresponds the appropriate moral entitlement. Since there exist obligations having a universal application, there also exist human rights, inborn and inalienable.

h) J.J. Rousseau. As mentioned above, the theory of the school of natural law is connected in some aspects with the concept of the "social contract," which found full expression in the ideas of J.J. Rousseau. The theory of the social contract is incomprehensible in abstraction from the concept of natural law. It presupposes a natural state of man in society and fundamentally stresses "the contract of authority" as well as the conditions of keeping this agreement. In this sense we encounter new moments of the "social contract" even in the work of the classical philosophers of the theory of natural law.

In Grotius a particularly important moment was the stress laid upon the obligation of keeping the agreement. This thought runs like a thread through the whole of Grotius' treaties, such that F. Stahl writes:

> The whole of Grotius' theory of natural law, although he was not aware of this, is nothing other than the recognition of the binding power of the agreement.[90]

Besides, Grotius himself, in the introduction to his work writes:

> And next, since the keeping of agreements is most closely connected with the law of.nature, (for there must have been some way for people to enter into obligations with each other, and a different natural method could not be thought of), civil laws derive from precisely this source, for those who have joined some kind of society or else have surrendered to the authority of one man or a certain number of people, have, in a distinct way, contracted obligations, or else, as follows from the nature of legal activity, they have pledged in a silent way that they will conform to what the majority of society has decided upon, or those to whom power has been given.[91]

Consequently, according to Grotius, too, social agreement is a "historical fact" (based, according to him, on the fundamental law of nature), which determines the form of the system and the legality of the norms of social conduct themselves.

Whereas Grotius himself did not recognize social agreement as a philosophical basis of the system, but only regarded it as a historical fact, another thinker, Hobbes, recognized the human being's egoistical state causing *"bellum omnium contra omnes"* as the primordial state and proposed the principle: *"pacem esse quaerendam"* (peace should be sought), as the supreme postulate; moreover, he stated that a real manner of keeping peace is the transferring of superior authority to the monarch. This authority, once transferred, is already an absolute and irrevocable authority, for it constitutes the social system itself.

Yet another new element in the theory of social agreement comes from Locke. Social agreement in Locke's work is a rational act which people carry out on account of mutual advantage, seeing the weak sides of their nature and trying to cope with this. Thus, they form a society and an authority, burdening the ruler with law and at the same time with the obligation of executing those tasks which an individual cannot carry out. Consequently, the moment of final cause is added in Locke's work in discussing the concept of agreement.

In the concept of the social contract, J.J. Rousseau's theory, which many philosophers and historians wanted to treat as a historical work, is crucial. A. Peretiatkowicz criticizes such a standpoint and claims that it is a philosophical theory. He quotes an early fragment of Rousseau's manuscript:

> There exist thousands of ways of gathering people together, but only one way of uniting them. ... I seek law and do not discuss facts.[92]

According to Peretiatkowicz:

> Rousseau's foundations of ethics (happiness and virtue), together with the chief social and moral postulates (freedom, equality) have been transferred to the idea of "natural law." This occurred as a result of accepting "utility and justice" as the foundations of natural law, and "freedom and equality" as the two chief legal-ethical postulates.[93]

Rousseau, recognizing the necessity of social life, poses the problem: in what way can we reconcile the fundamental demands of natural law in social life? Moreover, how can we

> ... find a form of association which would defend and protect with its whole might the person and the good of each associated person, and thanks to which everyone, uniting himself with all, would listen only to himself and remain as free as before?[94]

He finds the solution to such a problem in the social agreement, which guarantees equality and freedom at the same time:

> Each of us places himself, his whole person and the whole of his power at the disposal of the people under the chief direction of the general will, by which everyone becomes a member of the people as an indivisible part of the whole.[95]

In this way the ideal of equality was realized, for there is no such associated person on whom the same laws are not enforced in the interests of society.

The reconciliation of freedom with the content of social agreement follows from a special understanding of freedom:

> In vain did people want to identify independence and freedom. These are two things which are so different that they mutually exclude one another. If everyone did as he pleased, he would often do what does not please others and

then we would not have a free state. Freedom lies less in manifesting one's will than in acting so as not to be subject to the will of another. A truly free will is one against which no one has the right to resist. When there is general freedom, no one has the right to do that which is forbidden to him by another's freedom. True freedom is never destructive with respect to itself. In this way, freedom without justice would be a true contradiction.[96]

In *Contrat Social* (The Social Contract) I 8, Rousseau writes: "Freedom is obedience to the law which one has claimed for oneself." In order that freedom may fully be guaranteed, and that no one be subordinate to another, the legislative authority must not only be exercised by everyone, but must also apply to everyone. Laws must be the expression of the general will and also contain a universal object, applying to everyone. Rousseau does not admit the possibility of legal representation. The will must be revealed personally. For this reason, too, the referendum is the only legal form of functioning of the legislative authority. The executive authority, on the contrary, can promulgate only particular regulations and remains in constant dependence on the superior authority—the whole people.

For the concluding of a social agreement, unanimous assent is needed and nobody can be forced to accede to the agreement, whereas for the functioning of legislative authority, a simple majority suffices, which represents the "general will."

The theory of the social contract finally had its "consecration," as it were, in the Declaration of the Rights of Man and of the Citizen of 1789 in art. I 24:

> *Les hommes naissent et demeurent libres et égaux en droits. ... Le but de toute association politique est la conservation des droits naturels imprescriptibles de l'homme.*

> (Human beings are born and remain free and equal in rights. ... The aim of any political association is the conservation of the natural and imprescriptible rights of man.)

It must be noted here that the concept of the individual living in a primitive and wild state in the lap of nature, not bound by any ties, only later to enter into society through social contract, by his own free will, by virtue of laying down laws by way of a referendum, (also a contract), is something unreal, since the individual is not born socially undetermined; on the other hand, this does not explain the sources of the emergence of law-right. The contract itself is already a legal phenomenon and cannot arise merely on the basis of developed legal concepts. Here we ask: "what is the ultimate source of the coming-into-being of law-right?" The legal fact itself cannot be this source.

Two authors stand on the threshold between the old school of natural law and new trends in philosophy; they are I. Kant in Germany and Charles de Secondat, baron Montesquieu, known as Montesquieu.[97]

i) Ch. Montesquieu (1689–1755) published in 1749 his epoch-making work *De l'esprit des lois* (On the Spirit of Laws), in which he considered the natural foundations of law, examined its manifestations in the life of nations at different periods of time and at different stages of culture and reached the conclusion that, since even the wildest nations subject themselves to law, it must be the product of essential human needs, and on this account it is necessary for humanity. The spirit of laws is the content of laws eternally in accordance with the nature of relations regulated by them; *Les lois sont rapports nécessaires, qui dérivent de la nature des choses* (Laws are necessary relations which are derived from the nature of things). In this sense all beings have their laws, from the first Being, down through people and animals to the laws possessed by things. God is the general lawgiver and guardian of laws.

Rational beings (people) can, moreover, have their laws, but precisely this is also proof of the fact that they are subject to higher laws not constituted by them, for before people became intelligent beings, they had to have the possibility of acquiring this intelligence and certain laws, at least justice, had to safeguard laws. For this reason too, the view that only that which is the issue of positive law is just, is erroneous. There must, therefore, exist legal regulations which by necessity precede laws. Of course laws laid down by people are relativized to the history and culture and even to the climate of a given nation.

Different social systems have their specific virtues, for example for d e m o c r a c y the essential quality is a love of e q u a l i t y ; for a r i s t o c r a c y it is m o d e r a t i o n, to make possible equality with respect to law; for m o n a r c h y the leading idea is to be h o n o r a b l e ; and the idea of a d e s p o t i c state is expressed in f e a r.

Montesquieu is the author of the division of organs of one state authority into legislative, judicial and executive authority, that is, the government. He reached this concept on the basis of the analysis of the legislative state, the model of which he saw in the English state. The division of organs of authority is not a division of one indivisible state authority. The division of organs of authority is necessary, in his view, for the freedom of the citizens to last.

j) I. Kant (1724–1804). In relation to the widely branched school of natural law, at the same time recognizing social agreement as a fact standing at the bases of the organization of a really existing society, Kant is the one who in certain aspects breaks with this kind of concept. He recognizes the idea of the contract as a better way of organizing society. Moreover, Kant is—in his concept—the initiator of a new idealistic trend of the theory of law, but he accepts the natural foundations of law in the area of morality.

Kant's standpoint in the theory of law, as in the domain of theoretical philosophy, is exceptional. Legal concepts are closely connected with another "critical" period of his life, when after his criticism of pure reason he became more concerned with an analysis of morality.

In the domain of pure reason, in Kant's view, man is not dependent on empirical data and that is why he does not have knowledge of things in themselves, for everything takes place within the human being, is present for him in his spirit. Whereas in the theoretical domain the reason is bound by certain rules, in the practical domain we do not find ourselves in the field of necessity, but in the field of f r e e d o m and, deriving from freedom, *Sollen,* that is, the feeling of obligation. *Sollen* can ultimately be reduced to "moral sense," which is innate in each human being, both good and evil. Everyone knows that he has acted well when he has carried out an act from a feeling of obligation.

If, therefore, the individual has a feeling of obligation (a moral sense), then already by the nature of things he finds himself under the rule of some kind of law, which obliges him to carry out acts from a feeling of obligation. Kant, however, also differs from the philosophers of the law of nature in that he sees the regulation of this law not in some concrete, material form, but in a purely formal rule, which he himself calls the "categorical imperative of absolute duty," and which can be fulfilled only freely, from a feeling of obligation as obliging all people. It goes like this: "Act from a feeling of obligation in such a way that you might always desire that the maxim of your will might become a universally binding principle."

From the categorical imperative formulated above, Kant draws three commands as the fundamental principles of moral order: a) the command of freedom, b) the command of law, c) the command of punishment.

Without freedom the categorical imperative would be something absurd, for the human being would be deprived of the possibility of carrying out his own will with a feeling of obligation, for an act carried out under external compulsion is deprived of a moral nature. Without freedom the whole moral world would have to collapse.

Unlimited freedom can be realized only within the human being, that is, in the area of feelings, desires, appetites, views; for in this area one cannot really do harm to anybody. In the external sphere of life, on the other hand, the individual's freedom must be contained within certain limits, since otherwise the freedom of other people would be endangered at any moment and in such conditions the real possibility of fulfilling the categorical imperative of moral conduct would disappear, for without freedom one cannot live morally. Thus, it lies in the interest of the external freedom of everyone that there should also take rule over one's life the categorical command of apprehending freedom in certain limits, so that the self-will of each person may be reconciled with the self-will of everyone, under the provisions of general freedom. This categorical command is l a w . It is the shield of freedom; it is true that it partly encloses my freedom, but it does so in order to give others the possibility of keeping their freedom and in order to protect my freedom from even greater limitations which would come into existence in the absence of any legal order.

The natural consequence of an act is the feeling of satisfaction experienced by the person who has accomplished this act and conversely, the result of an unworthy act must be the sense of a certain regret. It is this regret which, as the necessary result of an immoral act, constitutes punishment, either a natural punishment, revealing itself in the form of pangs of conscience or harmful consequences, or else a judicial punishment. The latter is connected not with each immoral act but only with an illegal act (revolt against the law). It meets the criminal from the will of the state and must depend on the restriction of the external freedom of the criminal. The state, in dealing out the punishment, fulfills the obligation deriving from the categorical imperative. This means that the state only punishes justly when it punishes from a feeling of obligation and quite independently of the advantages that the punishment could bring the offender or the society. Then the offender will feel that, having fallen into punishment, he has only himself to blame, since he agreed to an act which involves a punishment foreseen by the law. The state, in punishing a criminal, will not derogate the human dignity of the condemned either. Respect for human dignity is an absolute command, since Kant formulated his practical imperative in the following way:

> Act so as to use humanity both in your person, as in the person of everyone else, always as an aim, never merely as a means to an end.[98]

Kant, leaving the regulation of the inner aspect of human freedom to moral norms, submitted to the rule of law only the external accordance of the act with a moral norm, irrespective of the motives which brought about this act. (*Rechtslehre* VI, 219). Dealing with external norms, he distinguished positive law, deriving from the will of the lawmaker, from the law of nature, contained in the *a priori* principles of the consciousness. For this reason too, the law of nature is always binding, even without positive legislation. It is discovered by reason. The law of nature is the basis and ultimate instance for positive law, since even if we were to accept only positive legislation, it would in any case have to be preceded by a natural norm which would justify the authority of their lawgiver.

Under Rousseau's influence, Kant reached the conclusion that the nobility of the human being determines his value to a higher degree than his wisdom, that humanity is something supreme, for it forms the whole moral world. Towards the end of his creativity Kant declared himself for the ideal of a cosmopolitan state (*Zum ewigen Frieden,* 1795), being the synthesis for a considerable length of time of discordant elements.

On his tomb in Kalingrad (formally Królewiec and Königsberg), there is a monument with a quotation from his work:

> Two things fill my soul with ceaseless admiration and wonder: above me the starry sky and within me—the moral law.

Kant's investigations, as Jarra writes,[99] resulted in the omnipotence of the state:

> The acceptance, as in Rousseau, of the fiction of a supra-empirical will of the people in general and such a will of the individual had to lead to the conclusion that the most absolute authority of the state does not oppose the freedom of the individual, being merely an expression of his own will. The recognition of the state, on the other hand, as the representative of the command of reason, led to the fact that state authority was proclaimed as infallible; citizens owe it outright obedience, and not only an open revolt against it becomes recognized as a crime punished by death or exile, but even a doubting of its validity and a passive opposition with regard to it. Since only God has such a standpoint that is characterized by the possession of rights without any corresponding obligations, as well as the ability to apply force without having to submit to it, then the state, endowed in Kant with the above attributes, becomes recognized by him as the incarnation of the Divine idea.

These words of Jarra apply even more to Hegel. Although the latter departed far from the tradition of the law of nature, it is, however, worth indicating some moments of his theory not so much of law as of the state and society.

k) G.W.F. Hegel (1770–1831) made the most farreaching radicalization in the domain of the theory of the state and law, for he takes his point of departure from his general still youthful principles that one must make oneself aware of the absolute spirit in oneself—as the absolute idea, which manifests itself in the most varied forms, for example the world and everything that the world is. And the whole of Hegel's philosophy is precisely making oneself aware of the absolute spirit in oneself.

The method of this process of becoming self-aware is dialectic, which Hegel discovered in the process of human thought and which develops by going through oppositions: from one thought, then moving through its negation, we reach an even more specified third thought, as the synthesis for previous states of thetic and anti-thetic thought. Moreover, things themselves do not appear to us as isolated, but on the contrary, as necessarily connected. Such a state of affairs led Hegel to the concept of dialectic, in which the idea goes from thesis through antithesis to synthesis, which in turn becomes the hypothesis for a further process of development.

Thus, the absolute idea, first appearing as if in the state of inactivity, develops by passing into its antithesis and emerges in the form of matter, as a mirror, as it were, which reflects it quite unconsciously; but, on the other hand, in the stage of synthesis it emerges in a form endowed with consciousness. The Absolute becomes a being for itself, in human consciousness.

At this point Hegel emphasizes freedom, which he identifies with the idea of the will. This will also goes through a dialectical development in the form of: a) abstractive law directed at acquiring for man (oneself) things that are subject to its rule—in this way property is produced and all that it necessarily involves; b) morality, in which the individual will no longer turn towards things over which it is to rule, but towards itself, insofar as it perfects itself—and here freedom arises; c) *Sittlichkeit* (customs), in which the will changes from individual to collective and is transformed dialectically into ever higher forms: families, civil communities *(bürgerliche Gesellschaft)* and states.

In the family, the absolute spirit expresses itself in the institution of marriage, the education of children, inheritance, etc. In the life of the civic community, institutions are set up which aim at satisfying the needs of life, bringing back impaired personal law *(Rechtspflege)* and averting danger *(Polizei)* from persons and things and bringing men together into organizations (Corporations) that are to work together for specific aims.

The highest form of the absolute spirit, however, is the state, which is God in his presence. God himself lives in the state. Each state constitution is rational, for in the state as the most supreme manifestation of the spirit, only that which is rational can take place. The best form of state system, according to Hegel, is the constitutional monarchy. The value of each individual is measured by his usefulness for the state, which is an aim for itself. No law can rule above the state.

The absolute spirit does, in fact, realize itself in different national spirits and manifests itself in different states possessing unlimited sovereignty. For this reason too, there is no power which might be able to establish and solve disputable facts between states. Only war remains. War is the objective "God's judgement" between states. The victorious state is absolutely right. Thus, Hegel in practice arrived at the principle that "force is above the law." For Hegel, the most perfect state was undoubtedly the Prussian state, and the "absolute spirit" was best expressed in the spirit of the German nation. The practical consequences of such a theory were concretely expressed in the policy of Hitler's Germany...4.

4. THE REACTION AGAINST "NATURAL LAW"

As a reaction against every kind of ideal law, including the law of nature, a new tendency appeared, which recognized only positive law as being a product

of the spirit of the nation, and it explained the emergence of this law on the
model of other products of the spirit of the nation, as, for example language, or
customs. From this aspect the question: "What is law in itself, or what is it to
be?" fell away, and it was replaced by the question: "How does law
develop?"

The first ideas of the historical school appeared in the work of an opponent
of the French Revolution, Edmund Burke, an Englishman, who believed that the
state and its forms are a product of evolution and an expression of the spirit of
the nation.

a) However, the true founder and initiator of the historical school is
Frédéric Charles Savigny (1779–1861), whose pamphlet *Von Beruf
unserer Zeit für Gesetzgebung und Rechtswissenschaft*, published in 1814,
became the "credo" of the historical school. He repeated the hypotheses of this
pamphlet in his famous work *System des heutigen römischen Rechts*
(1840–1849). After the Napoleonic period and its codification of laws, there
arose in Germany a dislike of Napoleon's legislature and also for the Napoleonic
Code, which had been introduced into some German states. More and more
people demanded a return to the old law *(Rehberg),* or that there be formulated
a new universal Civil Code for the whole of Germany *(Thibaut).* Savigny's
pamphlet was aimed at refuting the arguments of this latter view. Savigny
showed that law is a result of the spirit of the nation *(Volksgeist)* and that
any will of the lawgiver which is not in accordance with a historically based
legal custom is something inferior. Savigny raised to an incredible dignity the
"spirit of the nation," which is made up of history, culture and a whole series of
elements forming precisely "the nation." His thought was adopted by Georg
Frederic Pucht (1798–1846), who, still under the influence of Schelling's
philosophy, raised Volksgeist to the status of an objective power, producing
all manifestations of culture and also law, which has its roots precisely in the
spirit of the nation, while the forms of law and evolution are defined in advance
by the nature of the national spirit. People are merely passive vehicles of the law
which they did not create.

The historical-positivistic school of law found its distinguished expression
in the works of the French theoretician of law, L. Duguit and the Austrian neo-
positivist of law, H. Kelsen.

b) Léon Duguit (1859–1928),[100] Professor of Constitutional Law
in Bordeaux, and the author of numerous works from the area of the theory of
the state and law, regarded himself as a positivist, the continuator of A. Comte's
thought, and as such he took up the standpoint of cognitive empiricism, rejecting
other sources of human cognition. Hence, the problem of the existence of God,
of the human soul and its attributes, are for him a pseudo-problem; in relation
to these problems he is an agnostic. In the domain of the theory of law he rejects

the concept of natural law, but on the other hand, wanting to give a basis for social culture, he forms the concept of a "positive system of natural law," where the "social rule" and the "legal rule" become the basis of "positive natural law."

Duguit establishes the "social rule" on the basis of an observation of facts of human individual and collective life. From this observation he reaches the conviction that the human individual can live only in society, which, if it is well-organized, can reduce much human suffering. Hence the human being, if he wants to avoid greater sufferings and live in a better way, must, in his conduct, contribute to social solidarity. Thus, the hypothetical command emerges-the social rule: "One must do everything that is in accordance with social solidarity and not do anything that is contrary to social solidarity." This kind of command does not come from any power, or from God, but is a result of the pressure of facts. Social rule appears in three forms: 1° moral rule, 2° economic rule and 3° legal rule. There is, at the same time, a different intensity of the reaction of society in the case of the breaking of one of these three rules. When a moral or an economic rule is broken, the reaction of society is weaker and disorganized, or less organized. When, on the other hand, a legal rule is broken, society reacts in an organized way. Hence the value of this rule. The feeling of social solidarity is anchored in the human being, and the awareness of a social bond provides the basis for a greater reaction. In every person there exist two tendencies—an individual and a social one. Guarding the harmony of these two tendencies is precisely the social rule. The social rule, particularly important for human life, becomes a legal rule, and when it is transgressed we already encounter a specific social reaction. The social rule takes on the form of particular laws (legal rules), depending on what, in a given society in its majority, is regarded as particularly important for social life. Any positive law which would be contrary to the "legal rule" is only an apparent law and has no binding power. If, however, most of society recognizes that a social rule of some kind should become a legal rule, then quantity and strength (mass) is the determinant factor for the fact of a legal norm coming into being.

c) H a n s   K e l s e n,[101] the founder of the neo-positivist Viennese school of law takes his point of departure in his philosophy of law from the theory of cognition. Cognition is not merely reception; it has a creative nature. It is, at the same time, relative. Relativism is the consequence of his positivistic standpoint. The relativism of cognition is to justify the rejection of metaphysics, although Kelsen himself declares himself in favor of monism, together with a negation of divine transcendence. He considers that any transcendence is a result of the dualistic tendency in the human being, according to which we dualize the world, we dualize reality, we dualize value. The visible world is to be a reflection of the invisible world; values realized here on earth are to be a reflection of higher values; we form for ourselves a concept of God on the model of a concept of the state etc. Kelsen believes that the dualistic tendency in metaphysics is as erroneous as the whole of metaphysics. The only reality is the world as a whole, and the spirit of the individual is only an integral part of the spirit of the world. Kelsen called this pantheizing trend of his *die wissenschaftlich-kritische Weltanschauung.*

Legal problems in Kelsen are examined from the logical and formal points of view, as statements of duty of the same type as hypothetical statements: "If A occurs, then B ought to occur." If, therefore, an actual state occurs, for example when somebody has committed a robbery or a murder, then a legal consequence should follow: the murderer or robber should be appropriately punished. Thus, the legal norm connects the actual state with the legal consequence. Kelsen calls this connection between the legal consequence and the actual state a "r e c k o n i n g" or "settling of accounts."

Kelsen, under the influence of one of his pupils, Merkel, drew attention to the hierarchical nature of legal norms; he called this phenomenon *S t u f e n b a u d e s   R e c h t s* (a graded construction of law). In connection with this he posed the question: What is the ultimate cause for which constitution, as the highest norm of positive law, has binding power?

In response to this question he accepted the Kantian distinction into the domain of being *(S e i n)* and the domain of duty *(S o l l e n)*. Between the domains of being and duty there are no points of contact. From this it also follows that reality cannot be a basis for the binding power of law, since it belongs to the domain of duty. The only basis for law is the immanent domain of duty. Kelsen therefore accepts the hypothesis of the existence of a fundamental norm, *G r u n d n o r m,* which goes like this: "authority should be obeyed." He justifies this *G r u n d n o r m* by the fact that if we did not accept this norm then we would not be able to explain to ourselves anything in the domain of social duty. Thus, it is the highest norm and all others depend on it, for if we cannot base the domain of duty on the domain of reality, then we must base it on the fundamental hypothetical norm, which precisely declares that authority should be obeyed. Of course, accepting such a norm as fundamental, we recognize at the same time the omnipotence of the state, and this fact favors totalitarian and fascist interpretations of law.

d) T h e   t h e o r y   o f   "l e g a l   p s y c h e" as the first source of law, is closely connected to XIXth century psychologism, in which there appeared tendencies towards the elimination of the sciences and the replacement of them by psychology, in a broad sense, as the most general humanistic-natural science. According to Jarra[102] in opposition to theories attributing an artificial-conventional beginning to law, this theory sees, in a primal sign, a psychic property of the human being. Jarra connects this concept with historical positivism. He writes that the founder of the historical school, Savigny, proved that there exists an organic link between law and the nature of a nation; it develops with the character of the nation and disappears with it. The disciple and continuator of Savigny, Puchta, fell into legal mysticism, according to which law has a subsistent being in the depth of the national spirit, and becomes apparent in the form of customary law.

According to this concept, for a long time before conscious legislative activity developed, there already existed elements of law which satisfied the needs of primitively associated people. In this sense, therefore, law is the natural product of man's natural psyche, living collectively; it develops and changes depending on the conditions of social being.

L. Petrażycki made a deeper analysis of the theory of legal psyche. He too sought causal dependencies of the domain of legal occurrences in the psyche of people becoming aware of the fact that someone is obliged to do something and that something is due to someone from someone else. Such experiences exist, not only in organized societies, states, but also in gangs of people, and even in the area of children's games.

> As a result of investigations [Petrażycki] recognized these particularly legal experiences as certain wholes, in which so-called emotions play a fundamental part. Emotion—as apprehended by him—for example appetite, anger, fear, is a dual experience, a passive-active one, being on the one hand a certain passion (that is being acted upon), and on the other hand having the nature of an attractive drive (towards something) or a repulsive drive (away from something). Petrażycki imagined the legal phenomenon as the coming together of an awareness of specific situations between people and of a particular impulse towards establishing what is due to whom. Actions motivated by particular emotions are causally connected, according to Petrażycki, with precisely these emotions.[103]

In Petrażycki's view:

> law ... is a particular psychic factor of social life and acts psychically. Its action first of all consists in arousing or explaining the motives behind different factors and abandoned attempts (the motivational or impulsive action of law), secondly, in stabilizing and developing certain tendencies and features of the human character and in weakening and condemning others, in a word, in educating the social psyche in the direction that is appropriate to the character and the content of prevalent legal norms (the educative action of law). ... The system of legal norms binding at any given moment constitutes a transitory stage of social education and should be, as its educative function is fulfilled, replaced by another system of legal, motivational and educative action, adjusted to the already attained level of social psyche. The ideal is to attain a perfectly socialized character, the total rule of active charity among people.[104]

As to the foundations of law apprehended in this way, as well as its essential nature, Petrażycki outlines a method of political-legal thinking:

> The fundamental method of political-legal thinking is psychological deduction—conclusions drawn from psychological premises which are appropriate with respect to psychic consequences—motivational and educative ones—which should call forth the activity of certain legal principles and institutions, or else as to those legislative means which can bring about certain desired psychic consequences-motivational and educative ones.[105] ... As the proper and only possible mode of observation of legal occurrences, the method of self-observation, that is, introspection, should be recognized.[106]

> The introspective method—both self-observational and ordinary and experimental—constitutes not only the only means of observation and cognition of legal (and moral) phenomena in a direct and credible way, but at the same time a means without which any cognition of legal (and moral) phenomena whatsoever is impossible.[107]

The concept of legal psyche is merely a one-sided attempt at explaining the emergence of the legal system. Without doubt, law appears in the psyche, in which we become aware of its content. Law, however, is something objective, just as the objects of our cognition are objective, which also appear in the psyche. The fact that law appears in the psyche, however, is not yet an ultimate solution, since the appearance of law in the psyche is a subjective manifestation—the reflection of something that exists objectively beyond the psyche.

An attempt to reduce law and legal phenomena to passive-active emotions is the explanation of something that is of its nature rational by something that is of its nature irrational, and in consequence would lead to the negation of the essential nature of law as something objectively binding. On the other hand, the human psychological make-up is also something natural; it is a defined nature. To appeal to man's psychological make-up is then to refer to man's nature, and at the same time to stop mid-way, since it is man's psyche in the cognitive aspect which acts in such a way that it is directed by the contents of things apprehended cognitively but objectively real. Even the application of the somewhat naive method of introspection already reveals the connection between our consciousness and the state of things with nature, and therefore with nature as it is traditionally conceived.

As a result, then, various rational attempts at showing the sources of law lead to the revelation of the natural arrangement of things and to human reason, capable of interpreting the objective content of precisely this arrangement. All this means that reference is made to the natural necessitating sources ultimately directing (or influencing the direction) of human conduct.

The alternative to natural sources of law can only be the irrational command, the will, which does not mean that it is an a-rational command!

e) Thus, the complement and only alternative in relation to the concept of natural law is the theory of l e g a l   v o l u n t a r i s m,[108] according to which law owes its coming into existence to the w i l l of a principal head of society. This theory, which is accessible to the imagination of a simple man, has its long history, and to a certain extent is connected with the previously presented concept of the direct intervention of a god in the making of a law and also with the later concept of natural law, for usually the chief of the society would "reveal" the law, which was to be an expression of the will of the god himself. In earlier times the chief of the society himself had in himself something of divine authority or was even regarded as the incarnation of a god; he was "divine himself." Thus, the will of the chief of society was recognized as the concrete revelation of the law binding a given society. This conviction found expression in the principle of the Roman principate: *quod principi placuit, legis habet vigorem* (Gaius. *Inst.* I 2, 6), or in the formulas with which laws given by monarchs were provisioned: *car tel est nôtre plaisir.*

We find the philosophical justification of voluntarism in those authors who, basing their investigations on an appropriately understood concept of natural law, justified the passage from the state of a primitive society to a society with a chief authority by legislative privileges belonging by their nature to authority. For example in T. Hobbes, who though he sees in the state the result of an agreement, apprehends the agreement itself as the deprivation of sovereign rights of the individual in favor of the social sovereign; the latter, from the moment he assumes authority is absolute master, and his will—*voluntas summi imperantis;* the will of the sovereign—is the only source of law. Here, however, there immediately appears the varied context of the voluntaristic explanation. Is the will blind or rational? Is law binding because it is merely the command of a blind will?

NOTES

Chapter I. LAW IN GENERAL

A. The Theoretical Aspect

[1] I apprehend end and object interchangeably here, on account of the pre-scientific description of the phenomenon of activity. Of course, end or *telos* in the strict sense is the motive, which releases activity; object, on the other hand, is connected with the physical fact of activity, which terminates in some being.

[2] Cf. Levi-Strauss on this subject, *Natural Right and History*, Chicago and London, 1953, chapter III.

[3] On the subject of nature and its apprehension, particularly in Aristotle, cf. F. Solmsen: *Aristotle's system of the Physical World*, New York, 1960, pp. 92–117.

[4] "The nature of being"—its structure, its substance. Cf. on this subject my work: *Arystotelesowska koncepcja substancji*, Lublin, 1966, pp. 47–61.

[5] E. Jarra, *Ogólna teoria prawa* (A General Theory of Law), Warsaw, 1922, p. 118.

[6] *"HO GAR NOMOS TAXIS,"* Polit. IV 4. 1326.

[7] Cf. on this subject L. Bender, *Philosophia Juris* (The Philosophy of Law), Rome, 1947, pp. 63–78.

[8] Ibid. p. 66 ff.

[9] Aristotle. *Eth. N.* (Nichomachean Ethics) c. I. 1129b–1130. Cf. on the subject of *"debitum"* the comments of St. Thomas in *Contra Gentiles* II c. 28–29.

[10] The only possible answer is a negative one, for morality, as we shall later discuss, is connected with the experience of the person as a being for another "you."

[11] On the subject of relations, cf. my work: *Metaphysics*, pp. 304–312.

[12] The word "categorial" refers to one of Aristotle's categories and is to be distinguished from the Kantian "categorical" which has the implication of necessity.

[13] An individual in relation to other persons is the special subject of reflections in the next chapter.

[14] In E. Jarra's concept, morality is conceived as a particular indication of consciousness (E. Jarra, *A General Theory of Law,* Warsaw, 1922, p. 125), which of course is a simplification of the problem under the influence of XIXth century psychologism.

[15] I shall discuss the subject of "common good" below in the next chapter.

[16] This "binding power" is the characteristic of duty itself, for duty, characterizing the legal relation, is a special type of moral bond, conditioned by the structure of personal being and common good.

[17] Potentialization, that is, the dynamization of man's personal being, flows mainly from material conditions of be-ing.

[18] Assuming a standpoint of cognitive realism and accepting a transcendentalizing mode of cognition, we must recognize that there exists an objective arrangement of things and that there exists an objective hierarchy of being and good (real values). This means that in the order of being and good there exists an objective gradation, which the human reason can discern, and that not everything is to be reduced to a "subjective" point of view and subjective estimates. If, on the other hand, being and good are interchangeable, this means that the hierarchy of good corresponds to the ontic hierarchy. In consequence, the First Being, the Absolute, as the real reason of all beings, is at the same time the ultimate end of all striving towards a goal; that is, it is precisely objective, real Good.

[19] Cf. St. Thomas' analyses in his *Summa Theologiae*, 1a2ae q. 1, 2 and 3. All St. Thomas' articles and analyses constitute a "Magna Charta" of the sense of human life.

[20] The contents of legal norms are generally laid down by human beings; a legal norm itself, however, in its normativity, is already the contentual aspect of law as a relation of duty.

[21] Here we must, nevertheless, take into account all that has been said in section 2 of this chapter on the subject of "subjective law."

[22] These reflections are fundamentally drawn from the content of St. Thomas' solutions from *Summa Theologiae,* 1a2ae, 90.

[23] On this subject, see below, where the history of the concept of natural law is discussed.

[24] F. Suarez, *De Legibus*, London, 1679, c. 5.

[25] The analyses carried out should not, however, suggest an absolutization of aspects, for it is ultimately a person who is the author of a concrete legal norm, which, nevertheless "is justified" by the acting of reason, and not merely blind will.

[26] The problem mentioned here concerning how legal norms can have binding power when at the same time attainment of the Good has been in some way conditioned, is unusually important and is the key to a rational, human mode of existence, in the case where the individual finds himself or herself in various situations of coercion.

[27] On this basis the "competence" and authenticity of authority is and must be interpreted in a very wide sense.

[28] Cf. J. Kalinowski, *Teoria poznania praktycznego* (The Theory of Practical Cognition) Lublin, 1960, p. 9ff.

[29] J. Kalinowski, *Querelle de la science normative* (A Dispute on Normative Science), Paris, 1969.

[30] Ibid., p. 151.

[31] R. Ingarden, *Spór o istnienie świata* (A Dispute on the Existence of the World), Vol. 1, Warsaw, 1961, p. 97.

[32] All these "states," however, constitute an appropriate set of characteristics of the order of content, but they do not constitute a cognitive apprehension of really existing beings. Moreover, the expressions "really" and "existing" are also an appropriate "endowment" of quality–content in the language convention. Of course I am disputing at this point the interpretations of the phenomenologists.

[33] Between thinking (as a mainly post-Cartesian heritage) and cognition, there is the difference that thinking is a diverse "operation on the senses" already previously cognized, whereas cognition is a particular, precisely cognitive (primary reason) contact with the thing. Cognition embraces three spheres: the thing denoted, formal signs (aspectively apprehended senses of things) as well as the conventional signs of which language itself consists. I have discussed the subject of cognition more extensively in the work *I—Man; An Outline of Philosophical Anthropology,* New Britain, Connecticut, Mariel Production, 1983.

[34] J. Kalinowski presented comments, rightly and searchingly, on this subject in his *Querelle* (A Dispute), p. 113.

[35] Intentional being, in this interpretation, is characterized by the consequitive moments: non-subsistence, derivation, non-actuality. Such an object, though built by intentional acts of the consciousness, cannot be said to be a mere nothing, for it can be the object of truth judgements, which are inter-subjectively accessible; it can be concretized at the hand of the receiver and this concretization can be both cognitive and aesthetic. All this is right with the exception of some "be-ing," even the weakest. Be-ing derives merely from existence, and this existence is the existence exclusively of the subject. "Objective existence" is pure absurdity.

[36] I am expressing myself vaguely here, but we know from the context that "acts of cognition" refer to psychocognitive operations, to the extent that these are an emanation of the subject, coming into contact with the cognitive object in the cognitive process. We could call them "intentional acts."

[37] Earlier—already in the Scholastic period—scientists were aware, in a problem partly imposing itself, that *a posse ad esse non valet illatio* (there is no passage from possible states to real states). And precisely cognitive, universal contents (the sense of things) constituted the *"posse,"* as each universal concept "constitutes merely a potential state (precisely—not completely explained)" of the real contents of things. Kant, for noetical reasons (formal apriorism), negated the possibility of a cognitive apprehension of being in itself.

[38] As can be seen from the context, the cognitive act (that is, intentional act), p r e s e n t s the content of a thing. We cannot separate "empty intentional acts" from the content of things, for there do not exist some kind of "empty," "intentional acts," some kind of "nonbeings," on which "we hang" subjects, contents, "beings." Only in the works of some philosophers do such descriptions occur, causing very grave harm, for there are no themes in abstraction from the cognitive act, that is, from intentional acts which construct these themes.

[39] Cf. my article on this subject: "Intencjonalny charakter kultury" (The Intentional Nature of Culture) in *Logos i Ethos* (Logos and Ethos) Cracow, 1971, pp. 203–218.

[40] As has already been mentioned, non-subjective existence is equivalent to the acceptance of purely objective existence, and this is bound up in contradictions, otherwise we accept the equivocity of the term "existence." And generally precisely this expressly accepted equivocity became the cause of misunderstandings in this matter.

[41] But this does not mean that we reduce intentional being to psychic experiences. In this matter I completely agree with what Kalinowski wrote in *Querelle* (A Dispute), pp. 124–130.

[42] If contents "existed" because they are contents—the passage *a posse ad esse* would exist, and it would be sufficient to think about something in order for it to be realized. Or else we apprehend reality in a radically different way from commonsense data.

[43] Having in mind the essential distinction between universalizing language and transcendentalizing language, I would suggest completing the valuable and accurate analyses that Kalinowski made in *Querelle de la science normative* (A Dispute on Normative Science).

[44] More extensively on this subject: Krąpiec, *Teoria analogii bytu* (The Theory of the Analogy of Being), Lublin, 1959, part II.

[45] In the work mentioned, he takes into account above all the legal norm of positive law.

B. THE HISTORICAL ASPECT

[46] The very expression "natural law" is so ambiguous that its proper sense can be deciphered basically only in a historical context, when we take into consideration the theories of various thinkers. It becomes apparent that, in accordance with the various conceptions of "nature," we can apprehend "natural law" in various ways. And there are about twenty meanings of the term "nature," as Ph. Delhaye established in the introduction to his work *Permanence du droit naturel* (Permanence of Natural Law), Louvain 1967, p. 21. Depending on whether we regard "nature" as some (internal or external) factor of things or as the thing–object itself, various meanings of the word "nature" appear.

For instance, "nature" as the factor of things may be:
1. what the thing becomes – historical nature;
2. from the outside, ultimately, the creative factor is God,
3. or the non-ultimate is another nature giving birth.

Of the internal factors we should mention:
4. the essence of things, or that which has commonly been called strictly "nature," being the source of activity.
5. Sometimes the name nature was given to the internal component of things, that is matter,
6. or form,
7. or their combination. Combined matter and form is
8. a being in itself,
9. or substance.

"Nature" was used to denote some kind of things–objects, for example the universe, human being, God. Consequently:

10. sometimes nature is the universe (cosmos),
11. or the aggregate of created beings,
12. or that which can be created,
13. or some kind of material nature,
14. or the object of the natural sciences, and even:
15. all that which is cognizable by the senses.
16. God was also called Nature, insofar as He was set in opposition to the order of grace.
17. And that which comes from human instinct was called nature, although:
18. there were cases that nature was that which flows from reason and reflection, and:
19. there were times when the particular nature of the human being and its personal mode of reacting was designated by the word "nature."

Meanings of this kind formed against the background of different philosophical schools in the work of various authors; only some will be presented here.

[47] I do not intend to present here contemporary trends from the area of the theory of natural law. They are to a great extent a stronger emphasis on some aspects of theories already known. Opałek and Wróblewski (*Współczesna teoria*, p. 28) carry out a polemic with some modern interpretations of natural law, and at the same time in a particular way systematize: 1. the dynamic theory of J. Wilde's law of nature; 2. F.S.C. Nortrope's philosophical and anthropological theory; 3. C.L. Fuller's eunomy; 4. E. Cohn's psychological theory of the law of nature.

Besides, Opałek and Wróblewski do not deal with those interpretations of natural law which are connected with the concept of the Absolute: "We consciously exclude the whole group of theories of natural law which draw norms of just law from 'indirect or direct' acts of some higher essence. ... The basic methodological problematic has not undergone any change from the point of view of assumptions of criticism on which we rely in our work. It is widely known in connection with the criticism of the religious world–view. ..." Dynamic or philosophical and anthropological interpretations do not exclude the problem of God but they stress merely some aspects in the explanation of the world and phenomenon of law.

[48] I take up a strictly philosophical standpoint here, and not a theological one, in the sense of theology as the interpretation of the facts of Revelation.

[49] As W. Jaeger rightly observed, in *Die Theologie der frühen griechischen Denker* (The Theology of the Early Greek Thinkers) Stuttgart, 1953, p. 11, ancient philosophy is a particular rationalization of mythology; it is an evolution from *THESEI THEOI* to *PHYSEI THEOS*. This can easily be remarked on the example of the theory of natural law, which in the ancient world attained its culmination in Stoicism and Stoic concepts of the natural law.

[50] The formation of this group of conceptions of natural law is determined by the essential concept of being, fundamentally a common heritage of the center mentioned here. Moreover, such a concept of reality is connected inseparably with the concept of universalizing rather than transcendentalizing cognition. Human cognition, in a

universalizing aspect, exhausts itself in conceptual material: *a specie specialissima ad genus generalissimum.* The essentialist trend attained its highest formulation in Duns Scotus and Suarez.

[51] Descartes himself was fundamentally the catalyst of this standpoint and the person who expressed it in the most emphatic way; these tendencies, however, already appeared at an earlier period and in various cultural fields.

[52] A better understanding of the theories differing from the school of natural law requires the consideration of the very concepts of natural law, and in this sense, it is against the background of conceptions of natural law that varied, distinct concepts of the philosophy of law are built up. And therefore the concepts of the German Idealist philosophers and the representatives of positivism have been taken into account.

[53] Cf. note 48 above.

[54] Facts on the subject of ancient views are contained in the monographs on the subject of the history of philosophical thought, especially in the work of Ueberweg and Heinze, *Grundriß der Geschichte der Philosophie* (Outline of the History of Philosophy), 14th ed. Basel, 1957; A. Krokiewicz, *Zarys filozofii greckiej; od Talesa do Platona* (Outline of Greek Philosophy; from Thales to Plato), Warsaw, 1971; E. Jarra, *Historia filozofii prawa* (A History of the Philosophy of Law), Warsaw, 1923.

[55] As W. Jaeger rightly observes in *Paideia*, Warsaw, 1962, vol. 1, p. 177: "It would be difficult to mark out in history the line from which rational thinking begins: it would certainly already run through the Homeric epic, but the mixing of rational elements with 'mythical thinking' reaches so deeply that it is probably not possible at all to delimit them. ... The Ionian philosophy of nature draws directly on the epic."

But not only in the work of the Ionians do we find links with mythical beliefs; we also encounter them in Plato and Aristotle. "We still encounter the truest mythology in the basic philosophical concepts of Plato and Aristotle, as in the Platonic myth about souls, or in the Aristotelian doctrine that things love the immovable element which puts the whole world in motion." (Ibid.) Philosophical reflection, besides, could not arise and develop independently of other domains of literature, of politics and concrete life, first in villages, and then in the *"polis."*

It is commonly believed that the point of departure for philosophical and scientific thought is the discovery of "nature," that is, *"physis."* And although this *physis* was initially connected with the whole, with the question about the beginning of all things, nevertheless, the very appearance of the concept of nature derives from social-legal experiences. *Physis* was initially connected with the whole because in the Greek conception *"physis,"* the question about the beginning of all things, which bids us to go beyond the area of matters given to us in sensory experience forms a still indivisible whole, together with the attempt at embracing all that arose from this first source and now exists (*ta onta*) by means of collecting the concrete data of experience (histories). It was precisely this problem that was presented in a penetrating way by Lévi-Strauss, *Natural Right and History,* Chicago and London, 1953.

[56] Cicero, *De Legibus* (On Laws), 11. 4.

[57] For example Jarra, *Ogólna teoria prawa* (A General Theory of Law), p. 153.

[58] W. Jaeger, *Paideia.*

[59] Ibid.

[60] Ibid.

[61] Plato, *The Republic.*

[62] Cf. J. Wild, *Plato's Modern Enemies and the Theory of Natural Law,* Chicago, 1953.

[63] Compare, on this subject, the monograph of L. Lachance: *Le concept de droit selon Aristote et St. Thomas* (The Concept of Law according to Aristotle and St. Thomas), Montreal, 1933. The author excessively connects into one whole the theory of Aristotle and St. Thomas, for although many formulations sound exactly the same, nevertheless, the general climate and concept of being, as well as the concept of man in Aristotle and St. Thomas are different. As a result of this, the interpretation of even identically sounding formulations is rather different. However, the material concerning the theory of law, collected by Lachance, is excellent and is always highly informative.

[64] *Politics,* I 11. 1253a.

[65] Aristotle, *Nichomachean Ethics,* V 10. 1139b.

[66] Lévi-Strauss, *Natural Right and History*, Chicago and London, 1953, p. 148.

[67] Aristotle, *Politics.* I 4. 1252a.

[68] *Natura ius est, quid non opinio genuit, sed quaedam in natura vis insevit, ut religionem, pietatem, gratiam, vindicationem, veritatem. De Repub.,* Bk. II c. 53. 161.

[69] *Sequitur, ut eadem sit in iis, quae humano in genere, ratio, eadem veritas utrobique sit eadem lex, quae est recti praeceptio, pravique depulsio. De nat. deorum,* Bk., IIc. 31. 79.

[70] *Soli enim ratione utentes iure ac lege vivunt.* Ibid., c. 62. 154.

[71] *Quod honestum sit, id solum bonum esse. De finibus bonor. et mal.* c. 1.

[72] *Iustitia autem praecipit parcere omnibus, consulere generi hominum, suum cuique reddere, sacra, publica, aliena non tangere. De Repub.,* Bk. IIIc. 15. 24.

[73] *Est quidem vera lex recta ratio, naturae congruens, diffusa in omnes, constans, sempiterna, quae vocet ad officium iubendo, vetandum a fraude deterreat, quae tamen neque probus frustra iubet aut vetat, nec improbos iubendo aut vetando movet. Huic legi nec abrogari eas est, neque derogari ex hac aliquid licet, neque tota abrogari potest; nec vero aut per senatum aut per populum solvi hac lege possumus: neque est quaerendus explanator aut interpres eius alius: nec erit alia Romae, alia Athenis, alia nunc, alia posthac; sed et omnes gentes, et omni tempore, una lex et sempiterna et immutabilis continebit, unusque erit communis quasi magister et imperator omnium deus; ille legis huius inventor, disceptator, lator, cui qui non parebit ipse se fugiet, ac naturam hominis aspernatus, hoc ipso luet maximas poenas, etiam si cetera supplicia, quae putantur effugerit.* Ibid., Bk. IIIc. 23. 33.

[74] *Igitur doctissimis veris proficisci placuit a lege, audacio an recte, si modo, ut iidem definiunt, lex est ratio summa insita in natura, quae iubet ea, quae facienda sunt, prohibetque contraria. Eadem ratio quae est in hominibus mente confirmata et confecta, lex est. De Legibus,* Bk. I c. 6. 18).

[75] *Haec habemus in XII sane secundum naturam quae norma legis est.* Ibid., Bk. II c. 4. 10.

[76] *Ecquid ergo primum mutis tribuemus beluis? non enim mediocris viri, sed maximi et docti, Pythagoras et Empedocles, unam omnium animantium condicionem iuris esse denuntiant clamantque enexpiabilis poenas impendere iis, a quibus violatum sit animal. De Repub.,* Bk. III c. 11. 19.

Principio generi animantium omni est a natura tributum, ut se, vitam corpusque tueatur, declinet ea, quae nocitura videantur, omniaque quae sint ad vivendum necessaria, acquirat et paret, ut pastum, ut latibula, ut alia generis eiusdem. Commune etiam animantium omnium est coniunctionis adpetitus procreandi causa et cura quaedam eorum, quae procreata sint; sed inter hominem et beluam hoc maxime interest, quod haec tantum, quantum sensu movetur, ad id solum, quod adest quodque praesens est, se accommodat paulum admodum sentiens praeteritum aut futurum; homo autem, quod rationis est particeps, per quam consequentia cernit, causas rerum videt earumque praegressas et quasi antecessiones non ignorat, similitudines comparat praesentibus adiungit adnectit futuras facile totius vitae videt ad eamque degendem praeparat res necessarias. De Off., p. 4. 11.

[77] *... sunt namque ideae principiales formae quadam vel rationes rerum stabiles atque incommutabiles, quae ipsae formatae non sunt, ac hoc aeterna ac eodem modo sese habentes, quae in divina intelligentia continentur; et cum ipsae neque oriantur neque intereant, secundum eas tamen formari dicitur omne, quod oriri et interire potest et omne, quod oritur et interit. De diversis quest.,* q. 46 de ideis 2.

[78] St. Augustine writes: *singula igitur proprius sunt creata rationibus,* ibid., q. 46, 2 and that is why É. Gilson and Ph. Böhner (*The History of Christian Philosophy*) comment: "Augustine certainly never doubted that each human individual has its separate idea in God's mind." It does not appear, however, that this concept of the individual idea, where man is concerned, modifies his theory of legal obligation in the direction of analogical obligation, since Augustine did not have an elaborated theory of God's creative cognition through ideas. This was to be the work of St. Thomas, as we shall discuss in the next chapter.

[79] St. Augustino, *De libero arbitrio,* c. VI.

[80] É. Gilson, *The Spirit of Medieval Philosophy.*

[81] St. Augustine, *De Caveat. Dei,* II 22.

[82] Gilson, as above, p. 307.

[83] *S.th.,* 1a2ae, 90, I.

[84] Gilson, as above. Gilson also wrote in his *A History of Christian Philosophy:* "From this point of view, each particular thing has a two-fold existence—one in itself, the other in its own Divine Idea. In God the thing is God, just as a work of art is merely the artist himself as long as it exists merely in his mind. The thing created in itself is exclusively the copy of its model in God, just as a work of art is exclusively an approximation of what the artist had in mind when he was creating. This comment refers not only to species but also to each individual as an individual. For instance, every person has his idea in God." The last two Gilson's sentences are not equally correct. How can this be that individuals as well as species have their own ideas? Whether only individual human beings have their ideas but a sort of people does not?

[85] On this subject cf. É. Gilson, *L'être et l'essence* (Being and Essence), Paris, 1948, pp. 121–150.

[86] Cf. Jarra, *Historia filozofii prawa* (A History of the Philosophy of Law), pp. 135–138.

[87] H. Grotius, *De iure belli ac pacis,* II c. I cf. 10 n. I.

[88] Cf. E. Krzymuski, *Historia filozofii prawa* (A History of the Philosophy of Law), Cracow, 1923, p. 57; K. Opałek, *Prawo natury u polskich fizjokratów* (The Law of Nature in the Work of the Polish Physiocrats), Warsaw, 1953.

[89] Brief facts about particular representatives of the school of natural law are included in various works from the area of the history of the philosophy of law. I give them here as an illustration of the problem.

[90] F. Stahl, *Geschichte der Rechtsphilosophie* (A History of the Philosophy of Law), 1956, p. 167, quoted after A. Periatkowicz, *Filozofia Prawa J.J. Rousseau* (J.J. Rousseau's Philosophy of Law), Cracow, 1913, p. 99. Discussing Rousseau's concept I fundamentally base my discussion on precisely this monograph.

[91] Grotius, *On the Law of War and Peace,* as quoted above.

[92] As above, p. 128.

[93] As above, p. 133.

[94] Rousseau, *Contrat Social* (The Social Contract), I 6. Quoted after Peretiatkowicz, as above, p. 133.

[95] As above.

[96] As above, p. 136.

[97] Cf. Jarra, *Historia filozofii prawa* (A History of the Philosophy of Law), p. 177. The author notes: "Montesquieu, instead of following the example of his contemporaries and deriving law from reason, as an absolute and fixed principle, examines it in the context of historical reality and on this basis he is the first to categorically state its changeability and relativity, as results of the influence of physical and psychic conditions. ..."

[98] I. Kant, *The Foundation of the Metaphysics of Morals.* This practical imperative departs from Kant's ethical formalism and has heterogeneous sources.

[99] E. Jarra, *Historia filozofii prawa* (A History of the Philosophy of Law), p. 176.

[100] I present L. Duguit's theory on the basis of the work: J. Kalinowski. *Teoria reguły społecznej i reguły prawnej Leona Duguit* (The Theory of the Social Rule and Legal Rule of Leo Duguit), Lublin, 1949.

[101] I present H. Kelsen's theory after C. Martyniak, *Moc obowiązująca prawa a teoria Kelsena* (The Binding Power of Law and Kelsen's Theory), Lublin, 1938.

[102] Cf. Jarra, *Ogólna teoria prawa* (A General Theory of Law), p. 155.

[103] T. Kotarbiński, *Wstęp* (Introduction) in L. Petrażycki, *Wstęp do nauki prawa i moralności* (Introduction to the Science of Law and Morality), Warsaw, 1959, p. 8.

[104] L. Petrazycki, *Wstep do nauki prawa i moralnosci,* (Introduction to the Science of Law and Morality), Warsaw, 1959, p. 14ff.

[105] As above, p. 16.

[106] As above, p. 61.

[107] As above, p. 106.

[108] When we draw attention to the fact that legal norms are norms because they are the work of the reason, then at the same time we must admit that the functioning of the reason presupposes being, a natural arrangement of things and persons. This natural arrangement of things and persons, interpreted by the human reason, becomes the objective foundation of interpreting that which, in the thing itself (nature), is a good. And then, affirming the proper activity of the reason, we are fundamentally in the area of natural law, commanding us to do good. If, on the other hand, some "good" is recognized as a good because this was imposed *(bonum – quia imperatum; malum – quia prohibitum),* we find ourselves in the area of voluntarism. For this reason too, legal voluntarism can be recognized as the only opponent of natural law.

Chapter II

THE ANALOGICAL STRUCTURE
OF REALITY

1. PERSON AND THE WORLD

a) Existence

Although the human being "discovered" the universe long ago, in the VIIth century B.C.,[1] this was only the beginning of discovery and this process has not ended at all, both for the whole of humanity and for the particular individual. The universe—the world of beings—in which humanity is immersed and has its natural environment of be-ing, also constitutes the natural and at the same time the first object of cognition, which is the fundamental expression of human existence.[2]

Here it is not a question of a Heideggerian "existential," "involuntary casting of the person into the world" or being immersed in this same world, an immersion, which, being human, is manifested in speech, as the fundamental expression of existence, for the "expressing" of the individual by speech, even apprehended in the widest sense, is already a result of the more primeval connection of the humans with the world and its fundamental nature. Now the first knot tying man and woman to the world (in the specifically human sense) is cognition of the world; precisely cognition, and not "self-expression," not "thinking." All this is something further. And not cognition itself as an isolated fact, apprehended for itself, but a cognition of the world. And when we affirm the fact that we do know the world, it is not a question of universal, exhausting cognition, of precise cognition, but rather of cognizing the world as the beginning of a process of conscious being, and thereby also of being a human.

The process of cognizing the world, and thereby of cognizing oneself and of making oneself aware of oneself is extremely drawn out in the history of mankind, and it abounds in the most varied adventures, not only intellectual ones, but ones integrally connected with life, interwoven with cognitive, volitive and emotional experiences, woven out of truth and error, successes and failures, in a word, of all that constitutes the content of human life.

Something that is, however, prior to human life, is that which such life conditions in many ways: the world itself as the most widely and most deeply apprehended "human environment," that is, that which to a large extent is for humans their "reason for being." The world, reality, b e i n g , which is primarily given to us, are something not only genetically prior to the human being, but also precedes human experience epistemologically. This means that we cognize the world before we cognize ourselves and that the reason for cognizing ourselves and our most important matters is our cognition (of course correct and as little distorted as possible)[3] of the world itself, as a reality primary in relation to ourselves. That is why before making analyses of the foundations of moral human conduct, before an analysis of natural law, even before a reflection on the subject of the human being, the nature of human cognition, we must first become aware of the ontic nature of reality, of which we are a "part" that can fundamentally be understood on the basis of the general structure of reality.[4]

As we are born in the world and acquire not only consciousness but also self-consciousness on the basis of our "being-in-the-world," we experience ceaselessly and primarily that the world (as a reality) e x i s t s . The existence of the world (reality) is something absolutely primordial in all our human, above all cognitive, experiences, for in each real human experience connected with the content of being, existence is given to us primarily as a foundation of reality (often so evident that it is invisible, that is, it does not rivet our attention, although it can always be discerned). This existence of reality (a facticity which strikes us unceasingly) is precisely fundamentally that which we call b e i n g . It is on account of the e x i s t e n c e (fact) of things that something is really real; something is a being.[5] It is true that, fascinated by different contents of experienced reality, we pay more attention to the content itself rather than to its existential aspect (its fact—the fact that it exists) so that we tend to give the name "being" to each cognized content (what is more, we sometimes assign this name to some least real, abstracted content, which is often merely non-contradiction). Nonetheless, primarily being is e x i s t i n g content; an e x i s t i n g concrete (reality) in a really existing world.[6]

Primarily, therefore, to be a real being means to exist as a concrete individual content determined in itself. Content itself, on the other hand, abstracted from existence, is already a cognitive construct, that is, something derivative and more distant, produced by the human mind. It is precisely in the process of abstraction that we are capable of grasping a thing from some perspective and restricting ourselves to a cognitive contact with merely some attributes of the thing, even schematic ones, in abstraction from the rich context of realities which remains. First, however, the world "imposes itself" on us from the fact of its existence, which we can constantly check in ourselves. Besides, if it were otherwise, human life itself would not be possible, since it would not be known which contents are real and which are abstracted, that is, possibly false, as the result of a mental and psychic recasting.

The ascertaining of the fact that reality exists (that is the affirmation, in the most fundamental sense, of being) is spontaneously performed in us in an act of intellectual cognition, which is called an act of judgement, with the qualification that what we are dealing with here is a specific judgement, the so-called existential judgement, which possesses various degrees of cognitive intensity: from the simple prehension (grasp) that something (some thing) exists, that it is, which prehension is interwoven into the entire process of knowledge, to the formal existential judgement, as a separate cognitive act. The latter may be immediate, or even mediate as when, as the result of philosophical justifications I can state that, there exists, for example, God, although this is not given to me either in primary intellectual or sensory-intellectual experience.[7]

At the same time that I affirm that reality exists (the ascertaining of being) I am also, in a primordial way, given a very vague cognition of content as of the other aspect of reality, as the correlate of existence, for if I experience (and affirm) that reality exists, then it is the existence of s o m e t h i n g, which is a determined, though initially not cognized (or imprecisely cognized) content, being a set of "features," forming the nature of things. We can note this by taking a closer look at our visual-intellectual cognition: first I see that something exists. This something later becomes more distinct as I gradually cognize it better. And if I can make a mistake in the expression of content (for example it is a horse, a cow or a doe), I do not nurse any doubts as to the facticity and existence of something that is subject to a gradually better definition of content. And precisely because the cognizing of the content of an existing thing is subject to error, on the one hand, and on the other is the foundation of mastering this thing, the whole of human cognitive effort has become directed above all towards a gradually more precise grasp of the content itself, without paying attention to the very fact of the existence of things, since this is evident.[8] The fact of existence is obvious, and it is this obviousness which was to a great extent the reason why philosophers lost cognitive, and especially reflective sensitivity to the very act of existence. This involved catastrophic consequences in the area of philosophy (as a science which was to give an ultimate explanation of reality). Philosophy became the theory explaining not being (reality, on account of the fact that it exists), but the abstract thing, that is, being, on account of its arrangements of content, constituting in the cognitive interpretation the foundation of the " s e n s e " (meaning) of our expressions. No senses or meanings, however, are primordially given to us in the consciousness or in consciousness as such, but they appear as real senses because they are the contents of existing things.

Thus, the existence of the world (as a reality) is a more primordial "object"[9] for the human being, particularly for his or her cognition, which, as it is a constant process, does not stop at the very fact of existence, but at the same time aims at grasping that which makes existence real, that is, at grasping the content realized in existence. The world "strikes" us with the blade of its existence; however, the blade striking us is a blade of defined content, just as the blade of an axe is precisely its blade. However, it is thanks to existence that content becomes accessible in experience.

The primordial experience of the fact of the existence of the world can be cognitively objectivized and expressed in the form of the first and main statement concerning reality—"there exists something which is somehow determined in itself," which is a content determined in itself. This judgement is an affirmation of real being, and thereby it is a judgement about the relative identity of being, in which we discern primordially that it exists and also that it exists as a content in itself determined (cognitively even more determinable). Our cognitive grasp of being and the expression of it in a judgement on relative ontic identity can take on a dual formulation, in which we stress the affirmation either of existence or of a really existing content—it will always, however, be an affirmation of real being, which is real and actual, because it exists.[10]

The affirmation of existence as that aspect (act) which is fundamentally constitutive of reality is extremely important in the philosophical explanation of the real world, since at precisely this point idealism arises and all the menacing consequences of idealism which are well known to historians of philosophy. These are menaces not only for thought, but they undermine the many-sided character of our life-experiences. If we were to proceed to a "set daily routine" of a method of explanation, beyond the existential aspect of reality, we would lose contact with reality and our explanation would become perhaps logical and compact, but it would be of itself unreal, since it would not take into account the act of existence as the ultimate instance which is to ground the verifiability of cognition. This is precisely the case with a series of philosophical systems, which live only by their inner logic and the coherence of their hypotheses. Of course, logic and consistence are also values for thinking, but these alone, though they are derived from reality and initially grounded in reality, are not sufficient, since there arises the possibility that the mind in knowing may selectively connect certain features of the reality which it knows, and thus abstract from the way in which content is arranged in reality. When we affirm existence and consider the existential aspect we are forced to make allowances for existence and its role in being; we gain simply another task to be explained—to render free of contradiction the existential aspect of the being under investigation.[11]

b) Plurality

In our experience of the world, after its existence has been confirmed, the next matter is to discern the plurality of things. The world initially appears to us as the world of plural things. We notice this immediately from very early childhood. Developmental psychologists claim that a child already in the first month distinguishes his mother from other persons. In pre-scientific cognition the question of distinguishing things is so basic that precisely this pre-scientific cognition, ordered to everyday life, is fundamentally grounded in it. Even primordial definitions and names, the object of the ceaseless interest of any child who asks "What is this?," or what a given thing is called, are connected with the matter of the plurality of things given to us in our experience of the world. The search for connections between perceived things as distinct is something secondary and subsequent. In a word, ontic pluralism is given to us in a primordial way and in a more fundamental way than connections, or eventually the all-embracing connection that we discover between different beings in the cognitive process.

This primordial experience of ontic distinctness (the transcendental *aliquid*) requires a philosophical explanation, which in the history of human thought led to an ultimate negation of ontic pluralism, that is the negation of a very primordial experience of the world, giving explanations and theories priority over experience and real intuition, for as early as in the work of the first philosopher, Thales, it happened that philosophers, as they sought to justify the connection between numerically distinct things, reached the conclusion that plurality is illusory (on account of the superficiality of viewing, historical facts, various sources of cognition, etc.), and at the same time affirmed the actual monism[12] of reality.

Thus again, the matter is not trivial. What is more valuable: the primordial intuition of reality, or the logical theory of explanation, not verified by the perception of reality and the act of existence itself? The negation of the ontic pluralism that can be directly experienced in a cognition of the real world, in favor of, ultimately, monism, (though in the history of philosophical thought it was an attempt most often repeated, in different variations, at explaining reality), is not, however, justified when we measure it against the very task of cognition, and also with the fundamental mode of explanation.

All explanations aim at deepening our understanding of observed reality. Thus, the facts which are given to be explained cannot in principle be negated, unless it would be absurd to affirm existing facts, on account of some (not trivial) errors in perception or the necessity of negating fundamental principles (rules) of sound and correct thinking. If, on the other hand, the facts which are given in direct cognition are neither the result of a fundamentally erroneous cognitive perception nor are in opposition with basic rational order, we cannot negate these facts, which in this case would mean the negation of ontic pluralism, which we ascertain spontaneously both in relation to things existing in the world and in relation to ourselves, feeling the distinctness of human existence and consciousness irreducible to another "center." And moreover, when we consider that the monistic interpretation of pluralistic reality primordially given to us, is in conflict with the principles of identity and non-contradiction, we cannot recognize it as a rational type of explanation, but rather as an easy, perhaps even alluring, but fundamentally imaginative view of the world, not based on the rules of rational cognition.[13] In affirming monism we would have to accept that the same, unique, primordial element (in the historical or structural sense) is absolutely non-composite, if it is one, *monos;* and as it would have no other element beyond itself, it would become composite of itself, giving, as a result, ascertained ontic pluralism. If we negate the basic difference in a fundamental moment between "yes" and "no," between objectified affirmation and negation, we deprive such a mode of explanation of a fundamental law, a law which underpins all rational cognition—the law of non-contradiction. If we have dispensed with this law in one place, then we can arbitrarily make all assertions, since they will precisely be arbitrary, even though they may yield, in some moments of explanation, interesting and sometimes true effects. The truth, however, of imaginary hypotheses will not be the result of any basic assertion (in this case the affirmation of monism), but merely the ontic structure of thought itself, which lives by non-contradiction and in many cases will turn out to be in accordance with reality, in which it has its primordial source.

If, therefore, we affirm plural reality, then together with ontic plurality we must intellectually affirm all that which fundamentally renders this plurality free of contradiction, that is, that whose negation would involve the negation of primarily ascertained existing ontic plurality itself. Precisely this existing plurality of beings in the world is non-contradictory, when: a) particular beings are actually undivided in themselves, that is, they are one in themselves; b) they are divisible, that is, they are internally composed of elements ultimately non-reducible to themselves; c) they are ontically derived from absolute Being, which is a personal being, that is an intellectually cognizing being, acting through its will.

These matters require a rather profound explanation, since they constitute the foundation of the theory of reality.

2. THE STRUCTURE OF REALITY

Our affirmation of existing and ontically plural reality, being something primarily given, compels us at the same time to consider pluralism itself and to provide a non-contradictory explanation of the beings given in immediate human experience. Above all, the very act of existence, that is, the fact that there exists some content which is in itself determined, is universal. And although it is true that every being is different and appears as different, we do however ascertain the very fact of existence, acts of existence, fundamentally in each thing.[14] Furthermore, these things are plural, for there is more than one of them. How is it possible for a particular thing not to exhaust its whole content of being and thereby make possible ontic plurality?[15] These questions are nothing other than the effort to find a non-contradictory explanation in relation to primordially experienced reality.

The theory of explanation itself will go through an analysis of the three points announced. The first matter (after the existence of the world of plural beings has been ascertained), is to affirm the unity of particular beings: particular beings are in themselves actually undivided, which is expressed by the principle of non-contra-diction, as this principle is a cognitive (intellectual) interpretation of the fact that a given being is not divided into being, that is, "itself," and into still something else, which would not be this being, that is, "non-being."[16] If things are plural, then the very fact of plurality (existence of beings) is non-contradictory only when particular beings really exist as undivided in themselves and separated from other beings.[17]

Above all, beings are undivided in themselves, they are one, for the undividedness of being is nothing other than their ontic identity, expressed by means of negation, primordially affirmed in the very perception of reality, when we state that "something exists," that in itself is defined and ontically determined. The affirmation of the act of existence always involves the content made real in the act of existence and through this act. This content, when it exists, when it is a being, is not, at the same time, the negation of the same being. It cannot in the same aspects and at the same time be this being and non-being, that is, to put it in a general way: being is not non-being.[18]

The formulated principle of non-contradiction, constituting the backbone of what is called rational order, and in all rational operations being the ultimate instance of argumentation, is not merely an *a priori* or tautological formulation, but on the contrary, it is the interpretation of the content of a particular being. The structure of being, in its ultimate foundations, is such that it is not in itself divided into being (that is, that which concretely exists) and non-being, that is, the total negation of primordially affirmed being (that is, something concretely non-existing and not-something existing). The primordial affirmation of being as something concretely existing becomes, by way of reflection, if at the same time we affirm our perception of being, doubly strengthened: it is in truth being which is being; and our primordial cognition of it is real (anchored in being), since the existing concrete being is really an existing, affirmed, concrete being, and there is nothing in it that constitutes its negation, either in the aspect of existence or in the content connected with this existence.

The affirmation of being and the initial, fundamental, though very general interpretation of ontic "content," expressing itself both in the principle of real relational identity and in real non-contradiction, is, as was said above, the very crux of rational order, which is the order of the world, the order of things, the order of nature, and when it becomes known it also becomes the order and essential warp of c o g n i t i o n, as well as of t h i n k i n g derived from it. Hence, all reference, verification and argumentation will ultimately have recourse to the principle of identity and non-contradiction as the ultimate instances of rational cognition. On the other hand, that which removes the real principle of identity and non-contradiction will have to be recognized as a departure from the rational order of cognition, and thereby in the ultimate reckoning, as absurd.

Having, therefore, established the basic assertion on reality (this assertion is the intellectual interpretation of reality's content), we can make further analyses in the form of the posing of questions and the search for non-contradictory answers. The questions and answers presuppose, of course, what has already been said, and to a large extent constitute the clarification of the implied contents previously outlined.

If reality existing as plural is a collection of different beings, of which each in itself is one, that is actually undivided in itself, then the fact of pluralism thus perceived is only non-contradictory when particular beings in their inner structure are composite. This means that particular beings are one, undivided, but they are at the same time divisible in some real aspect.

The fact that beings are divisible is quite evident and given to us in life's everyday experience, for we constantly experience the fact of the division of particular beings, that beings undergo destruction, go out of destruction, and arise. All changes, in which we ourselves are also involved, involve as their conditions ontic composition, division and connection, an appropriate regrouping of ontic plural elements. This is obvious. However, understanding how things change and can divide is inseparably connected with understanding the inner composition of being, which is manifold, imposes itself on itself and is mutually conditioning.

One may not at first understand the assertion that any ontic composition, even the most obvious and at the same time superficial, of integrating, extensive parts, presupposes a fundamental composition without which all other types of composition would be something merely apparent, namely a composition from the act of existence and a determined concrete content—essence. For only the latter composition renders the pluralism of being free from contradiction,[19] and all other types of composition would not ultimately be real without the fundamental composition of essence and existence. There is a great uncountable quantity of compositions in being; only the domains, the large groups of fundamental compositions are few.

In the history of philosophy they revealed themselves slowly, as a result of the arduous investigations of the most eminent philosophers and thinkers. First, most generally, on the basis of the failures of different philosophical systems, Aristotle perceived that being is somehow in a manifold way composed of determined, potential elements, and of one moment organizing them, known as act. Hence, the composition of act and potency was the first "given," as it were, of the multiplicity of ontic composition and the first opportunity to part from monistic theories of being. Although Plato, by his theory of participation, attempted to give a pluralistic solution in the theory of reality, his participation was more of an *a priori* postulate than an interpretation given to us in the everyday experience of reality. Besides, for Plato this everyday reality was not even worth taking any special intellectual and cognitive effort concerning it. The only thing which held value for him was the world, insofar as it is the object of our intellectual, cognitive interpretations, which interpretations are expressed in the meanings of general terms. Plato, not yet acquainted with the theory of abstraction, was inclined to believe that everything which is the object of intellectual understanding somehow "is"; hence also the senses of general terms somehow "are," and they form "ultimate reality," since they are necessary, unchangeable, general, and thereby constitute, as it were, a separate "kingdom of fullness" of reality—a *PLEROMA*. Our material and changing world, the world of plural beings, of beings-shadows that are not the object of any true intellectual understanding but only of human experience, *DOXA*, that is only a reflection of, and a participation in the kingdom of the *pleroma*. Thus, the world of plural individuals was not a fitting object for real intellectual cognition.

If, however, we take up the standpoint that it is precisely the world of individual beings given to us in everyday experience, the material world, that is, the real, actual world, then the first matter to be explained is the very fact of ontic pluralism, particularly when we apprehend this fact on the basis of the history of philosophical thought, in which (not without justification), the dominating dispute is precisely the one concerning ontic monism or pluralism. Moreover, the very fact of many-sided ontic composition, as we have already said, is mutually internally conditioned, for there would not be the extensive-quantitative divisibility, given to us in everyday experience, if being were not composed from various real properties called "accidents." On the other hand, a set of properties without a real existing subject is absurd, when we become aware that to be a property is precisely to be a property of something, some being, that is, some existing subject (substance). The changes of the properties of one subject lead to the disappearance and emergence of other subjects, which would again be a contradiction and absurdity if the existing subjects themselves (real substances) were not internally composed of two things: 1) an element defining what this subject is and distinguishing it to the extent that it even becomes the object of clear, essential definitions, and 2) of a second element, a potential one, non contradicting precisely the transformation which is known metonymically as the "passage" of one subject into another, when beings disintegrate and re-emerge. It was precisely composition, which non contradicts the emergence and disintegration of really different existing beings, that bore the name of composition from matter and form, as non-independent ontic factors, mutually conditioning one another. And finally, the ultimate non-contradiction of the emergence and disappearance of really different beings is their composition from those factors which in the philosophical tradition bore the name of essence and existence.[20]

CARL A. RUDISILL LIBRARY
LENOIR-RHYNE COLLEGE
HICKORY, NC 28603

Although the problem of ontic composition from essence and existence has its rich history of errors, this history does not disqualify the problem itself, perhaps the most important problem in the theory of real being.[21]

We must take into account our terminology, first of all and in the very posing of this problem, and, connected with this, the nature of our language, for the terms "essence" and "existence" emerged in a different climate of philosophical language than that in which the very solution to the problem is given. St. Thomas' language, in his time, was mainly the language of Plato, Aristotle and St. Augustine, that is, a conceptual language, as a result of which St. Thomas' disciple Gilles of Rome (Egidius Romanus, doctor fundatissimus) in his work *Theoremata de essentia et esse* already reified both essence itself and existence. This was, by the way, an important cause for all other misunderstandings on precisely this subject, for if he claimed that *essentia* and *esse* differ as do *res* and *re*—a "thing" and "by, or with a thing"—the same formulation could have been made on the basis of exclusively conceptual language, which language fundamentally assumes only the determined structure of things, which can be adequately explained in numerically distinct concepts—which is quite untrue.

Next, our language, if it did not always directly involve the structures of things—numerically distinct structures—then it always involved being, since ultimately that which we cognize has being, or is conceived after the model of being. However, both essence and existence are infra-ontic factors. It is "from them" that concrete-individual being "is composed" in a way proper to itself; on the other hand, these factors, if they are taken separately from one another, are not existing at all. In real being we can intellectually and cognitively distinguish them as non-identical and non-reducible to one another, it is commonly said, really different. What we understand by this "really" is that we are not dealing with an exclusively mental distinction, one that is not grounded in being itself. On the contrary, it is reality in our intellectual (and thereby objective, real) view and interpretation which is such that in being itself there are factors called essence and existence, which factors are really ontically non-identical. This means that every real being, given to us in primarily empirical experience (but not only empirical being) has in itself a factor which "makes" it, constitutes it a real being, a being which truly exists independently of my cognitive apparatus and which compels me to affirm that it "exists" and is given to me independently of myself.

Moreover, as it is given to me as existing, it is at the same time somehow determined in itself to existence and I grasp this determination cognitively, at first in a very general and imprecise way. At a later stage, to a greater and greater degree, I elucidate for myself this determination, as something constantly identical. All this time I am aware that one aspect of a being is that which it is, and another aspect is (the fact) that it is, that it really exists. A moment of attention is sufficient for me to become aware of the fact that the issue "what a thing is" and the fact "that it really is, that is, that it exists," is not only my manner of cognition, but the very state of things, for if I believed that it was only a matter of my cognition, and not of things, by the very fact that I know more and more exactly "what a thing is," I would have been able to constitute the thing in its existence, whereas a gradually more detailed grasp of the content, that is, of the essence of a thing, does not yet constitute it ontically. It is true that every apprehension of content presupposes, directly or indirectly the very fact of existence, and that is why we are empowered to grasp the content of things ever more precisely. For this reason it may seem to someone that it is only a question of how we grasp: just as I suppose the fact that something exists and on this basis I grasp the thing's "essence," that is, its content, and cognitively discover it to a greater and greater degree, so also I would grasp the essence itself and in so doing I would be constituting it in existence. However, this route is not possible, for even the most intense thinking about money does not create it by the very fact of thinking; nor does intense thinking about a close deceased person bring him back to life. Thus, it is not mode of cognition which gives rise to the distinction between the content-essential and the existential aspects of being, but rather it is the very structure of reality which compels me ultimately to distinguish precisely these aspects of being.

Moreover, in philosophical reflection, several absurdities would be revealed to me if I really wanted to "reduce to each other" both these factors of the essence and existence of a concrete being and identify them with one another. It is sufficient merely to indicate some absurd consequences of such a standpoint to recognize that the essence of a real being is not the same as its existence.[22]

First of all, therefore, if to exist were the same as to be a defined content, then every time any content defined in itself were given, it would at the same time be real, it would always exist. In such a state of affairs abstracts, stories, myths would really exist, since these are all contents defined in themselves, and the assumption is that it is the same thing for something to exist really in itself and to be a determinate content. If we see that for example the existence of abstract things is absurd, then at the same time the real identity of real essence and existence is absurd.

Above all it is not by differentiating between essence and existence, but on the contrary, by really identifying them, that we would be led to absolute monism; everything would be merely existence, and existence of itself cannot be differentiated (it can be differentiated only on account of essence, existing content). Thus everything would be the same undifferentiatable existence. This runs contrary to the evident data which informs about the real pluralism of beings, which is a fact given to us for explanation. There is no such data in favor of regarding undifferentiatable existential monism (that is, that everything is the same existence) as a fact.

Finally, if existence and essence were to be really identified with each other in beings as it is given to us in daily experience, there would follow a host of consequences not in keeping with the facts. Thus, such ontic processes and occurrences as transformations, the action of beings on one another, efficient causality and even all forms of movement, would not be possible, for if one were to accept the hypothesis that everything is identical with existence, only one existing being would be possible and non-contradictory, to be more precise—only existence, which should be apprehended either as all-perfect, as something which cannot be lost, or else such that it would be in itself a collection and accumulation of all kinds of contradictions. In the first case (all-perfect existence) we would have to deal not with pantheism, but with the absolute itself. This is out of keeping with the inner experience of each one of us, and is also ultimately absurd. In the second case "we would fall out of" the rational order in general, and consequently the problem of explanation and meaning would be without any object.

What is the basis for both the pluralism of being, and for the various compositions in being, which we notice and experience? It is the fundamental composition—the composition which ultimately "grounds" all other compositions—which "grounds" pluralism, mobilism, all the various kinds of causality and influence. It is the composition in the real being given to us in experience out of e s s e n c e and e x i s t e n c e —elements which are heterogeneous, which cannot be reduced to each other in reality, and which are like the two sides of the same being. The relation of essence to existence is arranged according to the known Aristotelian theory of a c t and p o t e n c y , with the reservation that the act of being, constitutive in being, is precisely existence; whereas essence is the potency determining existence to "just such" an ontic state which we perceive in common experience, and which we submit to explanation in the sciences and in philosophy.

The composition of essence and existence is a condition for the analogy of being, that is, such an arrangement of the world in which essence and existence are realized in each being, in a way particular to that being itself, with the reservation that in each of these beings both the essence and the existence of this being are proper to it and "unrepeatable." Common to all beings is the occurrence of realization (the facticity) of essence through existence, and it becomes the basis of the analogical unity of the universe of real beings.[23] However, this occurrence of the realization of essence through existence, that is fact, is not ontically something abstracted both from the essence and the existence of a particular being, such that we cannot make facticity itself into some class of relations of existence to essence or vice versa. Existence is an act directly realizing essence and forming one real being together with it.

The analogicity of being and the analogical unity of being become the basis for analogical cognitive interpretations, which also cannot be conceptualized. And although we commonly speak of the analogical "concept" of being, we must always take into account that here "concept" itself is an analogical expression and it does not refer to the kind of concept that we possess in the case of universals; it is already a set of judgements which constitute the content of transcendentals as these are understood in classical (not Kantian) philosophy. The analogical unity of the cognitive interpretation of being is the condition for the objectivity and reality of metaphysical cognition itself. This cognition is specifically transcendental to such an extent that even universal expressions of colloquial language or of domains of cognition of other sciences in the area of classical existential metaphysics have an analogical, transcendental interpretation. This means that for instance the expressions "man," "quantity," "quality," used in metaphysics, do not mean merely an abstracted, more or less defined content, but mean contents existing in different individual cases of being, with the reservation that each individual as existing, and on account of his or its existence, constitutes a new, unrepeatable realization of being, in the ontic aspect irreducible to any other being, though it bears the name "man," "quantity," "quality."

Thus, the philosophical understanding of being takes place from the perspective of existence, with the ultimate comprehension that existence, as the act of a particular being is not only the basis for the existence of being, but also for its ultimate cognizability and comprehensibility.

3. THE WORLD AND GOD

Given such a structure of being as has been sketched out above, it is necessary to affirm the Absolute Being, who in the language of religion is called God. The fact that the Absolute, as being the supreme ontic fact, exists, is inseparable from the philosophical manner of explaining reality in terms of necessity (and so in ultimate terms, without having recourse to any other kind of knowledge). Reality is a certain (ordered) set of real beings, each of which is composed of the ontic "elements" of essence and existence.[24] This necessity of affirming the existence of an Absolute becomes immediately apparent to us when we draw attention to the fact that the world, being a collection of plural beings, of which each is composed of an essence particular for itself alone and of a proportional existence, does not have in itself any real reason explaining the fact of its existence (in any concrete being of the whole set of beings, nor in the whole set of these same beings).

The fact of real existence is common to the whole of reality, and the particular existence of a being, being different and irreducible to concrete content-essence, is not the "feature" of this essence; it does not originate from it, for if existence were a "feature," or were really explainable by a concrete essence which exists, then ultimately such an existence would have to be identified with some essence. Such a case is possible and necessary, and can at the same time only be one case: this ontic case is precisely the Absolute. He is being in its fullness, for in Him the act of being—"the very fact that He is"—and

His content-essence, "what He is"—are absolutely one and the same. Hence, we say in philosophy that only in the Absolute Being do essence and existence become absolutely identified, and that is why God's name is: "He who is." God's existence, as the ultimate necessary reason for real existence is indicated by every being which exists really, contingently, that is, in such a way that the existence of a given being is not identified with its essence. In metaphysics, to reject the Absolute means the same as to negate the fact that any beings exist at all, that is to abandon the rationality of cognition.

Thus, in the tradition of classical philosophy the problem of God is not given to us as separate from an ultimate explanation of existing being, which is given to us in everyday experience.[25] It does not, there, arise from any beliefs or convictions or other cultural facts found in society (although undoubtedly the idea of God is alive in culture), but in the area of philosophy there appears the necessity of affirming the Absolute, who is the God of religion, on the basis of the non-contradictory explanation of being itself, which really exists and whose existence cannot be explained by the inner structure of any one being in particular, nor by all beings taken together.

Yet we must also draw attention to the fact that affirming the necessity of the existence of God as a factor which renders the existence of contingent being free from contradiction, at the same time reveals His transcendence in relation to all contingent beings, also in that being which is "thought" and human concept—a fact which we should particularly bear in mind. This means that we cannot have a proper concept of God, but merely an analogical one, that is, we know that an Absolute Being exists, who is a being through Himself and from Himself, since His essence is existence, (He is, therefore, E X I S T E N C E) ; we do not know, however, and we have no ontic reasons to know, h o w He Himself is constituted in Himself. Even our knowledge about the fact that He is—being "The One who is"—is not a proper knowledge about God, but only a knowledge of the necessity of His existence, on the basis of the ontic structure given to us in sensory experience and understood in a metaphysical way. This means that, as St. Thomas Aquinas aptly said, we know that the sentence "God exists" is of necessity real, (when interpreted in ontic structure).[26] Hence, the transcendence of the Absolute is total and we cannot know any more about Him than that which is expressed in the very content of being, for if He is a being through Himself, then everything that the transcendentals express is realized in Him totally and fully, that is "being," "thing," "one," "distinctness," "truth," "good" and "beauty." We can say, therefore, that that which constitutes the content of being (truth, good or beauty) is realized in the Absolute in an essential way (if we may express it like this) and not only in a participative way or in any kind of limitation. He, as existing through Himself, at the same time is the reason which makes non-contradictory the existence of beings; therefore He is the ultimate source and beginning of these same beings, that is, as St. Thomas said: *per modum habitudinis principii.*

At this point it is worth recalling, in its most general outlines, St. Thomas' view of the problem of the cognizability of the Absolute, already mentioned elsewhere.[27] We can choose, as the basis of these reflections, article 1, question 13, part I of St. Thomas' *Summa Theologiae:*

> In Aristotle's view, names are the signs of intellectually cognized contents; on the other hand, intellectually cognized contents themselves are the similarities of things in themselves.

Consequently the path leads from signs (as particular symbols of our concepts), through concepts to the thing itself, and eventually even further, through things to their ultimate source—the Absolute.

The terms we use or, to take the matter even more broadly, our language (both natural and artificial language), are only signs or symbols of concepts and of the content of our cognition in general. There exists, then, a very large "distance" and an inadequacy of signs or symbols (and also concepts and judgements) in relation to what is being denoted. This inadequacy is all the greater because language signs are fundamentally instrumental signs, conventional signs. I can convey a content intellectually interpreted, such as "fatherhood" or "motherhood," by means of different words for different languages, that is in Polish, Latin, German, French etc.; I can express them, write them, paint or sculpt them, represent them in some kind of dance movement, and so forth. And each of the signs-symbols of fatherhood or motherhood mentioned here conveys somewhat different nuances of an abstract content, for the subjective-personal context is added to this. The inadequacy, therefore, of the signs-symbols of intellectually-cognitive experiences is great and, depending on the context, it can become greater still. When a content is unknown to us, we end up with a large lacuna where we should instead be able to convey content. When we convey cognitive contents to others by means of signs, we do so in a general way, and we prepare those who hear us or debate with us merely in a general way towards grasping this content, in a really analogical way, with their (that is, another person's) cognitive apparatus.

However, an immeasurably greater inadequacy can be noted between the thing in itself and the way in which it is apprehended in knowledge. Already in the early Middle Ages the distinction was known, between *cognitio apprehensiva* (a cognition which is very differentiated and is selective, either by its nature or through the person himself), and *cognitio comprehensiva* (which is accessible only to the mind of the Absolute). St. Thomas makes a distinction between: (a) the conventional nature of the sign *(signum)* that language is, in relation to cognitive contents; (b) the natural character of the sign—the meaning of the cognized thing, and (c) the thing itself, in relation to which the sign constitutes *similitudo.* Of course, this name does not solve the subtle problem of the relation between intentional being and real being, where *similitudo* is the aspective identity of the meaning of the cognized thing with the thing itself, but not vice versa.

When we draw attention to the fact that the cognitively apprehended contents of the thing itself are merely a very restricted and selected apprehension of a few features of the thing, (perhaps to some extent useful to human beings for life in the world), and the immense "remainder" of this contents is cognitively not apprehended, we can perceive how very restricted and superficial our cognition is in relation to the thing itself. It is true that we can say that there exists an identity of the cognitively apprehended contents of a thing and the thing itself in the aspect of apprehended features; however, the inadequacy between the thing itself, "rich in content," and our poor and selective apprehension, is very great.

Consequently, there occurs in our real cognition both a large distance and an "interval" between language and concept and also—even more—between the intellectual "copy" and the thing (which is rich in content) in itself. The cognitively apprehended thing is merely a very modest part of our material world, where there is a set of things, processes and occurrences which condition one another in unusually varied ways, forming the universe. While recognizing the existence of God as the Creator, the whole universe is only one of unlimited actually realized possibilities, since our universe is neither the only nor the best version of a world.

Thus, the "distance" between our cognition and God is infinite; God appears as a Being fundamentally transcendent for our cognition. All "easy" paths of reaching Him, seem only to be pseudo-paths.

In the article discussed, St. Thomas continues:

> We are able to name and express something to the extent that we can grasp it with our intellect. In this life God cannot be seen by us by way of His essence, but He is known to us from creatures as being related to them as their primal source, and by our attributing to Him unlimited excellence, and by way of negation—*secundum habitudinem principii et modum excellentiae et remotionis.*

Three methods are mentioned: a) *habitudo principii;* b) *modus excellentiae;* c) *modus remotionis.* St. Thomas emphasizes the first method but also accepts yet two further methods, as they played a similarly significant role in the tradition of Christian thought, although they are derived from Platonic and neo-Platonic sources connected with the essentialistic concept of being. The *modus excellentiae* is based on the Platonic concept of idea and participation. When Christian thinkers, particularly St. Augustine, employed the then scientific terminology of Platonic philosophy, they attributed to God all the perfections which can be perceived in the world and are a product of God the Creator. He

Himself, then, is to an unlimited extent Good, knowledge, life, beauty, and so forth.

However, such a concept of God as a God of unlimited good, wisdom, life, unity, justice, etc., particularly on the basis of neo-Platonic gradualism, could have given rise to the supposition that God is the unlimited perfect "base" of the world, or the ineffable spring (like Plotinus' One), from which the world is radiated and reveals, to a limited extent, unlimited Divine perfections. In such a concept of divinity, however, the danger of pantheism would arise, or at least pan-entheism. The transcendence of God would not be guaranteed.

Consequently, in the neo-Platonic Christian stream of thought, particularly in Pseudo-Dionysius, there arose the concept of apophatic theology, that is, a negative way of cognizing God. According to such a standpoint, God is so radically different and thereby transcendent in relation to the world, and all its perfections, that He is not anything that appears in the world. Apophatic cognition would cut itself away fundamentally from all forms of pantheism and would stress the transcendence of God in relation to the content of this world. Both methods of positive and negative cognition mutually complement one another, particularly on the basis of an essentialist concept of being, that is, such a concept in which it would not be existence but some type of unity (formal identity) which would constitute the be-ing of being (its reality). In such a concept only these two ways would be possible and at the same time real, as grasping the participative connections of God and beings "radiated" from Him, and also negating levels of being in neo-Platonic pantheism.

St. Thomas, however, having perceived that the act constituting the being of being is an act of actual existence, proportional to a given concrete essence, perceived at the same time that the ways accepted in the Christian tradition (positive and apophatic) are in themselves ineffective if they are not based on existential connections, that is, on a differently apprehended participation of beings. Only the first method, which stresses existential relations—*secundum habitudinem principii*—gives any real foundation for cognizing God via being. And when we take a closer look at St. Thomas' argumentation concerning the existence of God, then, in concentrating attention more intensely on the content of the reasoning carried out, we will be able to discern that here we have to deal with five modifications of one line of demonstration. This can be reduced to a demonstration of how some characteristic ontic states, accessible to a greater or lesser degree to human experience and not intelligible *per se,* become ultimately comprehensible and non-contradictory only when we affirm the existence of God as an intelligible being *per se,* since He is a being who i s existence.

The ultimate, ontic, basis of the assertion about the existence of an Absolute which makes non-contradictory the existence of the world, and characteristic ontic states in the world (such as changes, causality, contingent existence, the existence of perfection, order), is the existence of a being really composed of the non-independent components of essence and existence (non-independent with respect to being and to cognition), as the only (real) "reason" which makes ontic pluralism non-contradictory and also, in connection with it, the above-mentioned characteristic ontic states of movement, causality, order, etc. The negation of the existence of real composite being is presupposed by the negation of the existence of the Absolute. As É. Gilson[28] rightly remarks:

> Science can explain much to us in the world; perhaps it will sometime in the future explain to us everything that the world of phenomena is. But why (thanks to what) does anything exist at all? Science does not know and this is precisely because it cannot even pose this question.

Here, it is of course a question of the empirical sciences built up on the model of Comte's teaching. The only possible answer to this, the most important of questions ("why" is a synonym for "question"), is that each concrete existential act, each concretely existing thing depends for its existence on the pure Act of existence. In order to become the ultimate answer to all existential questions, this most important cause must be absolute existence, that is, existence through itself and not by virtue of another existing being.

Thus, there can only be one stream of thought in philosophy, that which explains the world in terms of existence, that which affirms God as pure existence, and thereby also as a personal being, (if true and good are transcendental values of existing being, for true and good presuppose that existing reality is ordered to the intellect and will of the Absolute). This means that the rationality of being, revealing itself in the form of first principles, just as being itself, given to us primarily in sensory experience, is derived from the intellect since, as it does not "explain" its being through itself, it does not at the same time "explain" its comprehensibility, which is the participation with intelligibility *per se* and with the intellectuality of the Absolute. Likewise, the contingency of being presupposes that it exists, because it is "desired" to exist. This desiring of the existence of being is an inner necessary relation of being to the will of the Absolute.[29] Thus, the transcendental properties of truth and goodness indicate the Absolute as a personal being.

Ontic participation and its dependence on Absolute Being, particularly in the order of comprehensibility, are connected, in the history of human thought, with the Platonic theory of ideas, later grafted by the neo-Platonic philosophers from the *pleroma* onto the divine intellect of the Absolute, for, as we know, Plato assumed the standpoint, in a particular historical-philosophical context, that human beings have two not equally valuable modes of cognition-*noetic* and *doxal*. He did this, seeing on the one hand the radical changeability of the material world, and on the other the necessity of human conceptual cognition, while at the same time not knowing the concept of abstract thought and yet wanting to make the heritage of philosophical schools from the Eleatic and Heraclitean circles valuable.

The *doxal* mode of cognition, as less valuable, would have as its object the world of changeable beings, whereas the *noetic* mode of cognition, a purely intellectual one, must at the same time also possess its object, that is ideas; ideas are located somewhere in the order of fullness and perfection, for the general expressions (terms) of our language indicate "senses" which are necessary, unchangeable and general, and thereby scientifically fully valuable. They cannot n o t be non-objectivized. Thus, their objects, known as ideas, somehow a r e ; the intellect (the intellectual soul) interprets them and lives by them. These ideas are ultimate reality, and their reflection and "participation" is in fact the world of plural and changeable things.

The Platonic theory of ideas, in spite of Aristotle's criticism, has passed to the history of human thought as its permanent heritage, a heritage which is fruitful to this day, grounded in the philosophical concept of God. The Absolute, being internally "simple," non-composite, necessarily existing, reveals itself as the effective exemplar and final cause of composite being, that is, contingent being. This means that, on the basis of an interpretation of contingent being, we are compelled to recognize that contingent being (the world) is not only really contingent, (that is, it does not have its reason of existence in itself but beyond itself, ultimately in the Absolute, which alone can have and must have the reason of its being in itself alone, as it is a "being through itself"), but is also ordered to the intellect, that is, it is derived from the Absolute intellect and at the same time is ordered to ultimate, absolute good, that is, to the Absolute. This absolute objective good can be identified with the objectively and ultimately apprehended "common good," which we will discuss below.

If being is derived from the Absolute according to the order of His intellect, then we are forced to recognize that the Absolute possesses some kind of "plan" for the existence and activity of the world as derived from Himself and ordered to Himself. This "plan" is nothing other than the set of Divine ideas, that is, eternal models for contingent beings, as is well known from the history of philosophy. Divine exemplarism, introduced into Western European thought by St. Augustine, was known in its changed form in the work of the neo-Platonists (the ideas of things were found in the *Logos),* and it had its source in the epistemological speculations of Plato. Divine exemplarism, insofar as it directs the activity of contingent (created) beings, was called by St. Augustine the "eternal Divine law"—*ordo divinae sapientiae secundum quod est directiva omnium actuum et motionum* (the order of Divine wisdom, insofar as it directs all the movements and all the activities of beings).

Thus, the ultimate justification for the rationality of the world and of all its parts is the intellect of the Absolute, to the extent that this intellect inscribes the marks of its intelligibility into beings "produced" by itself by virtue of creativity itself (derivation). This rationality, which is fragmentary in the measure that being is fragmentary or partial (for being is contingent), has its ultimate explanation in the Absolute, (that is, the Person-Intellect), which is rational through itself. We call this rationality, insofar as it is the source of the emergence of beings and their activity, divine exemplarism, in accordance with philosophical tradition; that is, we speak of ideas in the divine intellect as of "divine eternal law."

From the pluralistic and at the same time realistic philosophy, the problem of divine ideas as developed in the works of St. Thomas Aquinas, is utterly different than in Plato, St. Augustine, Duns Scotus or Suarez; and in the same way the whole of the scholastic tradition went in this same direction.[30] After all, scholasticism was the continuation of the thought of Duns Scotus and Suarez, and not of St. Thomas, even in the work of such Thomists as Cajetan and in the mainstream of traditional Thomism, which, while battling with Scotism and Suarezianism, did however accept from these systems terminology, and a way to present problems which did not exist in St. Thomas' system itself.

In the old Platonic-Augustinian stream of thought, divine ideas were thought of as univocal specific models for things, which are realized in matter and assume individual natures, as a result of which it was possible to speak of "species," which have their ultimate explanation in divine ideas. Thomas, on the other hand, differentiates between the mode of divine cognition and the object of this cognition. God—the Absolute—cognizes in His divine way, in accordance with the nature of the Absolute. To be the Absolute means to be a unique being, non-composite and fully perfect, but not in the way perfection is realized in contingent beings: perfect in the manner of pure act, pure existence. Hence, the activity of the Absolute, in this case cognition, is equally perfect, non-composite.

Translating this into the language of ideas, the Absolute, when it is a question of the m o d e of cognition, cognizes through the one idea of His own essence. God in Himself and through Himself "sees" e v e r y t h i n g in the most perfect way, as He is in the aspect of being the r e a s o n o f e a c h c o n c r e t e ontic fact.

Plato and St. Augustine thought, on the other hand, that there were many species-ideas, since they did not clearly become aware of the difference between the m o d e of the Absolute's cognition and the o b j e c t of His cognition.

When, however, considering the object of Absolute's cognition, then it is He Himself, as He is the total reason of being who cognizes everything that is being; that is, if we translate this into the "language of ideas," in God there exist as many ideas as there are diverse beings forming the world. And since to be a being means to be a concrete, real, existing content, as a consequence there are as many ideas in God as there are individual existing beings: thus God cognizes everything that is being, insofar as it exists.[31]

This kind of solution, as given by St. Thomas, was something new, even though he was basing it on both the Platonic-Augustinian and the Arab theory of ideas, to be more precise, the Aristo-telian-Averroistic concept of *pronoi* (Providence). Plato, who did not yet know the concept of abstract cognition, could not have introduced a differentiation between the mode of cognition and the mode of existence of things. Perceiving that we cognize "generalities" by our reason, he had thought that precisely these "generalities"—that is, ideas—"are," and that they exist independently of our thinking. Such a presentation of the matter in hand was required by the objectivity of cognition, at that time, as it had to contend with the subjectivism and relativism of the Sophists. The generality of the objects of cognition was, however, something secondary, derivative and dependent on the mode of cognition.

Aristotle drew attention to the fact that when we cognize abstractively, we cognize generally, while things in themselves exist individually, since they exist materially. However, our intellect does not cognize matter, for it does not have in itself—in the Stagirite's opinion—the conditions which make it intellectually cognizable. Accordingly, it was necessary to seek, in the thing itself, elements that were constant and general of themselves, and which did not become individual until they were connected with matter. Such a constant and (of itself) general element of things was precisely the form of things, which became individual by being connected with matter. Thus, according to Aristotle, changeable things in connection with matter exist in an individual way; we cannot, however, intellectually cognize an individual thing as individual. Besides, the cognition of an individual thing is unnecessary, for precisely the "non-material" element (form), being of itself general, is the basis of the intellectual cognizability of things. The human mode of cognition is general, although, according to Aristotle, the basis of this generality is an objective state, namely the very form of a thing. It is true that Aristotle, too, had doubts in this matter, for he accepted the concept of individual form, even though the individuality of form constituted a real drawback in his system and did not fit into his concept of rational cognition.

It was precisely this that became the reason why Arab commentators on Aristotle assumed the standpoint that individuality in general, even if it were form itself, is uncognizable for the intellect. And that is why God or Providence does not cognize details or individuals, for precisely individuality cannot be an object of cognition for any intellect. Thus, a theory of Providence was created, which was merely responsible for the general course of the world, responsible for general laws, and completely non-responsible for individual states of things, which were something accidental, not fitting into the general scheme of law or forecasts of Providence.

Platonic ideas were held to be the confirmation of this, as they were generalities, and it was precisely these generalities, that is, ideas, which could only be an object of the divine intellect. This was convenient for the concept of "law of nature," to the extent that in this way a very solid foundation for the unchangeability of general laws was obtained—all law is, of its nature, general, since they were founded on divine ideas. Lawgivers, having authority as well as a "closer" contact with God, could mark out general laws which were meant to connect all people univocally, just as a general essence of species univocally "connects" particular essences, that is, individual "instances" of a general nature.

St. Thomas stresses, however, that to be a being means to exist as a concrete, individual essence and not to "be-identical-with-oneself," as was commonly accepted following Greek philosophy (both Platonic and Aristotelian), for if "to be a being" meant "to be identical with oneself," then the factor marking out being, constituting its beingness, would not be concrete existence but the form of things, which of itself was general, according to the whole Greek tradition. And then the concept of general ideas would have its ontic foundations. Yet "to be a being" means to exist individually, concretely. Consequently God—when He cognizes particular concrete beings in Himself in a divine, non-composite (that is, "simple"") way, cognizes the individual ideas of things. Generality, as St. Thomas continually teaches, comes not from the states of things, but from the imperfection of our spirit, our mind, for the human mind is not so perfect that it can know the essences of things in a concrete manner, just as they exist. It cognizes them abstractively, that is, generally. Generality is a product of schematization. Generality is the characteristic feature of our human cognition. The human mode of cognition *(sc.* conceptual cognition*)* has become the source for the myth of the existence of general essences and general ideas. In a word, the concept of general ideas, according to St. Thomas, was simply a projection of our own mode of cognition of the object itself. The fact that we cognize conceptually in a general way has become, in the history of philosophy, the cause of the emergence of the concept of the existence of general ideas. This concept, connected with the theory of the cognition of God has, in turn, become the cause of the anthropo-morphization of the cognition of God, and, in the concept of natural law, it has become the basis for totalizing legal tendencies.

The change in the concept of divine ideas introduced by St. Thomas Aquinas had, of necessity, to bring about a change in the interpretation of natural law and eternal law. And here again, we encounter in St. Thomas Aquinas' writings an interesting phenomenon (which still confuses those who read his texts merely "materially," without a deeper understanding of them), namely, St. Thomas employs the same definitions which were forged by his predecessors, Aristotle, Plato or St. Augustine, but he gives them a new content, which we must interpret in the context of the whole of his doctrine. This is so, also in the case of St. Thomas' concept of eternal law and natural law. Here he accepts the definitions forged by St. Augustine, both of eternal law *(ordo divinae sapientiae, secundum quod est directiva omnium actuum et motionum)* as well as of natural law *(participatio legis aeternae in rationali creatura subsistens),* but he gives these definitions a new meaning, in accordance with his new concepts of being and of cognition.

We shall have to go back to these problems when explaining the nature of natural law. It is important at the outset, however, to become aware of the philosophical context of the whole question, in order to be able to explain more specifically, on this basis, the very concept of natural law which binds human persons analogically, just as their ontic structure is analogical and the nature of divine ideas is analogical. However, in accepting the philosophical nature and the metaphysical context of the explanation, we must at the same time also draw people's attention to the fact that the use of natural law in practice does not imply the necessity of its philosophical understanding. It is in reality thus (speaking *grosso modo)*, that matters in fact stand, for each human being is directed by natural law in his conduct, in the same way that he uses speech in a language, and employs *volens nolens* the grammatical rules of the language in question. However, the matter of a philosophical understanding of natural law is one thing, and its actual recognition is another. Here we are concerned with an ultimate understanding of natural law, and that is why we extensively outline the philosophical basis of the explanation of the phenomenon of law, even though we shall have to pay particular attention to the fact of actually recognizing this law in the domain of human conduct.

NOTES

Chapter II. THE ANALOGICAL STRUCTURE OF REALITY

[1] This "discovery" of the universe by the first Greek thinkers, Thales, Anaximander, Anaximenes, Heraclitus and others (on this subject cf. Jaeger, *Paideia,* Vol. 1, pp. 176–208) is connected with the beginning of science as reflected, necessary, general cognition, justified by commensurate factors that can be discovered by the reason and that belong to the universe. This appeal to certain commensurate natural factors (from the macro- or micro-structure of nature) is seen as the fundamental difference between mythological and philosophical knowledge. The reference to the gods, even cosmic ones, was slowly rationalized, while nature has become the fundamental explanatory factor. Nature, as a being determined in itself, acting regularly, in accordance both with its inner structure and with the structure of other things, becomes the ultimate instance in the process of rational justification.

[2] Here I am stressing human, that is, conscious being. In this sense cognition is always a fundamental expression of human being. It is this expression all the more in relation to the first object of cognition.

[3] This is more of a postulate than a statement.

[4] We must distinguish here the issues of the philosophical cognition and the spontaneous cognition of some things, for it can happen—and normally does happen—that we spontaneously cognize some specific objects earlier and independently of philosophical cognition. If, however, we want to cognize a matter in a philosophical context, we are obliged to indicate the foundations of cognition and to reflect on the fundamental context. We shall still return to this problem.

[5] It is just at this point, in a proper understanding of being, that the roads of philosophical thinking part, for the following question is always relevant: "thanks to what" is something really a being, a reality? The history of philosophy provides various answers, so that the very expression "being" or "being as being" is very ambiguous, for the world was really real for Parmenides thanks to the law of identity; for Plato it was real thanks to ideas, revealing themselves in the form of meanings of general expressions of natural language; for Aristotle it was real thanks to substantial form; for Avicenna, thanks to the "third nature"; for the materialists, thanks to matter, etc. Each, from such (or similar) understanding of reality immediately affects both the concept of reality and the philosophical system. If we take note of the fact that being is real, due to existence, we are put in a really real and at the same time neutral position. On this subject see by Krąpiec and Kaminski, *Z teorii i metodologii metafizyki* (On the Theory and Methodology of Metaphysics), Lublin, 1962, pp. 96–143.

[6] É. Gilson (Being and Essence, Paris, 1948) presents this matter very well on the basis of the history of the concept of being.

[7] This matter has been well presented by Z.J. Zdybicka in *Partycypacja bytu* (The Participation of Being), Lublin, 1972, pp. 98–110.

[8] This is also connected with the process of conceptualization and the practical use of clear and distinct concepts.

[9] I understand the expression "object" here in a wide sense—as that which initially imposes itself on my cognition.

[10] Cf. on this subject see: Krąpiec, *Metaphysics*, New York, Peter Lang Publishing, Inc., 1991, pp. 104–203.

[11] In the course of this work we will more often encounter this type of expression characterizing the essential moment of philosophical proof. That is, what we want here is to explain an important fact; that to negate such an explanation will be either to resign from giving any explanation at all, or it will lead us to admit the absurd; for if I have a fact which, for important ontic reasons, requires explanation, then we must in the process of reasoning indicate such a factor necessarily connected with the fact, the negation of which factor is at the same time the negation of the fact itself.

[12] By monism we understand here the theory of reality according to which everything is the manifestation of one being, which being is necessarily internally non-composite; it is simple in itself.

[13] It is not difficult to show that truly consistent monism is in contradiction to the facts, that is, to ontic pluralism, for if there existed primordially only one being homogeneous to the being given to us in cognitive (empirical) experience, and this being were absolutely non-composite, then ontic pluralism would not develop from it. Non-complexity (simplicity) does not give complexity as a result.

[14] For in each real being we perceive: a) the act of its existence (facticity—the fact that it is); b) some concrete content, which, because it is individual and concrete, is in itself determined to the ultimate (only intentional beings are nondetermined, on account of the selectivity and perspectival nature of their apprehension by the cognitive apparatus); c) the ordering of content to existence. All three moments in each being are different. Common to them is the "fact-of-being," that is, every concrete content (individually different) is completely inwardly ordered to an act of existence appropriate to itself, which is also different in each case, being ordered to a content commensurable for itself. If the act of existence of a particular being is really non-reducible to content (essence) and is really different from it, and in spite of everything actualizes this content, then the question arises: Why (thanks to what) does a given being exist rather than not exist? And this is a basic metaphysical question against the background of the fact of the existence of plural beings. The existence of beings (the fact that being is) is not to be explained by the content (essence) of these same beings (what they are), since the aspect of essence (what being is) does not "cause" the fact that it is.

[15] St. Thomas, in *Contra Gent.* 11. 15, makes significant analyses on this subject, about which I wrote in *Teoria analogii bytu* (The Theory of the Analogy of Being), Lublin, 1959, p. 145.

[16] Cf. my work: *Metaphysics*, pp. 122–131.

[17] Ibid., pp. 138–143.

[18] Ibid., p. 123.

[19] Z.J. Zdybicka has devoted her monograph *Partycypacja bytu* (The Participation of Being) to the problem of the decontradictification of the pluralism of being on the basis of the theory of participation specified by herself.

[20] I have elaborated this problem more extensively in my *Metaphysics*, part II.

[21] A classical elaboration of the problem of the essence and existence of contingent being is the work of N. Del Prado, *De fundamentali veritate philosophiae christianae*, Freiburg, 1911.

[22] The various possibilities of absurd consequences coming from the negation of the composition of essence and existence are analyzed by Del Prado. Ibid.

[23] On the subject of analogy see my work *Teoria analogii bytu* (The Theory of the Analogy of Being), Lublin, 1959.

[24] The ontic foundation of the necessity of affirming the existence of God is precisely real composition from essence and existence, for it is not the same to exist and to have an essence. All other foundations known in the history of philosophy are not based on an analysis of being in itself.

[25] Cf. on this subject my discourse: *Filozofia i Bóg* (Philosophy and God) in: *O Bogu i człowieku* (On God and Man), edited by Bishop B. Bejze, Vol. 1, Warsaw, 1968, pp. 11–55.

[26] *S.th.*, 3a4ad 2: *Scimus enim quod haec propositio quam formamus de Deo, cum dicimus Deus est, vera est.*

[27] Cf. the cited discourse by Krąpiec, *Filozofia i Bóg* (Philosophy and God), p. 35ff.

[28] É. Gilson, *God and Philosophy* in *Being and Some Philosophers,* Toronto, Pontifical Institute of Medieval Studies, 1949.

[29] Cf. my *Metaphysics*, the Chapter on "Transcendental Good."

[30] Cf. *S.th.*, 1a q. 15 passim.

[31] St. Thomas explains the necessity of the existence of ideas in the following way: "It is necessary to assume that there are ideas in the mind of God. What is called an 'idea' in Greek, in Latin is called a 'form.' Thus, by ideas we understand forms of other things existing beyond or apart from the things themselves. Now the form of a thing existing apart from that thing can play two roles: either that it be the exemplar of that whose form it is, or that it be the principle by which that thing is known, just as the forms of knowable things *(cognoscibilia)* are said to be in the one who knows them. On both accounts it is necessary to assume that there are ideas, which becomes clear in the following way. In all things which are generated (which come into being), not by chance, it is necessary for there to be a form which is the end-goal of every generation. The one who acts (the agent) would not act on account of form except inasmuch as the likeness of the form is in it. This can happen in two ways. In certain agents the form pre-exists before the thing which is to come into being according to natural existence, as for example, a man begets a man, and fire gives rise to fire. In certain other agents the form pre-exists by way of intelligible existence, as in agents who act through their intellects: for example, the likeness of a house pre-exists in the mind of the builder. This can be

called the idea of the house, since the craftsman intends to make the house similar to the form which he has conceived in his mind. Since the world has not arisen by accident, but has been made by God acting through his intellect ... it is necessary that in the divine mind there be a form according to whose likeness the world has been made. The meaning of ideas consists in this." *(S.th.*, 1a, q. 15 a. 1).

According to St. Thomas (q. 15 a. 2) there are as many ideas in God's intellect as there are individually existing things themselves, since every thing possesses its own idea. "In God's intellect there are proper ideas, as the reasons of all things,' which in turn is not in contradiction with the absolute non-composition of God (as postulated by the neo-Platonic philosophers who, in order to keep this non-composition, held that God possesses only the idea of the first creature and that this creature possesses the ideas of further creatures), for the multiplicity of divine ideas exists in the manner of something o n e and i n d i v i s i b l e. The idea of that which is done is found in the intellect of the doer as that which is understood, and not as the species by which it is understood, which is the form which brings about understanding. The form of a house in the mind of the builder is something understood by him. He forms a house in matter according to the likeness of this form in his mind. And it is not contrary to the simplicity of the divine intellect that he understands many things. But it would be contrary to his simplicity if his intellect were to be formed by many species. That is why many ideas exist in the divine mind, but as cognized by Him. This can be clarified in the following way: He knows his own essence in a perfect manner, and therefore in all the ways in which it can be known. His essence can be known not only inasmuch as it exists in itself, but also inasmuch as it can be participated in by creatures according to a certain manner of likeness. Each creature possesses its own proper species (specific perfection), insofar as it participates in some way in divine essence. Thus God, to the extent that He cognizes His essence as being imitable by such and such a creature, knows His own essence according to its proper reason and as the idea of this creature, and likewise for other creatures.

Chapter III

THE DRAMA OF NATURE AND PERSON

The general understanding of the ontic structure of the person constitutes not only an unchanging condition of the understanding of law, its nature, its binding power and scope, but it is a factor which renders this same law free from contradiction in various aspects. Depending on an appropriately understood ontic structure of human conduct, both individual and social, as well as of ultimate human destiny, there develops a differentiated understanding of law as a factor which fundamentally regulates human acts.

That is why we must here call upon philosophical anthropology, which allows a deeper apprehension of the person in important cognitive contents of life—emotional, volitive, moral religious, social and above all, of the fact of human death. These matters are necessarily presupposed here. However, despite that, we must recall, to an absolutely indispensable extent, the person's fundamental ontic structure and its social context, on account of their direct connection with the fact of law.[1]

1. THE HUMAN FACT (PHENOMENON)

When we explain, in philosophy as in other sciences (though in a very special way) the facts given to us in everyday cognitive experience, then we must, in the area of philosophical anthropology, show above all the HUMAN FACT. However, it is no easy matter to understand this fact, since it is composite in itself and can also be presented as part of different types of cognition, both scientific and pre-scientific.

It seems to many that the HUMAN BEING can become precisely the desired objective given FACT for philosophical explanation only when seen through science, since we must, in philosophy, make use of everything that is said by science, as Carrel postulated long ago, in order to show the model of the human being in all its aspects.

However, to be sure, such a postulate is anti-scientific, since the model of the human being, as it is outlined in different sciences by different methods, would in principle "hinge upon" the cognitive acts of each respective science, which would, as a result, make it impossible to form such a model that would be truly one and indicate the r e a l   f a c t . That is why the road to cognition is different here. As every science is based on a person's pre-scientific cognition, according to how he or she is educated in a particular epoch, so too is philosophy, for if a confrontation of contemporary science can take place at all—in any era—this probably happens only in the human mind. We presuppose, therefore, that the philosopher has some basic acquaintance with the results of the science of his or her generation.

However, which of the elements of a composite fact should be emphasized? Owing to a tradition which is over two thousand years old, scholars have recognized in the human being both a specific set of biological factors similar to those in other mammals, and what is generally called spirit or reason. Already in Aristotle's Lyceum the human being was defined as *ZOON LOGIKON*—an animal endowed with reason. It was commonly and traditionally objected that this generally named (and demonstrated) fact is too general, that it is inadequate and schematic, but the new propositions put forward, particularly those made recently, are subject to even greater reservations, and moreover, they constitute only an incomplete and fragmentary moment of the traditional general view of the human being, which moment presupposes, at the same time, the general understanding of the human being as an ontic fact. What is more, it so happens that, in the history of human thought on the subject of the human being, the models for understanding the human being proposed by philosophers or philosophizing scientists generally constitute some kind of reification, either of the biological aspect of the human being or of its spiritual aspect.

And yet, if some intelligent extra-terrestrial visitor came to our planet, it would perceive a very strange creature which, while being bodily similar to other animals, is at the same time even biologically distinct from them—a creature having a p o t e n t i a l i z e d organism which has functions connected with something other than purely biological aims. This animallike creature employs t o o l s made by itself for supra-biological aims; it employs s p e e c h as a system of conventional signs which are accepted and understood by others in its society; it conserves t r a d i t i o n and nurtures p r o g r e s s . Speech, as a system of conventional signs, testifies both to a c o n c e p t u a l cognition (this cognition is above all at the service of technology), and a c o n t e m p l a t i v e cognition (this is at the service of humans, as the creator and fulfiller of their highest functions). And one of the most characteristic moments of the "human fact" is human s e l f - k n o w l e d g e and reflection, not only on one's own acts but also on the meaning of one's own life and one's human destiny.

Precisely these moments, which contribute to the "fact" of being a human, require an explanation and a philosophical interpretation, whose aim would be the construction of the kind of reflected-upon model of the person which, on the one hand, will ultimately explain human being in the context of his most important function, and will, on the other, enable the explanation to be of a certain kind. The explanation given will have to be such that its eventual negation or rejection would of necessity result in a negation of the human "fact," given to us in pre-scientific cognition, and would therefore negate the perceived important elements of the human fact. When we consider the outlined human "fact" in a twofold way, as it appears to us: a) as "nature" (the biological though specific aspect of the human being), and b) as "spirit" (whose moments are technology, language, conceptual cognition, contemplative cognition, self-knowledge, society), then we perceive that in the history of the concept of the human being one of these two aspects would be emphasized and developed theoretically, and the other would not. Thus, in history as well as at the present moment, the human being is for some people either *res naturae,* a more or less complicated product of nature, to which he or she is ultimately reduced (whether in diachrony or synchrony), or a spirit, a transcendence of nature, its demiurge, potent or impotent. Yet the analysis of the elements of the human fact indicates the need for a different model of the person, which is outlined when reflecting on the facts of direct human inner experiences, accessible to every human being. A man or woman, on the basis of such an analysis, is a personal self who "expresses himself" or "expresses herself" as a unique being in matter (nature) and through matter.

Of course, the general outlines of the concept of person must be clarified, specified and modified, on the basis of the particular theories which formulated and presented their own particular models of the human being.

2. SOME THEORIES OF HUMAN NATURE

Perhaps the most "natural" concept of the human being was presented by evolutionism, based on the natural-biological sciences, according to which the human being is the last great link in the chain of evolution of the world of living matter, and even of the whole universe.

However, evolutionism, whether "blind," as in J. Huxley, or "directed," as in P. Teilhard de Chardin, although it explains a great deal about the history of life on earth, does not explain the elements of the "human fact" described above, particularly the elements of human transcendence over matter, which humans organize for extramaterial aims. Moreover, in the exclusively evolutionistic interpretation itself, as a possible, u l t i m a t e theory of explanation, we encounter a strange irrational assumption, that of explaining something "greater" by something "lesser." The reason for the emergence of more perfect creatures are less perfect creatures; the reason of being is supposed to be non-being. That is why the evolutionary theory can only be an auxiliary theory, functioning in the context of other complementary theories, in which the error of explaining being by non-being is avoided. Of course, I am not going into detailed discussion here with Teilhard de Chardin, whose vision of reality, from the methodological point of view, is an amalgam of observational statements, statements from the area of the theory of a science, as well as statements of the type dealing with belief, while all these types of statements, and indeed diverse ones too, are employed in the construction of a new theory, a vision in which the person appears almost as a cosmic god.

Even more interesting, in fact, were those theories which also reduce the human fact to a merely biological aspect, but which undertook the analysis of the shallow human "I" (that is, the human personality conceived as a center of disposition in relation to the world of things), in the light of medical or economico-social sciences. Freudianism and Marxism come to mind here.

If we were to reflect on the model of the human being shown in Freud's work, then we would above all perceive that his concept of human personality is a theoretical "background" for psychoanalytical therapeutic operations on the sick, neurotic "I," conceived not as being, but as a certain profile of activity. The "I" appearing in this way becomes comprehensible by reference to factors that are genetically prior, that is, by reference to the history of the individual in childhood, as well as to earlier pre-conscious forces (libido, eros, thanatos). Having probably borrowed the concept of pre-consciousness from Hegel, Freud recognized that the fundamental basis and reservoir of forces is the "id" (which is "libido," according to the first theory, and a combination of the antagonistic forces of eros and thanatos, according to the second). The specific development of the "id" leads to the appearance of consciousness and consequently the "ego," which, by interiorizing the arrangement of socio-cultural conditions, educates the "superego." All three stages of the development of fundamental forces are connected with either a normal or an abnormal outlet for basic instinctive drives (conversion, frustration, etc.) and, as a result, they thereby constitute a normal personality or one that deviates from the norm.

Such a theory allowed psychoanalysts (and, after Freud, psychoanalytical models of neurotic man became very differentiated) to carry out therapeutical operations. And in this sense the model of the human being presented here can sometimes be useful. However, with respect to its truth value, this conception is inadequate and erroneous, since it grasps the human fact very selectively (in fact, it does not even apprehend the individual as a being and subject, but as a personality-self, *Selbst*), which takes the neurotic "I" as its starting-point. The method applied to selected facts of the consciousness could not lead to the kind of theory of the human being which would be adequate for the human fact and at the same time non-contradictory with the fundamental elements of this fact.

Similarly the Marxist concept, although it is immeasurably deeper, also ultimately reduces the human being (in the historical aspect) to a creation of nature, even though consciousness and work in social conditions distinguish the human being from this same nature. This "distinction" from the background of nature is, however, a phenomenon of dialectical development. Moreover, it seems that the human consciousness as interpreted in Marxism, refers not so much to self-knowledge as to the aspect of "being in the world," that is, it stresses the "I" as the center of dispositions in relation to the environment, whereas the problem of the human being (as we shall discuss below) appears in the self-knowledge of the "I" as the subject which subjectivizes "my" acts.

The last link in the chain of anthropological thought, in which the human being is planted firmly in nature, and which reduces the human being to belonging to nature, without any possibility of transcendence, is an appropriately interpreted theory of structuralism. Although structuralism is a very interesting and fertile method of ethnological and cultural enquiry, its epistemological assumptions and the consequences flowing from its application are extended to the human being, and how humans are to be ultimately understood. Besides, C. Lévi-Strauss himself, the main creator of this theory, made unambiguous suggestions in the direction of precisely such an understanding of the human phenomenon; nevertheless, several very eminent contemporary philosophers have in fact grasped the philosophical implications of structuralism.

At first sight, the direction of structuralism seems to be a return to ontological positions; for here we recognize the permanence of fundamental ontic structures, which are to become the ultimate basis of the explanation of the fluid, historical phenomena of human life and of the human being, who, in different variations of existentialism, was generally recognized as the one and ultimate subject explaining the most varied manifestations of reality. Ultimately, human awareness-existence, through the act of creative cognition, gave every being its m e a n i n g . However, structuralism, with its recognition of the permanence of structures, with its rejection of history, of the human subject and of the primacy of consciousness, is, in fact, an attempt to ultimately explain human reality by r e d u c i n g it "to its base," to biological structures, while biological structures are subject to a further reduction to the state of matter. The latter is explained by the "law of accidentality," as the most universal law of being.[2]

Lévi-Strauss formulated his philosophical views on the human being not only on the basis of ethnological investigations, but directly, in a discussion with J.P. Sartre, whose aim in life was to create a new anthropology, which was no longer to be based on the *cogito* of thinking, but on the *cogito* of empirical experiencing. Lévi-Strauss writes:

> Descartes wanting to create physics, cut the human being off from society. Sartre, wanting to create anthropology, cuts his society off from others. Firmly set in individualism, the empirical *cogito,* which is to be simple and naive, loses itself in the blind alleys of social psychology because it exposes the secondary incidents of social life—the strike, the sports match, the queue—which do not reveal the foundations of such life.[3]

In discussing Sartre's position, then, and his emphasis on "I" as the subject, we must first of all, according to Lévi-Strauss, negate this subject as a basic ontic structure, for subjectivity can be reduced to wider, more general and primary structures. As Freud, Marx or Hegel to a large extent affirmed, the human "ego" is only a reflex and dialectic buckle of the "whole," covering opposite trends.[4]

For Lévi-Strauss, the stages needed to reach a fundamental structure are: a) language; b) psychoanalysis; c) biological mechanisms; d) the basic law of accidentality, leading to stable cognosticism.

Ad a) Lévi-Strauss believes that:

> linguistics puts us in the presence of dialectic and totality of being, which is, however, external with respect to the consciousness and will. Language, a non-reflective totalization, is in a certain sense a human mind, which has its reasons, and a human being in fact does not know them. And if someone puts forward the reservation that it is only for the subject, which is a speaking subject, such a solution is excluded, for the same evidence which reveals before him or her the nature of language, also reveals to the subject that this nature was the same when he or she did not know it ... since what is said is not and will never be the result of a conscious totalization of linguistic laws.

Thus, the "I" is the result of the use of language rather than its creator:

> There would be much to say on the subject of that reputed totalistic continuity of the "I," which we regard rather as an illusion kept up by the demands of social life, and therefore as the reflection of the exterior onto the interior—than as the object of irrefutable experience.[5]

Ad b) Freudian science requires that the explanation of more composite structures take place through less composite structures—and on this basis, we see the reduction of psychic phenomena to biological ones:

> From the moment we attain an understanding of life as a function of inert matter, we discover that this matter possesses properties completely different from those that were previously attributed to it ... and consequently, in our apprehension "I" does not oppose "you" any more than the human being puts himself or herself in opposition to the world: the truths we reach through the human being are of "the world." The person who begins by plunging the self into alleged obviousness of the "I" can never extricate himself from there. The cognition of people sometimes seems easier to those who have allowed themselves to be caught in the trap of personal identity. However, in this way one shuts for oneself the gate to knowing the human being. The basis of all ethnographical investigations is written or involuntary "confessions."[6]

Consequently, the "I," just as the neurotic Freudian "I," can be reduced to forces more fundamental than those which manifest the "I."

Ad c) These more extensive and more basic forces are a manifestation of the "whole." The ethnologist, in order to understand the meaning of the human being, attempts, in the face of different cultures,

> to put himself in the place of the people who live there, understand the principle and rhythm of their intentions, perceive the epoch or culture as a meaningful whole. ... Dialectical reason ought to lead the humanistic sciences to embrace reality, which only it can make accessible to them, whereas scientific effort in the strict sense consists in the sharing of reality, and later putting it together again according to a different plan.[7]
>
> We would define ourselves, therefore, as a transcendental materialist and aesthete. A transcendental materialist, because dialectic reason is not anything other for us than the analytical reason, nor is it anything that could be the basis of an absolute originality of human order; dialectic reason is something more in the womb of the analytical reason itself: it is a necessary condition for this reason to dare to begin resolving what is human into what is non-human. An aesthete, since Sartre uses this term to define those who want to examine people as if they were ants. But disregarding the fact as such, it seems, is the attitude of every scientist, since he is an agnostic. It is not a compromising attitude at all, since ants, with their artificial cultivation of fungi, their social life and chemical stimuli already put up a sufficiently strong resistance to the operations of analytical reasoning. We agree to the name aesthete, then, insofar as we believe that the ultimate aim of the humanistic sciences is not to constitute man but to dismember him in order to solve the enigma of man.[8]

Ad d) Lévi-Strauss wrote that:

> Man's wisdom consists in looking at oneself as experiencing "I" with the awareness (but in a different register) that what he experiences (so fully and so intensively), will present itself as a myth to people of a future century and perhaps to himself in a few years' time, and will not reveal itself at all to people of a future millennium. Each sense can be justified by a lesser sense and if this regression finally comes to recognize the "law of coincidence," which can only state "that it is so and not otherwise," then this prosepct does not contain anything alarming for the mind, which is not disturbed by any transcendence, even in a larval form; for man will receive everything that he might rationally wish for himself, if he succeeds—under the condition that he bends before this law—in defining his practice and placing the whole remainder in the sphere of comprehensibility.[9]

The negation of subjectivity, as the larval form of transcendence, structuralism, the reduction of everything which is governed by the law of contingency to basic structures, leads to agnosticism and the negation of the foundations of all theism. This comprehensibility is a comprehensibility à rebours.

Another trend for understanding the human being, favored by contemporary anthropological concepts and denoting the aspects of consciousness and spirit, is derived from Hegel's standpoint.

Hegel's theory, too, did not emerge "from nothingness," but is an important link in the philosophy of the subject, deriving from Descartes and finding its distinct mark in Kant's creativity. It is the cognizing subject and the facts of consciousness—whether concerned with content or function—which are something fundamentally valuable, something that must be analyzed and interpreted. Since Descartes' time, the "I" (as a spirit present to itself, as something cognitively indubitable, since it manifests itself in thinking—*cogito*) is constantly the area or "field" in which the drama of the experience of consciousness takes place. And even if this "I" were to disappear, as a result of criticism (as in some systems: Hume), or become reduced to a function awaiting empirical facts (for example, the analytical reason in Kant), cognitive contents or laws of consciousness still become the "reality" analyzed by various philosophers and raised to the dignity of "object of consciousness" or even to "everything" or "the whole."

Hegel, too, grasped the object of thought as "everything" and "the whole," which, being contradictory in itself, does not "exist" but b e c o m e s, according to the law of dialectic, "yes" and "not-yes," as well as "not not-yes." This last negation of a negation is a synthesis in relation to the thesis and antithesis of previous states. The developmental dialectic of the object of thinking reveals in Hegel the "absolute spirit" through development from unconscious, pre-conscious states, through the subjective spirit and the objective spirit. In the human being, from the moment a state is reached in which the human being starts to philosophize, the absolute spirit achieves its fullness, not only in itself but for itself. The individual is, however, only a reflex, a dialectic moment in the development of the "whole." The human being, together with his subjective spirit is only a stage of the revelation of the absolute spirit. The human being is not a whole in itself, a being in itself and for itself in the full sense of this word, but only a function of the whole. This whole ultimately gains its self-understanding as a being in itself and for itself in the absolute spirit, and develops dialectically in the necessary stages or phases of development established by Hegel.

It is not surprising that the reduction of the person's role to a function of, stage in, or only a dialectic moment of, the development of the "whole" provoked the opposition of some of Hegel's students, particularly S. Kierkegaard who, perhaps also under the influence of the Christian religion (he himself was a Protestant Pastor), perceived the exclusivity of the individual existence of the human being, his experiences and the drama which takes place in the depths of his personal consciousness. The person as an individual, experiencing this drama consciously, thereby finds himself in an exceptional (existential) border-line situation. None of the objective and great systems, like for instance Hegel's, can justify or make sense of human existence. Only the affirmation of Jesus Christ, who has overcome the tragedy of death and sin, can help the human being to experience the fear of danger. The choice, either of Christ or of nothingness, is the only alternative given to human beings. The alternative that a choice exists, in the terminal, conscious, tragic situation of existence, also appears in the work of other existentialists, but with the reservation that the choice is directed, and will lead, towards nothingness, as for instance in M. Heidegger and J.P. Sartre.

Among the existentialists, perhaps the most original and at the same time controversial philosopher is M. Heidegger, who draws upon classical philosophical concepts in many areas. Concerning the problem of the human being, he too uses categories which were already elaborated in antiquity. Above all he draws attention to the fact that we cannot place the human being within the framework of the Aristotelian category of substance, as existing in itself in an unchanging way, for the human being ceaselessly changes from within. And if we could define the individual, then perhaps it would not be so much by means of categories, but rather through "existentials" (precisely because they are specifically human modes of being), for the individual human is born completely immersed in the world. That is why his fundamental mode of being, his "existential," is precisely *Geworfenheit* (a passive "being thrown" into the world), in which the individual must express himself or herself in a human way, consciously, by philosophizing. This passive "being thrown" into the world—and immersion in the world—are expressed in a threefold order: a) in relation to objects, b) in relation to other people, and c) in relation to one's own mode of "being-intime."

Thus, above all, the human being finds himself or herself in the role of a user in relation to objects, particularly inanimate ones (but also living ones, that is plants and animals). Objects, (that is, the surrounding world), interest man and woman insofar as they are u s e f u l, insofar as they are accessible, "ready-at-hand" *(zuhanden-sein),* or as they can be used in the realization of a personal aim. For this reason every human being builds a "pyramid of usable values" for himself or herself. In a word: the individual expresses himself or herself consciously in the form *sich besorgen,* in relation to objects of this kind. The human being is a concerned user of the object.

However, we live surrounded by other people, who require our special existential attitude, a mode of being that is not indifferent but involved, a mode of being "concern-with"—*fürsorgen.* The other person actively involves me in some way, either in a positive or in a negative sense. And I cannot, in relation to ... the other person living side by side with me, be "objective," uninvolved.

Above all, the human being itself (apprehended in itself) is the "place" in which being expresses itself, in the one who builds in precisely "this way," and in whom existence fulfills itself in time—*Dasein.* Existence fulfilling itself in time is essentially ordered towards death, which is what gives the human being his or her ultimate expression, or personal and unrepeatable "countenance." In the face of death, human "temporary being of this kind" is expressed—in the proper sense—in the form of experiencing care—*S o r g e*. However, at the same time the prospect of death gives meaning and intensity to human experiences, of which the fundamental cognitive experience is the apprehension of being. It is in human *D a s e i n* that being appears thematically as *das Seiende* concretely experienced in a conscious way—as the meaning of being as it fulfills itself in the individual. Being itself, beyond human *D a s e i n*, is inaccessible, and that is why man and woman become the place in which Being is joined to such being. To be more precise, he and she become the manifestation of Being under the appearance of such entities.

The human being is an exceptional creation in whom the sense of being appears. He or she is, as it were, the common good of various shades of existentialism. Of course, the mode in which the meaning of being appears in each of the existentialists is perceived and expressed differently in each case. For Jaspers, the essential meaning of being is expressed in the privileged judgement "I am," in which there is an immediate affirmation, from within, of the "mystery" of existence, since all other judgements which state the existence of objects or other people are already "reifying" statements, making a mere object of a living person. The same motif also appears in Sartre, who magnificently describes the function of "reifying" another person. The sense of being, for Marcel, is ultimately revealed in the act of love and loving trust. ...

Everywhere, however, the human being is the place "which is central," constituting the "sense" or "non-sense" of being. The "I" of the existentialists, when grasped as consciousness which is fulfilling itself in time and constituting the meanings and subjects of being, is the transcendence of all "I" in the presence of the whole of nature; it is also the "reason for" our strangeness in the world, it is the source of unfulfilled (unfulfillable) aspirations and tendencies, the source of a tragedy from which there is no escape, since it is impossible for one who is a person (who expresses himself or herself in the conscious "I," which "I" produces the meaning and meaninglessness of being) to leave consciousness.

3. THE HUMAN INDIVIDUAL—A PERSON

The various explanations of the human being proposed here by way of illustration, are instructive, as they constitute, in the main, a selected, periodically occurring grasp of aspects of reality, a grasp of reality which occurred in history in different variations. The classical stream of the philosophy of being dominates extreme conceptions, but we are aware of the fact that being itself is very diversely understood, and that is why there were different systems even in the classical stream, to the extent that it stresses the twofold aspect of human being: its material structure, and at the same time its spiritual appearance. This found a distinctive expression in the concept of the person mentioned by Boethius, when he defined the person, having undoubtedly in mind the human being, as *rationalis naturae individua substantia* (an individual substance of a rational nature). It is true that this definition also applies to God and the angels, according to Boethius' thinking; nevertheless, the guiding concept in its construction was undoubtedly the cognitive grasp of the human being. And if the human being was conceived as a p e r s o n , in the Christian tradition, then we must seek the foundations for a more adequate understanding of the human being precisely in the analysis of the concept of the person (perhaps even in the early theory of the person), as the supreme ontic formation in general, and we must do so also for a synthesis of these aspective, sometimes even contradictory, formulations about the human being.

It seems that we can, in the light of the achievements of the philosophy of the subject, express Boethius' definition as the "I" of a rational nature; for what Boethius understood by the expression *individua substantia* must briefly be called the analogically conceived "I." Individual substance deriving from rational nature (undivided in itself) precisely manifests itself as the rational, conscious "I." Thereby, this "I," understood analogically (that is, "I" as the fulfiller of conscious contents in each being of human nature), better expresses unrepeatability (of the "existential" type) than the schematization of Aristotle's thought *individua substantia*, which M. Heidegger rightly criticized.

We are witnesses to the fact that, in the history of philosophy, there appeared—cyclically, as it were—two streams of thought, stressing two aspects of human being: the Orphic-Platonic trend, which stresses the human "I" as an independently existing divinity, which is connected rather with the matter of the human body, which body is more of a "tomb" than a help in the inner perfecting of the spirit; the second stream, on the other hand, stressed the role of nature, the role of the body, its connection with the whole of nature and the universe.

The Orphic-Platonic trend of understanding the human being proceeded from directly given human psychic experiences, particularly higher spiritual ones (religious experiences, higher aspirations, conceptual cognition, reflection, love etc.), which indicated the transcendence of the human psyche, which in a fundamental way dominated nature and changeable time-space conditions in such a way that, in the cultural context of the time in question, the human "psyche" could be conceived merely as a mythological god, who is immortal and lives by exercising spiritual values. This awareness of transcendence in relation to nature was at the same time connected with the redemptive function of philosophy (for only philosophy made man or woman realize that he or she was a divine being who must spurn and liberate the self from the material conditions of being "imprisoned" in the body), which seemed to exclude the need for religion, especially soteriological Christian religion. St. Augustine, fundamentally accepting the Platonic concept of the human soul, had to make an enormous intellectual effort to be able both to accept philosophical ideas and affirm the Christian faith.

Together with the Orphic-Platonic stream, there appeared, almost simultaneously, a second more naturalistic (and naturalistic-legal) attitude, operating on the concept of nature *(physis)* on the basis of the discovery of the universe. What is more, the human being was conceived as a certain defined nature, and the universe as a set of ordered natures which are subsistent beings, having an ordered, permanent, rational activity. The human being as a defined nature is the same object of rational philosophical investigations as the whole universe. And the whole of the human being's exceptionality, which was undoubtedly perceived even by Aristotle and the Stoics, gained its ultimate explanation by calling upon the rational, material context of the universe and not upon some supra-cosmic transcending gods. The human "I" was to be merely a particular discharge of the cosmic nature—how momentary that makes it!—for although the human being is endowed with thinking, neither Aristotle nor the Stoics were able to say whether this real capacity for thinking was actually caused by the human immanent p s y c h e , or whether it was the activity of a pure intelligence or of *natura naturans* itself.

4 . THE HUMAN BEING—A PERSONAL BEING

The starting-point, in a philosophical explanation of the human being, can only be the immediate facts of our cognition. When we speak of the "immediacy" of cognition, we thereby exclude not only all emotional mediators, (all objective cognition, particularly the scientific kind, requires this), but also those connected with the nature of systematic cognition of a similar type to the premises of a syllogism, which help cognition to come to its conclusion. The Classic philosophers called this an *ex quo* mediation. We also exclude the mediation of all symbols, known as *medium per quod,* even of the kind represented by human speech employing conventional signs as expressions; (metonymic symbolism is *a fortiori* excluded here). What is more, where really immediate cognition is concerned, any *medium quod* is also excluded, that is, a mediation of the type that we constantly encounter in our conceptual cognition of a real thing. We cognize the contents of a thing by apprehending its meaning—the cognized meaning is a concept—which in fact connects us with the thing itself, apprehended aspectively, and is the reason why it can be truly known, but which meaning can at the same time be "abstracted" from the thing, since we can take meanings themselves as the object of our analyses when we abstract them. In fact, we possess extremely few acts of immediate cognition. Immediate cognition can probably be reduced to the kind of cognition we carry out through existential judgements (when I recognize that this particular John exists), as when we cognize what is consciously happening in us, that is, when we cognize our inner states or conscious existential processes.

The immediate facts of our consciousness are something fundamental and indubitable in the process of the interpretation of the human being. All hypotheses gained as a result of interpretation (philosophical or scientific) in relation to immediately given facts of consciousness, but not in accordance with them, must be rejected as false, for any interpretations whatsoever are something secondary in relation to immediately given ones; they are something given indirectly, something gained precisely by means of a process of thinking, whereas immediately given ones are primary. However, precisely these immediately given ones must be further submitted to ultimate explanation, taking into account their nature appearing in the consciousness, that is, the kind from which we cannot refer to some further science.

Thus, in all our conscious experiences, we experience that "I" am the one who fulfills functions and acts of the most varied content, both material and non-material. "My" acts experientially connected with matter (such as physiological functions, as experiencing a headache, a stomachache, heartache, etc.) as well as acts which in their structure turn out to be nonmaterial (such as acts of conceptual and judgemental cognition, as reflection, acts of reflection, love, etc.), have a varied structure. When we consciously experience what is "mine," and in all "my" acts fulfilling these acts of the "I," we witness the p r e s e n c e, the i m m a n e n c e of the "I" in all that is "mine," as well as the fact of the transcendence of the "I" over particular (as well as combined) acts of "mine." This has fundamental theoretical consequences. We also have an immediate inner experience of the presence of the "I," the e x i s t e n c e of the "I," but we do not cognize its (the "I's") nature. The "I" is immediately given, as c a u s i n g my acts, which acts are diverse in content; it is given merely from the aspect of its existence and not from the aspect of its nature. We perceive here both the correctness of Hume's investigations and at the same time the tragedy of his error, for he, criticizing Descartes, was completely right in claiming that we do not possess any idea or any impression of the "I," and consequently, he believed that it is some kind of psychic construction, some kind of psychic habit. It is true that we do not possess an idea of the "I," since we have no experience of its nature, but it is also true (and we are certainly conscious of the fact) that the "I" is p r e s e n t, that the "I" exists and supports in their existence all contents experienced by the "I." That is why we give existence to all "my" contents, whether material or non-material; they exist, "live" a life of the "I," present and conscious in all "my" acts. And a condition of psychic normality is precisely the awareness of the existence of "I" in "my" acts, being caused.

However, at the same time we do not know the inner content, we do not directly cognize the nature of our "I." We know and we are aware of the presence and existence of "I" animating all that is "mine" in my acts. If, however, we wish to cognize the nature of "I," we are compelled to take, with this purpose in mind, a roundabout way through the analyses of the structure of "mine" and come to conclusions about the nature of "I" through interpretations of that which is "mine." We constantly proceed in this way. We cognitively establish the content of our "I" by making arduous efforts, liable to error, to analyze the content of acts ("of mine") fulfilled by our "I."

Thus "I" and "mine" are given to us immediately in our experiences of consciousness, with the reservation that "I" appears to us only from the existential aspect, from the aspect of fact and presence in all that is "mine." We have no experience of the content, that is, the nature of "I" itself, whereas we are directly given the experience of the content of that which is "mine," which can be, and is, both material and spiritual.

We can, therefore, state that the "I" appearing to us from the existential aspect, from the aspect of me who is present in "my" contents, occurs as a s u b s i s t e n t s u b j e c t w h i c h i s p r e s e n t and at the same time the author of "my" acts, having a content which is also evidently given. The nature (structure) of these contents of everything that is "mine" can indicate to us, and does indicate to us, the nature of the "I" itself as a subsistent subject and one that nourishes all that is "mine." And if this "mine" is both material (the contents of physiological experiences) and non-material (the acts of intellectual cognition, love, etc.), then the "I" itself will be in its nature simultaneously material and non-material. Thus, the observation of directly given conscious experiences puts before us the problem of the existence of the kind of ontic structure of the "I" which is at the same time material and non-material.

Of course, philosophical interpretation has now reached the point where, on the strength of it, we must "construct" a true model of the person. What is important here is that the structure of the human being, appearing as a result of explanation, be completely in accordance with the immediate facts of our consciousness and that it may, at the same time, ultimately explain why precisely we experience "my" material and non-material acts as having their subject in the same "I."

A theoretical solution to this strange phenomenon was suggested by St. Thomas Aquinas,[10] who skillfully employed the general Aristotelian concept of the human being, and which he included in his original theory of being. St. Thomas' solution transcends the Platonic and at the same time the Aristotelian view of man; it avoids their extremes and at the same time coheres with the immediate facts of our consciousness.

Having, on the one hand, the "I" which subjectivizes "my" acts, and yet on the other hand, precisely those acts "of mine" have material contents (physiological acts) and non-material contents (higher psychic acts), we must keep the ontic identity of the subject "I" immanent (present) in both groups of acts, and at the same time see them as groups of acts of the transcending "I," since we directly know that "I" (subjectivized) am the author of these acts; I transform them, and thereby experience that I am not—"I" is not—a construction of acts, but on the contrary, acts radiate from the "I." This "I," which transcends material and non-material acts and is at the same time present as the same subject (being) in both types of acts, is somehow "composite." As the reason of being for spiritual, non-material acts— non-contradiction from the aspect of the subject—there is the spiritual "part" (aspect) of the "I", which I call (in accordance with tradition) the human soul. Consequently "I," immanent in "my" acts, is given immediately, to me, and not proved; the "soul," on the other hand, is the result of proof, which renders free from contradiction; it is a systematic construction, necessary for explaining the fact of the immanence of the "I" in my material acts. This soul, being the subjective reason of being, for spiritual acts, is not independent of the body, but on the contrary, is essentially connected with it, as can be seen from the mode of functioning of spiritual acts. The bonding of the soul with the body is essentially non-contradictory only when the soul and the body, forming a unity, are to one another in the relation of act to potency, to be more precise: of form to matter (Aristotle already perceived this). There is, however, in the person, the important moment that the soul, being a form of the body and organizing for itself the matter for being a human body, exists subsistently.

Hence, the human soul exists not because it is a form, because it organizes, but, on the contrary, it organizes because it subsistently exists, although it came into existence at the moment it became an independent organizer, that is the form of its body. Thus, the human being exists by the soul's existence as the form of the body. The subsistant soul-form constantly organizes for itself the matter which is to be the human body, precisely because it is organized. The human being, then, is not a real being as a result of the organization of matter, but on the contrary, the organization of matter takes place as a result of the fact that the subsistent soul is at the same time the organizer (to the extent that it exists), that is, the form of the body. The organizing of the body by the soul is not something added to the soul, but belongs to the soul's inner nature. Matter is constantly organized by the "soul-I" and the soul is the reason why we experience ourselves as of the same being.

St. Thomas' solution, as has already been mentioned, appeared as different both from the Orphic-Platonic and from the Aristotelian one, for the human soul, although it subsists (and the soul is entitled to existence in a proper manner, and not just in "the whole" that is man or woman, as the composite of soul and body), did not, however, exist previously through the body (organized by itself); nor is its relation to the body merely "external" but, on the contrary, as it is the form and organizer of the body, the soul is essentially connected with matter organized by itself. Matter is for the good of the "soul-I" itself, since only the "soul-I," by means of the matter which it organizes, can express itself, can come into contact with being, can perfect itself, for only it ("the soul-I") subsists. In a word, matter organized by the soul is organized for spiritual aims, for transcendent aims. And here St. Thomas' concept differs from the thought of Aristotle who, also regarding the soul as a form of the body, accepted the fact that the soul itself is not entitled to being, but that only the whole which is composed of soul and body is entitled to it; in a word, the human being, according to the Stagirite, emerges a s a r e s u l t o f o r g a n i z a t i o n and his being is fundamentally the b e - i n g, not of the soul but of the whole. Consequently, the disintegration of the whole is at the same time the disintegration of the soul. According to St. Thomas, it is correct to say that the disintegration and death of the organism does not yet destroy the soul, which does not exist by the existence of the whole but by its own existence, and the body only participates in the existence of the soul insofar as it is organized. Thus, the fact that it may cease to organize some greater or lesser amount of matter still does not affect the existence of the soul, for, although it exists together with the body (to which it "grants" existence), it does not exist as a result of the fact that it forms the body, as in Aristotle's system.

St. Thomas' solution, therefore, is very specific. It avoids the shallowness and one-sidedness that appeared in the history of anthropological thought. The personal moment of the soul, of its own existence, is stressed in this solution, which recalls the analyses of the existentialists which emphasize the individual's exceptionality. On the other hand, by accepting the concept of human n a t u r e, the moment of the organization of the body by the subsistent soul, we can perceive in a much deeper way that which was unilaterally, and thereby falsely, stressed in Aristotle and the modern structuralists; for the fact that the human being is a determined n a t u r e, the fact that matter enters the essential composition of this same human nature, that through matter organized for the good of the soul itself the human being is "relative" to the whole of nature and has essential connections with it, all this still does not deny the actual transcendence of the human personal "I."

The necessity of matter for the soul-I—for being a human and coming into existence (though not for being "of" matter)—can never be too strongly emphasized, for only the universe, nature, and matter, allow the existence, the activity and perfection of the human person. Without matter and its essential ontic function, human being would not be possible, for a human being does not exist previously as a spirit-soul, but the soul obtains its existence precisely at the moment when it is empowered to become the form-organizer of the human body. And, together with the function of formation, it obtains its own existence, which in turn it grants, through the act of formation, to the human body.

Having the immediate, ascertainable existence of our own "I," always present in all psychic and conscious acts, the "I" as the fulfiller of the content of our acts, we immediately perceive the transcendence of this "I" in relation to all experienced contents. These contents are, as it were, "threaded onto" the being of the "I." They are m i n e because I animate them, I give them my being. It is true that they, too, "construct" me in a particular way, ultimately enriching the nature of my "I," but it is I who called them to being.

In this light, too, the p e r s o n a l aspect of the human being reveals itself more clearly. A human is a personal being, and not merely an example of a specific species: *homo sapiens*. To be an example of a specific species means to receive one's existence through n a t u r e, to which one belongs. The existence of an individual of specific species is the result of being organized to a definitive nature. The human being, on the other hand, receives existence as a soul which organizes matter and constitutes species through this organization of matter. To be a person means to receive existence—life without the mediation of nature, for personal existence (in this case the existence of a human being) is not a result of nature, but on the contrary, nature is the result of the subsistent existence of the soul, which is at the same time a form of the organism. The existence of the person is, then, a unique existence, which organizes nature for itself. Having in mind the relation of the subsistent subjective "I" and of "my" acts being fulfilled, we perceive, as if *in fieri,* in the act of being formed, the relation of person to nature described in the classical philosophy of being. Precisely the subsistent "I," c o n s c i o u s in "my" acts (both spiritual and bodily), is nothing other than the sought-for p e r s o n, which St. Thomas spoke of as being EXISTENCE PROPER AND PROPORTIONAL TO A GIVEN INDIVIDUAL NATURE. We perceive that the "I," transcendent and at the same time immanent in all "my" acts, is an expression of the transcendence of the person over nature. It is the person as a subjective, subsistent "I" (given to us in cognition from the existential aspect), who organizes, that is (as expressed by Aristotle, and St. Thomas after him) f o r m s for himself or herself an individual n a t u r e as a concrete, individual source of human rational activity.

Of course, this organization of a person's individual nature takes place fundamentally through spiritual acts, since we are concerned here with nature conceived as a source of human activity in the purely human aspect. It is not a question of myself organizing, as I fancy, my bodily nature, which is given to me to a large extent by the system of my genes. The organizing for myself of my material body and nature is also dependent on biological and material laws, and on all those determinants which constitute natural order. The person, as the fulfilling, subjective "I," is entangled in the laws of nature when it forms and organizes the body. Having a primacy over the organized body, it nevertheless needs it in order to express itself, to make itself aware of itself, in order to be a human being. In all that manifests itself through the body and in the body, the human being is "related" to other products of nature and is subject to the laws of conduct which have been discovered in nature.

In spite of this, however, the human being transcends nature and manifests his or her personal characteristics of activity. These are the result of a formed personal "nature" (conceived as a source of activity), which can roughly be identified with human personalistic profile constituted as a result of hierarchizing spiritual acts. And in this sense "I," as a subject which exists to a higher degree than does the organizing of the body for myself, transcend the contents of spiritual acts and their permanent mode of activity. I select for myself my acts, through which I express myself and enter into the world I find.

It is I who select for myself (choose and reject) in my acts of decision the acts of a specific content which suit m e. The appropriate selection of acts for oneself (always with a specific content, having an influence on the nature of "I") is precisely the forming for oneself a personal nature, the construction of a personal "face." And that is why the human person is a potential personality, that is, the kind that through its acts perfects itself, constructs and fulfills itself; that is, it reaches fullness. In all these acts, matter is necessary for the human person; but the aims of such "reaching fullness" are far beyond material ones, yet marked by the nature and laws of matter. The aims of the person are internal, personal: the enrichment of cognition, the enrichment of love, the gaining of a higher state of freedom in relation to all determinants, whether internal or external. Through such a type of inner enrichment the person transcends nature, although he or she is at present in it through his or her acts of life, particularly psychic acts. The person reaches auto-affirmation and development mainly by developing in himself or in herself a mode of being "for-the-other-person." Ultimately, a person actualizes his or her personal potentiality through the moment of death, conceived actively, when he or she gains the full conditions for making an ultimate, complete, precisely personal decision in relation to the Transcendence, which appeared in the course of a changeable life rather as a problem than as an irrefutably intruding reality, in relation to which he or she would have to assume a standpoint. That is why the human person as a "being-towards-death" fulfills himself or herself ultimately as a person, that is, as completely free, cognizing in a direct way and capable of the highest love precisely through actively conceived death, which is the keystone of the whole of life's "construction" of the personality.

5. THE CHARACTERISTICS OF THE PERSON (TOWARD THE THEORY OF THE PERSON)

In the classical stream of philosophy, it was customary to distinguish the characteristic features of personal being; these are: intellectual cognition, love, freedom, the subjectivity of law, completeness and dignity. An analysis of them would give, as a result, the fundamental framework of the theory of the person, and thereby of philosophical anthropology. Each of the features, when analyzed (as is almost self-evident), constitutes a specific synthesis and, as it were, a dialectic coupling of the moments of person and nature (determinants usually deriving from a material factor), with the reservation that the transcending of the former ones is regarded precisely as an expression of the soul, (the specific—human—soul), in the personal being. At the same time it is stressed that the first three features (that is, cognition, love, and freedom) distinguish the human being, as a personal being, from the rest of nature. The latter three, (the subjectivity of law, completeness, and dignity), on the other hand, emphasize the transcendence of the person in relation to society.

a) H u m a n c o g n i t i o n constitutes in itself an immense subject to cover and analyze, especially when we take a look at this problem in the light of the varied discussions that have accumulated around it in the course of centuries. It is not possible here to make even introductory and general remarks on these subjects. Let us draw attention, however, to some which are more closely connected with the nature of personal being. Above all, we perceive an essential difference between human and animal cognition. The latter, restricting itself merely to the world of the senses, is connected inseparably with reactions of movement, which fundamentally aim at conserving the life of the individual or the species. The human being, however, interprets the content of being, apprehended in various aspects, when cognizing, rather than merely what is necessary for purely biological aims. Apprehending being, in cognition—whether conceptual or aspectively judgemental—one simultaneously u n d e r s t a n d s apprehended reality and expresses this understanding externally to other people. In the act of cognition, therefore, one links together three "levels" of signs: conventional signs, for example; general expressions, symbols, etc.; natural signs, for example the comprehended meanings of general expressions; and the thing denoted, which is itself apprehended cognitively, aspectively. Thus, cognition is a ceaseless "making contact" with being, with the thing itself, and not an independent conscious experience of the senses, nor an operation based merely on conventional signs, as occurs in the case of computerized "thinking." When linking, in the act of cognition, three levels of signs, the human being carries out only one cognitive function, though it is inseparably made up of the different threads of the structure of the senses and the reason. And although an analysis of particular cognitive structures is necessary and indispensable for a better understanding of the process of our cognition, what is exceedingly more important is to perceive the functional unity of our cognition, which at different stages is more or less satiated with matter (the cognizing senses), or with non-materiality and freedom. And if the analysis of the structures and sources of our cognition indicates a factor o f n a t u r e , which is extremely important for understanding the act of cognition, its relation to reality, and its content and mode of being, a closer look at the function of cognition (its fact and mode of activity) shows us a non-determined and personal mode of human be-ing.

We perceive, in the human being, who cognizes a twofold selectivity: one that is innate, as it were "given" to an individual together with nature, and another that is free, deriving from choice and personal fancy, that is, linked with love and freedom. The selectivity of our inborn cognitive apparatus, flowing from nature, expresses itself in the fact that we make cognitive contact with being, insofar as it is entwined in matter, or else we construct for ourselves a concept of being on the model of material being. Although it is true that "what we cognize" is being (and that is why we are capable of cognizing any being) it is, however, also true that we cognize this being as the "essentiality of material things," that is, "the fact of how we cognize" is characterized by materiality. The object specifying our thought is the "essentiality of material things," while the matching object is being as being. The human being, therefore, can cognize anything, but at the same time will apprehend anything cognized on the model of material things. "Apprehending" even non-material things—God, too—we apprehend on the model of material things, for the person, immersed in existence in the world, and emerging from the world, needs the world of matter to express himself or herself cognitively. Thus, the person apprehends the being of things, but under cover of apprehending matter. And this is human natural cognitive determination. Just as a receiver is adjusted to receive certain wavelengths, so too the human being is "regulated" to the essentiality of material things. And the person can effectively employ language, though "ontic" but characterized by an ordering to matter, to the essentiality of things cognizable by the senses.

Apart from this natural selectivity given to the human being together with nature and its history (the making of tools throughout the centuries, even stone tools, is significant here), there exists in the human being as a personal being a cognitive selectivity deriving from free will and freedom. It has long been noted that we better cognize only what we love (what we like, at least) and what we want to cognize, but not what we are forced to cognize. Cognition, love and freedom, are mutually conditioned and complement one another like the three sides of a triangle. This does not mean, though, that they have the same measurements and that the intensity of one side of life draws the intensity of the other two sides, since great love can exist in spite of the other person's being poorly known; but there is always a mutual conditioning of the acts of cognition, love and freedom.

The selectivity of our acts of cognition, on the basis of love and choice, manifests itself above all in our education, and then in our particular cognitive interests. Ultimately, we ourselves, freely, and fundamentally out of liking, choose an "occupation" for ourselves, and thereby we cognitively specialize and become more aware of certain domains, even theoretical, cognitive ones. When we specialize in one domain, we are capable of cognizing it in a better, deeper way than we do another. Our love for one area of knowledge increases our cognitive capacities to such an extent that strong involvement (love and freedom) allows even the intellectually weaker to go further than those who are uninvolved though more capable.

b) When it is a question of l o v e (as the act towards which man's and woman's personal life is aimed, and through which it is fundamentally fulfilled), the moment of initiative, the moment of freedom and transcendence, is very visible. Whereas in animals "love" is an instinct that is completely at the service of the species and is at the same time blind, necessary; in the person the domain of love has an extremely wide scope: from sexual love, through various forms of solidarity and human friendship, to love and friendship with God.

The very nature of the act of love, however it is conceived—whether in an Aristotelian way, or according to St. Thomas' theory, or finally G. Marcel's— shows an inner connection both with cognition and freedom. This is because, in order for love to exist, some kind of cognition, at least imperfect cognition, is needed. Moreover, this act is inwardly interwoven with freedom, with choice, since in love we always encounter the affirmation and choice of a good—person or being (the name and terminology used by differing philosophical trends varies, but does in fact yield the same moments, despite various languages and a diverse cognitive apparatus), which we love and through which we bind ourselves no longer just intentionally but really, thereby establishing a new mode of be-ing, that is, for the other person. For this reason, too, St. Thomas conceived love on the model of a permanent inner activity, which orders us to the object of our love, quoting St. Augustine's well-known expression: *Ponderibus aguntur omnia. Amor meus pondus meum - eo fervor quocumque feror.*

The act and state of love, while completing cognition, constitutes the person into a small microcosm, as it were, in which everything is contained, for, if through the act of cognition we become intentionally connected with being and express the content of this being in ourselves, then we may give ourselves to the other person in the act of love, when we are thus inwardly enriched, giving, together with ourselves, our whole inner richness.

The act of cognition and love is, as it were, a double arm, with which we connect ourselves with the world and another person, making possible the objective "circulation" of ontic values. In the act of love, which requires a specific analysis (which takes into account its causes, structure and results), two moments must be stressed: the moment of freedom in love, and the moment of the mode of being for the loving person.

The first matter, freedom in love, particularly in its supreme expression, which is the act of friendship, is connected precisely with the personal aspect of a human being. Through love we not only affirm the cognized good but, at the same time, in friendship, we co-create this good of the other person, and in the other person. And personal love does not cease as a result of the changeableness of the partner, but being free, is simultaneously loyal. Thus, personal love takes a different course from that which happens in nature on the basis of "instinctive love." Love, causing a specific state of being "for the other person," fundamentally constitutes the significance of life and personal activity. G. Marcel, expressing himself in rather an exaggerated way (but in his language this expression is the proper one), rightly drew attention to the fact that love belongs more to the category of *être* (to be) than to *avoir* (to have). Love causes a new state of personal being, a relational state which deeply penetrates the structure of personal being. Through love, a person exists for another person.

And in fact it is difficult, about impossible, to separate such a mode of being from personal being. Thus, love conceived in this way is the basis of social harmony and the ultimate, optimal model of social relations.

c) The third moment characterizing personal being l e a d s to f r e e d o m. The foundation of freedom is undoubtedly the intellectual capacity to cognize being, and the capacity to come to love being in itself and for itself, as a good in itself, a good called, in the tradition of classical philosophy, a just good, as opposed to a useful good, which is desired on account of a different aim, and a pleasurable good, desired on account of itself as acting and possessing the very function of the "happening" of love. If a person can intellectually cognize every being, then the human being can at the same time come to love it as a good, and that is why none of the concrete goods determines an individual, so that that good will be desired by necessity. The horizon of being and good, being infinite, is the reason for a merely necessary (not free) desire for good in general (similar to "happiness" which is not defined more closely). Concrete good, on the other hand, always appears to a person as inadequate, in relation to good in general, and that is why it can always be loved or rejected; it does not have in itself the power to coerce us into loving it.

However, the very drama of human freedom takes place in our practical cognition and choice of the kind of practical (or practical-practical) judgement which concretely determines human activity. I c h o o s e for myself the kind of judgement (not necessarily the best, or the wisest, or the most convenient), through which I will determine myself to action. This choice of a practical judgement determining my activity is the moment of my human auto-determination and freedom. Thus, freedom takes place within the human being. In relation to the external world we can merely be i n d i r e c t l y free—through auto-determination. In the act of free choice, which is identified with the act of choice, we fundamentally constitute our freedom not in relation to the world of things, but in relation to our own selves, as the subjects acting and fulfilling ourselves through our activity. The world of things, the world of matter, is basically "dense" with determined beings, which govern themselves by necessary material laws. The personal world, as the world of the spirit, requires auto-determination, and thereby requires inner constitution of itself as an acting being.

Through the act of freedom, manifesting itself in free d e c i s i o n, we fulfill ourselves as a person, that is, as a subject acting rationally from within. In the use of practical reason (practical judgement, through which we are auto-determined to human activity), we express ourselves as a human being concretely synthesizing into one all our structural elements. In the act of decision we fulfill ourselves as a personal being, selecting for ourself a concrete, personal "face" through our acts. We cannot free ourselves from the act of decision in any way, we cannot transfer this act to anyone else. In a word, in the act of decision—presupposing both cognition and love—we express ourselves as a human beings, in an essential and fundamental way. Not everyone is capable of understanding other kinds of acts (for example, theoretically cognitive ones), but everyone is capable of making rational decisions. What is more, since we cannot avoid this act of decision nor transfer it to another person, it is the only moment that is analogically common to all human persons. All this indicates that the human being fulfills the self as a personal being through acts of decision, as acts that are the most human. For this reason, too, such acts are the objects of particular concern both to societies (natural and religious ones) and to the great reformers of humanity. Acts of free decision also focus in themselves the moral aspect of human life, and they are regarded in all religions as the main carrier of personal responsibility which dominates all changeable conditions, even a person's death.

Besides the three acts mutually complementing one another, acts of cognition, love and freedom, through which the person dominates nature, we must, in turn, draw attention to three further features of human personal being: the subjectivity of law, completeness and dignity. They also, in a way, mutually complement one another, at the same time presupposing cognition, love and freedom.

d) The subjectivity of law. Considering personal being, which is free and determines itself through the free choice of its cognitive acts, we perceive that before making an act of decision and auto-determination, it is (we ourselves are) undetermined and thereby incapable of activity. Rational auto-determination is not possible without an intellectual understanding of the concrete good which we are to fulfill through a determined act. The understanding of a concrete good is nothing other than a first glimpse of the content of natural law—"good should be done"—as we shall discuss at a later stage. The doing of a concrete good, through self-determination of oneself, contains of necessity a relation to another person, to another "you," since it presupposes the act of love, constituting us in a new mode of being "for-the-other-you." Each real act of love (and a real act of love is also a choice of one option for action in decision, as its constitutive essential factor) contains in itself an ordering to the other "you." If, therefore, I constitute myself as a free person through my free decision, then this same act of decision virtually contains both natural law and a bond, through relations with other persons. And this is nothing other than precisely the subjectivity of law. Although a closer understanding of law will be established still further on in our analysis of the fact of law and our analysis of the definition of the content of law, we already perceive, if we define this subjectivity in general outlines, that: a) it occurs on the basis of realizing a personal good (also called in another context "common good"); we are concerned with the fact that the human being is inwardly ordered to development through intellectual and moral development; b) this development, however, being the property of each human person, cannot take place in abstraction from another "you," since my development cannot eliminate the development of another person; c) the realization of personal development in human conditions is possible only through the transformation of matter as a means of "expressing oneself" and perfecting the spirit. Matter must be proportionally divided among persons perfecting themselves, in order to make possible this perfection (for example, study, an honest life). Thus, there exists a relational connection between acting persons, insofar as their activity (or inactivity) is mutually d u e to people, (duty is the characteristic feature of an interpersonal legal relation), on account of the fact that each person is necessarily ordered to perfecting himself or herself, that is, to fulfilling common good. The subject of these interpersonal relations can only be personal being, open both to the world and to other persons, because it is free in itself, merely subject to auto-determination.

e) The w h o l e n e s s or c o m p l e t e n e s s of personal being occurs in a very contrasting light, depending on different theories of the human being and society in which the individual is either exclusively a constituent factor of the whole, superior to the self, or a moment, reflex, or part of this same whole, or finally someone (something) secondary and second-rate in relation to society. It is enough to become aware of such concepts of the human being as the Stoic one in ancient times, and the Hegelian one in modern times, for the set of problems concerning the relation of the individual to the whole to take on at once a sharper expression. Similarly, an acquaintance with the kind of theories of society that Plato advocated in antiquity, T. Hobbes in modern times, and Fascism today, brings into sharper relief the problem of the relation of the person to society as a different type of "whole."

If we consider the structure of the human being, and the specifically human, personal nature of its activity, we will become aware of the fundamental anthropological assertion that I, being a person, transcend matter, both in being (which exists not as a result of the organization of matter, but by coming into existence in matter as a subsistent soul, which in turn organizes this matter for extra-material ends), and in specifically human activity (which manifests itself above all in intellectual cognition and love, as a fundamental act of the will). If a human being were to come into existence as a result of the organization of a "whole" which is superior to the self, then he or she would not be a subsistent being. Yet the human person is a being which has the most perfect mode of being: he or she exists as a self-conscious subject, that is, as a being in itself and for itself, which ceaselessly manifests itself in the relation "I" to "mine," in the immediate facts of our cognition. As I am a being-subject, I am no longer subjectivized in another being, and that is why the human being cannot be conceived as a "part" of this "whole-to-be." The human being is an autonomous subsistent being who does not gain existence from the "whole," that is, nature and society. Yet this does not mean that our existence is not conditioned by nature and society, that we exist independently from them, but it means that both nature and society do not constitute an adequate reason for being of our existence!

What is more, human cognitive activity is of the type that "fills" people with the richness of content that is around them. Through this ceaseless enrichment "from within," the human being becomes a "whole" or "realizes himself" or "herself" in a personal aspect of his or her life, constituting himself or herself a new world, almost a "universe" superior to the cosmic reality, because it is self-conscious and open to universal communication with another person, as another distinct "world." Acts of love supplement cognition in interpersonal communication, constituting the person as a "being-for-another." This communication, however, exhausts itself in categorial relations, presupposing the existence of being as a subject, in itself and for itself. Hence, there no longer exists, beyond the personal being, another subsistent being, whose part, element, moment or reflex would be personal being. Personal being is, therefore, a complete being for itself, forming the highest ontic whole.

Of course, on this basis there arises the problem of establishing concrete relations between personal being and society. These are problems of a concrete policy, which cannot nullify the fundamental statement that personal being—being a whole—is superior to society in his or her personal life, whether this society be natural or supernatural. And each society, being a personal mode of existence, is ordered, is f o r the person, as its aim. And the better the society, the more it makes possible personal development, creating real conditions for the essential moments of personal life, (which manifest themselves in spiritual acts) to develop more and more fully. In this state of affairs we must emphasize the transcendence of the person over all social creations, as groups of nonindependent relations, which presuppose the existence of beings-subjects. Yet we must also note that a human being's transcendence over society (in personal moments) does not eliminate the ordering of a man or a woman to society in all the other moments, which can be apprehended as a means to realizing personal life and, through them, to realizing the common good. Thus, the person in his or her various aspects is ordered to society and conversely orders society to the self, in which is also expressed the drama of person and nature ever present in the human being.

f) Finally, the last feature characterizing the human person is his or her d i g n i t y , which manifests itself in the fact that the person, being the aim of all conduct, cannot ultimately be explained through a set of "thing-relations" (through nature), but only by reference to a different person (another person) ultimately to the transcendent "Thou" of the Absolute, for the human states that are the acts of love or decision and conscious activity in general, cannot adequately and sufficiently be explained by reference to a complex or set of "thing-relations" expressed in the language of physics, chemistry or any other science as a science. I do not love or make a conscious decision because I have at this moment such and such a chemical composition of the blood or such and such a nervous state. On the contrary, "abnormal" nervous states explain only the pathology of decision or activity. The reason for being, of my human activities, is ultimately the person as a being in itself and for itself, as a being-end, and not as a means to an end. And even if in some immoral act I were to conceive the person as a means to a different end, then this other end would always be the person, that is, being in itself and for itself, for if the opposite were true, we would regard these acts no longer as "immoral," but only pathological, inhuman. This thought about human dignity as the end of all conduct was excellently expressed by Immanuel Kant, when he stated: "Act in such a way that you employ humanity both in your person, and also in the person of everyone else, always as an end, never merely as a means."[11] As he correctly wrote in his *Critique of Practical Reason,*[12] the person is an end in itself, and ought never be treated by anyone (not even by God) merely as a means without being, at the same time, an end, and therefore humanity must be sacred for ourselves in our person; for it is the subject of moral law and thereby all that is sacred in itself, and only on account of it, and in accordance with it, can anything be called sacred at all. ...

Of course the basis of this dignity is not only the subjectivity of moral law, but above all the kind of personal being which transcends all other natural and biological forms of existence.

The dignity of the person is indivisibly connected with a religious mode of activity, for if human life and the meaning of its essentially human activities cannot ultimately be explained by the laws of nature as a set of "thing-relations," but, on the contrary, is to be explained by interpersonal relations characterized by the "reason for being of the significance" of these human activities, then the person fundamentally finds himself or herself in a "religious climate," that is, the kind of climate in which we justify the significance of our human activity by referring to, and ordering our life to, another person, another "you"—ultimately the "Thou" of the Absolute. The other person, who gives meaning to human life and activity, is idealized as a god or divinity. When we think back in time to ancient Greek literature, we immediately notice this strange and at the same time very symptomatic way in which the Greeks reacted. Nature, putting up a barrier to human activity or its purpose (or helping to fulfill human purposes) immediately became personified, became an appropriate divinity. Thus, springs, rivers, the ocean, the air, etc., became divinities for the Greeks, who by using their common sense, instinctively sensed that a justification for human conscious life cannot be sought in a sphere that is lower than man, and a justification for being cannot be sought in non-being. That is why the context of human life was usually transferred into the sphere of the gods, who alone could somehow justify human activity and conduct. This reference to another person as justifying particularly the purposefulness of human conduct (but not only that), introduces us into the domain of religion (which synthesizes all acts of personal life), particularly into the domain of religion that has as its object the reference to a personal God who is the Absolute, that is, a being in Himself and through Himself, and thereby Good, True, Beautiful.

The ordering of one person to another, (particularly the "Thou" of the Absolute), constitutes in a fuller sense the mode of personal life that "being-for-another-person" is. It is significant that this characteristic mode of personal life, bound by an interpersonal relation establishing a constant ordered mode of activity, finds a very interesting fulfillment and exemplification in the theological concept of the Persons of God, where the pure relation, (categorial in the human sense), becomes a relation constituting the person of God, for the Father is wholly ordered to the Son, is "FOR-THE-SON," and so forth. The subsistent relationship of the Persons of God would be an interesting "confirmation" of the concept of the human person who fulfills the self and perfects the self by the mode of being for the other "you," in abstraction from which he or she loses the meaning of activity and life. In all this, the personal being appears as not only being in oneself and for oneself, but being such, he or she is at the same time a being for the other person and the aim of moral conduct. All this is only an explanation of what we call the dignity of personal being.

The theory of personal being, through a clarification of the latter's fundamental characteristic traits, will contribute to a fuller understanding of the person as a member of society, the carrier and subject of law, particularly natural law.

6. TOWARDS SOCIETY

In human activity, as in being, the characteristic "link" of nature and person can be noticed, for the determining moments of nature (and of the body) occur, both in the cognitive order and in the appetitive-aspiring order, as well as the moments of the spirit (and personal ones, transcending in it and expressing themselves through it).

The very cognition of the human being, structuralized and organically composed of the senses and the intellect, although it is only one function, is in some stages more saturated with matter and natural determinants, while in others it reveals the transcendence of the spirit, so characteristic for the person, which is manifested in the structure of acts of intellectual cognition. Likewise, volitive acts, though anchored in the emotions, nevertheless transcend these emotions and sometimes even radically oppose them. A more detailed analysis of human activity is at the same time a detailed illustration of the unceasing drama of nature and person in human existence.

This is clearly brought out in the act of decision, which is an act of our freedom, for it becomes apparent upon closer analysis that, when we make a free choice, we choose for ourselves a practical judgement, by means of which we determine ourselves to activity (auto-determination), constituting ourselves a free source of activity, because we really determines ourselves to activity; for without determination there is no specific source of activity. It is a free source, since through the act of choice I myself accept from within the judgement that I want. It is not always the best judgement, nor the only effective one, nor the easiest, for in the process of practical cognition the choice of judgement is free, though it is usually inspired by inborn or acquired tendencies (dispositions or predispositions) of the human being. However, these tendencies do not destroy freedom. Hence, in making a free choice, we do not fundamentally choose external things, an external good; we do not fundamentally change the deterministic course of nature, but we choose within ourselves the kind of judgement which determines us to activity. Activity itself will set in motion external forces, and the deterministic mechanisms of nature will, through them, express its spirit outwardly. The person's free choice, being the basis of this freedom, is also an illustration of the link of freedom with nature, that is, the determination of the world of nature.

Presupposing a general acquaintance with the mechanisms of human activity and the structure of spiritual acts, through which an individual takes on characteristic features of personality, we must pay closer attention to the interpersonal actions of man and woman, insofar as the potential (dynamic) aspect of personal being actualizes itself in them and reaches its fulfillment. In order to constitute a truly human life, a mere individual activity (restricting itself to the individual) is not sufficient; nor is the organization of life along the lines "I-you" sufficient: the kind of relations that denote "us" as a beginning of society are also necessary.

Of course, society will not eliminate the relation "I-you"; on the contrary, it will make it more distinct, as the essential context of human life, for what is "you" for me, if not a particular extrapolation of "I," if not a treating of the other person as a second "I"? There occurs a very significantly different relation of "I" to the world of nature and to the personal world of other people, as "you." Although both nature and other persons are beings, that is, some kind of subsistent subjects, we do nevertheless construct for ourselves the being of persons differently from the being of things. At the same time there is a great danger of treating the being of persons on the model of the being of things, which Martin Buber warned us against. I cognize the being of things through activity manifesting the inner properties (features) of things. That is why a natural being is for me above all a set of features, a bundle of necessary elements, which exists; it is the o b j e c t of my activity. I must know the features of things in order to take account of reality, which is sometimes harsh for me, in my activity. In a word, a thing of nature is above all for me an "object" of my activity; it is something constituted by the sum of features-elements.

How differently do I myself see myself. I conceive myself above all as a living, subjectivizing s u b j e c t, as "I," who subjectivizes all that is "mine." I perceive in a vivid way that no act, nor all acts taken together, as yet constitute "I," for I am on no account the SUM of these acts. I transcend them; I perceive their inadequacy in relation to "I." That is why seeing myself "from within," I always have for myself a different measure of estimation than for being, which I view "from the outside" and which I perceive above all as the sum of features somehow existing in it, and not as a subject "radiating" from itself, in activity, the features which it can change.

And precisely the recognition of another "you" is what surmounts the changing of the other person into a thing or object, that is, to conceive of the other as a subject who acts and not simply as a set of characteristics forming an object.

The richness of personal life does not exhaust itself, however, along the lines "I-you," for all the values that are necessary for human development and which the human person does in fact produce cannot be consumed or produced here. Let us take, for example, the cognitive goods that are constituted by various domains of organized science, various domains of extra-scientific, artistic, religious cognition—libraries, churches, scientific institutes, laboratories, and so forth—and we perceive that the whole domain of human culture is based on cognition. However, the cognitive aspect is not the only aspect of personal life. The domain of love, the domain of what is called "sacred," etc., is also the amassing of the great values which the particular person in the relation "I-you" neither created nor is capable of appropriating. For this, a concordant and organized group social "we" is necessary, based precisely on objective good transcending individual life, and on life going by only in the relation "I-you." This good is already a c o m m o n g o o d of many persons (and not only the restricted "we" situated in the relation "I-you"), who, joining in the most varied inter-personal relations, produce and appropriate common values, developing, each in itself its p o t e n t i a l i t y of personal being. This actualization of personal being, this inner development of every human being, is also the indubitable common good of the whole. Thus, the c o m m o n g o o d appears as the basis of being able to create a new form of human being—the social form. What, however, is this common good which founds society?

Before we take a closer look at the very concept of common good as the ontic reason for society, we must, continuing the analysis of interpersonal relations already begun, take a closer look at the very concept of society, on the basis of the dynamism or the potentiality of human personal being, already mentioned. This will, in a way, concern the understanding of the common good; however, it will not draw us away from the fundamental course of our reflections.

Consequently, perceiving along the lines of the relation "I-you" an openness of our personal being, we thereby ascertain a lack of natural determination (which is undoubtedly something positive, although it is expressed in negative language). On the other hand, this allows us to enrich ourselves with all the values which constitute the content not only of the world of things but also of living persons. This intentional enrichment (of the cognitive order) is, as it were, a starting-point for real communication of acquired values, in the act of love.

Let us note, however, that both the very process of acquiring cognitive values and the process of communicating to another person through acts of love, are not only slow and long, but above all c o m p o s i t e (manifesting the compositeness of being), and that they are subject to the development of different types of "skills"; above all, that they require the existence of a group of other y o u ' s , on account of specifically contingent, potential human nature. This means, above all, that the human person, being precisely a contingent, potentialized being, is not capable of actualizing its nature immediately through activity proper to itself and without the participation and help of other persons, actualizing various aspects of the potentiality of the person.

If every subsistent concrete contingent being, being the object of our empirical-intellectual cognition, is a composite being, in spite of the fact that it is a real, single, one, actually undivided, being, then the person, as the most perfect being given to us in experience, is also in the highest degree the "bond" of necessary (and, considering its ontic aspect, transcendental) relations, constituting him or her as one being. We perceive in the person a whole series of "constitutive factors-parts" of the same type as for instance "integral parts" (constituting the body), "essential parts" (such as matter and form—the soul), "substantial parts" (substance and accidents), "essence" (nature), and "concrete," individual existence.

Here it is sufficient to draw attention to two types of composition: (1) from "integrating parts"; and (2) from substance and properties-accidents. As a result of such composition, particularly of substantial parts and those concerned with properties, the human organism finds itself in a constant movement and flow of matter; since a whole series of new cells emerges in it, a whole series of them disappear. The organism develops from embryonic states to a fullness of maturity. This development takes place slowly. At the same time the human being, a composite being, is also one concrete substance, the subject, which acts through its properties—the "powers of activity," that is, the cognitive powers (the intellect as well as internal and external senses); volitive powers, (appetitive and propulsive), which determine the emotional-aspiring aspect of man and woman; the motive powers, as well as the vegetative powers which make biological life possible—the receiving and assimilating of food, and reproduction.

Ontic-material conditions are merely one aspect of the potentiality of personal being as well as the reasons explaining the relation of a person to a group of other persons, to society. The human being, as a concrete, individual *compositum* (in which the material-sensory elements and the rational-volitive ones constitute a closely bound unity, a dynamic unity subject to constant development and perfection), can reach the fullness of personal life by the actualization of his or her potentialities. The slow development of all the powers of human nature—in many stages and conditioned in many ways, the "non-independence" of human existence, which embraces nearly a quarter of a person's life—makes him or her dependent on various groups of other persons and constitutes one of the bases of the fact that human beings organize themselves into various kinds of social groups.

Potentialization concerns the whole of human life in its various aspects, and so the nature of interpersonal ties connecting man and woman with various social groups is often also appropriately varied. What is essential in each of these ties is the fact that human beings are i n t e r d e p e n d e n t, while each human individual arrives at the fullness of the development of his or her personal being—at least this is so in intention. The whole of the human composite structure constitutes the basis of the coming into existence of the relation "person-society." The human person, although constituting a certain whole and complete "world in the self," cannot develop—as has already been mentioned—cannot realize the possibilities or rights that precisely constitute the "completeness" of the personal "world" without acting together with other persons, and this not only along the lines of the relation "I-you," but of the group of other persons, communicating in common good and constituting from this aspect some kind of "we."

It is easy, therefore, to note that the independent human individual "is formed" precisely in the course of this many-sided interpersonal interaction. He or she is a "being-in-itself"—an independent, complete one—to the extent that he or she is at the same time a "being-for" others, a social being. The potentiality of human nature explains the essence of the social bond in the aspect of "internal causes," which constitute the personal being as "this here" individual concrete being. However, the fundamental explanation of the essence of society as a being-relation between persons requires, on top of this, a consideration of the aim, that is, of the "common good" as the ultimate reason for the coming-into-existence of society itself.

We must, however, draw attention to some concrete forms of social life (by way of illustration), and also to the general concept of society, and finally to the "common good" as the ultimate, final reason for social life. This will make clearer the structure of the human potentialized person, who is at the basis of the legal fact itself and also of the binding nature of natural law.

7. Basic Social Groups

a) The Family

Already Aristotle, in Book I, Chapter 1 of his *Politics,* wrote correctly on the subject of investigating various societies:

> The best method of investigation is, in this case as in others, to follow the emergence of certain relations from the very beginning. First, then, it is a necessary thing for beings who cannot exist without one another to unite with one another, that is, the female and the male, for the purpose of procreation; this happens not of free choice, but as in all animals and plants under the influence of the natural instinct to leave behind another being of the same kind. ...[13]

Natural instinct does not, however, hinder the free mutual choice of husband and wife. Children are the natural result of marital union, and they are connected naturally—as an effect is connected with its cause—with their parents, together with whom they form a family.[14]

It is the family which constitutes the smallest social group, conceived as the "union between parents and children." It is the natural form of social life and at the same time its basic cell. In general, all philosophical trends recognized the family as the basic form of social life and the fundamental developmental "niche" for man and woman. The nature of the family determines to a large extent the nature of larger forms of social life, to such an extent that there have been theories that societies are not constituted by "citizens," but rather by families, as being more basic cells of life. And although this opinion does not seem to be true in its strict interpretation, it is nevertheless true that the family fundamentally educates the human being to become a member of higher societies, and that the laws of the family for educating the human being cannot fundamentally be conveyed to other social creatures.

A discussion on the question of the family appears to involve several problems, the consideration of which would require separate studies. However, some of them should be mentioned here on account of formulations occurring in the concept of natural law, concerning both the definition of law itself and of some of its forms.

The first problem in this matter is the very concept of marriage, its biological and psychic basis. We are concerned here with such aspects of the problem as the difference between the sexes, penetrating the human being totally both from the somatic and the psychic aspect. As a result of such a state of things, the actualization of the potentialized human personality takes place a l s o (but not exclusively) through an actualization under the direction of the essential human factor, the reason for sexuality, and in fact all that is inseparably bound up with the sexual aspect of the human being. This is linked with human beings personal development through real love for another person, as well as the development of society through giving birth to, and bringing up, children born in love. That is why we should stress the indissolubility, in marital human life, of the moments of reason, love and sex, and also the personal, indeed precisely human, perfecting of oneself. In the normal natural course of affairs the uniting, and not the excluding (as extreme trends of thought and religion sometimes advocated), of all these moments of human life lies on the path of the actualization of human personality.

Another problem is the question of monogamy and the indissolubility of the marital bond, which is connected with this. Attempts were made to solve this matter by referring to history, that is, to its developmental forms. We are concerned here with the theory of matriarchy as a primary system.[15]

The concept of matriarchy contains elements of conviction that the family is a certain evolution of more imperfect and primeval forms of human life, such as the horde, polyandry, polygamy, and finally monogamy as the highest form of human life.

Advocates of the concept of matriarchy, wanting to explain the variety of forms of social life and taking as their starting point certain assumptions from biological evolutionism (which latter was extended to the domain of the social sciences), are of the opinion that each perfect form of social life is derived from imperfect and more primitive forms. The social life of the human being is also subject to the law of evolution. Early social life arose from the sexual instinct, which urged people to unite in unstable relationships, in which sexual disorder or hetaerism were dominant. These relation-ships were characterized by license and instability of relation. As a result—in such a state of affairs—of the uncertainty of fatherhood, the offspring grouped themselves above all around the mother, beside whom—as a strong male at the head—stood the mother's brother as the central "head" of the family.

The patriarchal theory, established by Westmarck,[16] and then confirmed by W. Schmidt's investigations—which is perhaps not completely objective and grounded, since it was not based on materials that had been personally examined, but on special reports from missionaries,[17] advances the view that the primordial form of family life was monogamy and patriarchy. These concepts (like later theories concerning the belief of primeval peoples in God) derive from a statement, supported by the observation of primeval manifestations of cult among peoples of the most primordial degree of development, that both non-monogamic forms of marriage and non-monotheistic forms of cult are a perversion and degradation of "pure" ethical-religious forms. Westmarck expresses the firm view that primeval man, the hunter, was most probably a monogamist, since he could note such forms of life in animals lower than himself, and animals closest to the human being in development are precisely monogamic. Wundt, in *Völkerpsychologie* (Book VII), regards the ascertainment of the monogamy of primeval man as the most important discovery in the history of the development of human society. The problem of the history of family structure is to a great extent a hypothesis, dependent above all on primeval premises of a more general nature, either philosophical or religious and theological, for we do not have any clear traces of the prehistory of marriage.

Reference to ethnology or prehistory does not ultimately solve the problem of the monogamic indissolubility of marriage, but here we must have recourse to purely theoretical arguments, drawn both from the structure of the family itself (and its essential welfare, which includes the bearing and education of children), and from the structure of personal love, which finds its essential realization in marriage.

Above all, then, the normal social aim of marriage lies in giving birth to, and bringing up children, by creating for them conditions which favor their psychic-personal development. When we consider that educating a human being for independent life takes up roughly one third of a human life, that is, about 21 to 25 years (if we take into account the conditions needed for attaining full psychic maturity), and when we also take into account the fact that in a normal marriage there should be no fewer than three children, (for the very fact of social reproduction), we will perceive that this educational task, in the usual course of affairs, takes the married couple about 30 years of their life, that is, as long as the period of fertility lasts, on average. If, then, when considering only the good of society and of the family, the whole mature period of human life is needed (in the normal course of events) for the bearing and educating of children, no basis occurs for a monogamic marriage to fall apart after it has completed its essential function, for in any case it is impossible to make a new marriage to educate a new generation. The essential marital function, therefore, seems to be monogamy and the indissolubility of the marital bond, in the normal course of events, of course.

When we consider that the second, no less important and equally essential, function of marital life is expressed in the development of personal love, involving the human being totally, then from an analysis of the nature of human love it can be seen even better that real love, offering "itself" to the other person without reservation, also requires the same response and the continuation of this "dialogue of love" through one's whole life. For if human beings are to reach personal perfection, they can do so only through real love towards another person. Real love demands a "departure from oneself" (towards the other) and an offering of oneself to the other person. Of course we are not speaking here of the renunciation of married life through celibacy, on account of religious, scientific or artistic values, for these values are also a service to the other person. A better execution of these values, and a better service to other people sometimes requires a resignation from married life for the purpose of intensifying the service itself, which also purifies the person involved and removes selfishness, and thereby contributes to the forming of higher personal values.

Thus, real love towards another person is, in normal circumstances, a total involvement, without time conditions, since the very spiritual experience of love is beyond time, and one of the essential conditions of love is that it should last "always." In such a state of affairs, marriage based on totally involved love has no basis for breaking up, since it is not merely a contract for specific material purposes, but is an expression of inner consent to (and an involvement with) human life "for the other person."

Consequently, monogamy as well as the indissolubility of marriage and thereby the stability of the family and its fundamental grounding, are supported by considerations of social and personal good. We must treat all eventual separations, faults and failures as coming from secondary considerations, and not from the essence of the very nature of marriage, for the nature of marriage points towards its monogamy and indissolubility.

The monogamy and indissolubility of marriage are connected in an essential way with other very important "goods" of the family. We generally include among these the community of family life, the community of its material goods, the family's right to bring up children, the family's right to obtain social care from the State, which, according to the "principle of assistance," cannot abolish family laws but must protect them and help the family as the basic social cell. This help, of course, is expressed differently in different historical and economic conditions.

Against the background of family problems, it is also usual to discuss the rights of unwed mothers and widows to obtain care from the State, and the rights of children, especially orphans, to have universal social care.

The family, then, universally recognized as the basic unit of society, is the first necessary community which actualizes in the most fundamental way the potentiality of the human person.

b) Extended Societies[18]

If the family is the smallest human community, then, in a normally functioning society, we perceive "extended societies," being, as it were, a family conceived in a wider sense. It is usual to mention, going in the direction of ever more perfect communities, the following social creations (of course without going into their evaluation from some special point of view): the clan, together with its legal and non-legal members, for example, slaves or servants, in the past; the small municipal administrative district *(gmina),* conceived in a restricted or wide sense as an extended neighborhood; the social c l a s s ; the t r i b e ; the n a t i o n and finally the S t a t e , as the most perfect form—so far—of the social system.

It is difficult, of course, to discuss these problems, since they do not fit into the framework of a lecture on the philosophy of law. However, on the other hand we cannot fail to notice them, on account of the fact that all these forms of social life are a concrete expression of the real life of human persons who are involved in them in various sections of the historical or geographical area. A detailed analysis of them is made in sociology, philosophy and social ethics, and also in other domains of the human sciences. From the philosophical point of view, (the philosophy of law), the only important fact is that such communities exist, influence the development of attitudes and character of particular people (the actualization of potentialities), and thereby are the expression of some kind of conscious and binding nature of law, for each of these social groups has an awareness of its distinct right, directing its functions.

It is difficult, in our European society at present, to speak of clans and their servant or slave members. Undoubtedly, however, such social creations existed in Europe, and they can also be encountered in societies at a different stage of their development, for example in some countries of Africa and Asia. What is, on the other hand, more socially binding is the t r i b e (particularly in some African countries), being made up of a group of people having an awareness of their distinctness, which is usually based upon: a) the conviction of coming from a common ancestor; b) the similarity of language; c) the distinctness of cultural forms, which create exclusivity in the form of a religious cult, the way houses and estates are built, the way of acquiring means of subsistence, defense, and so forth.

Generally, and in connection with the analysis of the concept of the tribe, there also appears the problem of a common place of residence and tribal organization, whose representative is a common Chief, having a more or less centralized authority. Tribes found in the less developed forms of social life (for example, in the young countries of Africa) are, however, considered as a transitive form of life, subordinate to the State.

A higher form of social life, closer to the meaning of tribe, is constituted by the n a t i o n,[19] which usually has its origin in the tribal community. There are two widely known theories of the nation:

1. The n a t u r a l theory sees the emergence of a nation from tribal communities living in the same or a close territory. According to the assumptions of this theory, the nation was formed through tribal communities as a result of the similarity or else the "identity" of cultural experiences, which included a common language, a common religion, common traditions, a common history, etc. Such a theory of the nation emerged over a hundred years ago (1851, Mancini), and was later harshly criticized. Particular attention was drawn to the fact that there are no pure tribal groups concerning the aspect of race; that communities of language, religion and cultural traditions cannot be isolated and do not constitute one nation, since cultural factors must be, and in fact are, common to many nations, for instance concerning the Germanic nations and those of South America.

2. The theory about the c u l t u r a l conception of a nation views the essence of nationality in a group of people united by a conscious community of historical destiny. According to Renan, the nation is a fundamentally spiritual unity, connected by a common history in the past, the present and the future. A special part is played here by the common awareness of this community among the members of the nation. Distinctions of origin, tribe, or religion can obtain. In this way, for example, one American nation was formed. A nation in this sense is a group of people united by conscious ideas of a community of historical destiny.

It appears that the phenomenon of the nation is a comparatively new historical category. For the Ancients of society, the concept of nation was not yet known; that is why it is difficult to speak of the "Greek nation" or the "Roman nation." It is also difficult to speak of nations in classical medieval times—the origin of nations dates from the end of this era—and the factors which greatly contributed to their emergence, besides blood ties, communities of speech, economic interests and cultural forms, were also wars and conquests, which obliged people to unite in ever wider tribal groups.

When, until the end of the XVIIIth Century, national States emerged in Europe, their spokesmen were Kings, Princes, or a dynastic Oligarchy. Since the French Revolution, however, the idea of the nation has been a factor in organizing States. Precisely this idea of the nation developed in the Romantic period, as the main motive force of social life. It is sufficient to draw attention here to Fichte's activities *(Reden an die Deutsche Nation)* or to Polish Romantic poets.

The XIXth Century witnessed the emergence of many national States in Europe. In this century, there also appeared the first ideas of racism and the supremacy of the white race, on the basis of the Colonial conquests made by England. The concept of the unity of race or the unity of blood led, in the course of time, to the mysticism of blood and of race, and the far-reaching social perversions connected with the acceptance of precisely such a point of view. It is sufficient here to mention the Nazism of the Third Reich.

The concept of the nation is connected with the problem of one's native land, and in general what is called the "homeland," which in a certain sense presupposes the settlement of a given nation in a specific territory, even though, as was noted earlier, the matter of specific territory is not connected in a necessary way with the concept of the nation. On the other hand, it is difficult to demand that there be mentioned merely the essential and necessary constituents of the nation, since the nation itself is a kind of moral unity of people; consequently, the constituents mentioned here—such as common speech, religion and history, common territory, a common culture inherited from one's ancestors and created in the awareness of precisely "national" unity, a common will for unity, and so forth—also constitute the nation in a moral sense.

The acceptance by society of the idea of some kind of nation, and the acknowledgement of nationality, took two fundamental forms in history: patriotism and nationalism. The boundaries between patriotism and nationalism, when viewed from the side of a member of another (uninvolved) nation, are immensely difficult to disentangle, since everything that looks like a patriotic experience for a member of one nation, can, for a stranger, appear to be nationalism. And it is difficult to give any objective indications about patriotism or nationalism. We can judge these phenomena only on the basis of the results of experiencing these values as particular persons. If national values contribute to the ennobling of the person, we can then speak of the experience of patriotism; if, on the other hand, national values experienced by someone deform and debase the person in question, we would then undoubtedly have nationalism before us. Thus, the actualization towards good of human potentialities through a specific society, is always the essential destiny of every community.

When we draw attention to other culturally more developed forms of social life, there appear before us three basic social groupings in particular: the small municipal administrative unit, class, and the State. Strictly speaking, these three groups may be distinguished even in the existing State, since specific municipal administrative units and social class did not appear independently of the State. Although in ancient times town-states *(POLIS)* existed, they were rather more of a state than a municipal administrative unit.

Since the municipal administrative unit and social class are smaller units than the State and act within the State, it is sufficient to pay only general and passing attention to them.

Social administrative units are small units (a village, settlement, town, county) which develop in the State and form in the domain of (very differentiated) state legislation separate administrative, economic and cultural units. Their autonomy is relative and very varied, depending on the concept and system of government of the State itself. They are a stricter form of social life and at the same time a school for living as a State. The human being becomes aware of social and state ties by becoming aware of law and its binding power precisely in the life of the administrative unit of which he or she is a member.

If the administrative unit is always connected with a specific territory within which the State organizes social life (or finds an organized social life), the social c l a s s is a general phenomenon within a State, or even an international phenomenon. The very concept of social class comes from the socio-economic investigations of Karl Marx, who made people aware of this idea. However, he writes about himself to Weydemeyer (5. III. 1852):

> As far as I am concerned, I have not the merit of discovering either the existence of classes in modern society or the merit of discovering the struggle between them. ... The *novum* that I introduced consists in proving: 1. that the existence of classes is connected only with specific historical phases of the development of production; 2. that class struggle inevitably leads to a

dictatorship of the proletariat; 3. that this dictatorship is itself only a passage to the abolishing of all classes and to a classless society.

Lenin gave the following definition of class:

> We call classes great groups of people, differing among themselves on account of the place they take in a historically defined system of social production, on account of their relation (usually fixed and legally expressed) towards the means of production, on account of their function in the social organization of work ... on account of the method of obtaining, and the dimensions of the part of, the social richness which they have at their disposal. Classes are such groups of people of which one can usurp the work of another, thanks to the difference of the place that it takes in a specific system of social economy.[20]

According to this concept of class we can always distinguish a class possessing means of production from a class not possessing these means. Hence, a constant antagonism and necessity of conflict, ending in dictatorship and "de-classing."

After the Marxist concept of class, others appeared, indicating the following class-forming factors:

(a)   the opposition of interests within social groups;

(b)   a moral tendency towards social justice, for groups of people having similar work in the economy;

(c)   biological factors, as it were, or the commonness of functions carried out by a specific group of people;

(d)   political factors (historical ones) such as wars lost and won.

Considering all these factors, Messner[21] gives the following definition of class: "We call classes social groups whose members unite in a common and similar effort aimed at either change or the keeping of a given social order." Depending on the concept of class which we accept, we can speak of its rights or of its anarchy.

c) The State[22]

The most important and so far the supreme form of social life is the State. In dealing with the problem of the State, we must draw attention to its elements or essential features, to some theories about how the State was formed (which illustrate its nature), as well as to the role of the State with regard to society.

Many concepts of the State are known in the history of social philosophy. In Greece, the early State was really a town-*polis*, together with its surrounding villages. In Rome, the concept of the State grew to exceeding dimensions. It was made up primarily of citizens *(cives),* who, mainly by means of conquest, captured territories accessible to Roman culture. In medieval times, "land" (usually under Royal sovereignty), was added to one's own, as a characteristic element of statehood.

The State as a perfect society was defined by Aristotle, who also included in his definition the moment of purposefulness, besides formal elements constituting the perfect, self-sufficient society (autarchy).

> Finally, the full community made up of a considerable number of village administrative units, which have in a way attained the limit of universal self-sufficiency, is a state; it arises in order to make life possible and exists in order to make life good. Each state, therefore, arises by means of natural development, like the first communities, for it is the aim towards which they aspire, whereas nature is precisely the attainment of the aim. The property that each creation attains at the end of the process of its formation is called its nature; this is so with reference to a man, a horse and a family. The attainment of the aim (to which it aspires) is the acquisition of full perfection, while self-sufficiency is the attainment both of the aim and of full perfection.[23]

In this version, the State is an association of settlements, having the complete self-sufficiency (autarchy) necessary, to afford citizens the best mode of living. The autarchic association ordered to the common good was regarded, for many centuries (especially in the period of the dominance of Aristotle's influence) as the essential constitutive element of statehood as a social organization. This theory also has many adherents today, particularly in the scholastic stream of thought.

In today's development of the State, however, we perceive that autarchy is inaccessible, even for big State organisms, for human needs have increased and, as a result of applying modern technology, the whole world has "shrunk" exceedingly, in relation to what it was for the ancient world, the medieval one, or even the world of modern times. In principle, there are no longer any fully self-sufficient State organisms in today's world.

That is why we must draw attention to and stress other essential elements of statehood: a) a social union, b) endowed with a superior authority, c) in an appropriate, specific territory.

In the social union, awareness and a feeling of State unity are required. The feeling of social unity is particularly stressed as the fundamental element of the cohesion of the State organism. The size of the population does not come into play here: it can be very high, as for instance in China, or very low, as in Malta.

In spite of this, however, the feeling of social unity is sufficient for the people living in a specific state territory to feel that they are the population of precisely this State, as opposed to what foreigners might feel when living in this same territory.

An essential element constituting statehood is supreme authority, and in particular the population's conviction about the necessity of the existence of precisely the authority which is governing at the time. It is not required that the population should accept this authority of its own free will, that it should agree with this authority, but only that it should be convinced that, in the given circumstances, it is this supreme authority which is a necessary authority, and that this is why it must be recognized.

The concept of a superior authority was formulated for the first time by Bodinus in the XVIth Century. In ancient and medieval times, the concept of a superior authority (as an element constitutive of statehood) was not so strongly marked in people's consciousness, since authority was either completely imposed, without any participation of the population, or it was distributed among the disputing powers of Empire, Church, Princes or Kings. Some of the more modern authors (Duguit) believe that the concept of authority is senseless, for the State represents a bond between the governing and the governed, and that this alone is sufficient for understanding statehood.

As far as territorial determination is concerned, the matter can be treated in various ways, depending on historical conditions. Territory is usually defined by the frontiers of the State. The sea—the area of coastal waters—is also included in the territory of the State. It has not yet been established to what extent aerial and cosmic as well as underground areas belong to anyone's territory. These matters come within the scope of international law and are at present the subject of intense discussion.

One's conception of the State depends upon which theory one accepts concerning how the State arose. These theories have changed very quickly, so it is not necessary to quote and analyze them here. By way of illustration, we can indicate some of the theories, in order to testify to history on the one hand, and on the other to indicate that each of them stressed, in some aspect, that feature of the State which corresponded to the chosen model which functions in a given theory of the state.

Well known to us are, for instance, theories of the religious beginnings of the State, according to which statehood was a divine creation and the result of the direct action of a god, or of his indirect intervention. We should include, in the first concepts in the history of systems, all the myths left to us by history about the beginnings of the Babylonian, Assyrian or Egyptian States. Biblical stories about the statehood of Israel are also a result of the conviction that God directly intervened in building the Jewish State. The nature of these States was based on theocracy as the basis of the authority which really bound people together.

The theory of the so called the indirect intervention of God in forming state organs ("all authority comes from God") is expressed in the belief that the natural condition of human society is that it have the character of a State, whereas nature is the result of God's creative activity. Since human nature is such as it is and comes from God, it follows that the necessary forms of manifesting this nature also come from God. State creations are such a form. That is why the medieval scholastic thinkers were convinced of the indirect derivation of the State and of authority from God (St. Thomas Aquinas, Suarez and others). This indirectness of derivation from God, however, is in fact, a strong affirmation of the natural character of the State.

Besides religious-theistic theories, the theory of the social contract has been formulated, according to which the State arose as a result of the agreement of people amongst themselves and the conclusion of an appropriate pact. This was formulated particularly clearly in the theories of Hobbes and Rousseau. People, as they were enemies to one another *(homo homini lupus),* and in order to save themselves, placed their autonomous rights in the hands of the monarch in an ultimate way; the Sovereign has since then possessed absolute authority over everyone and everything.

This conception is vividly linked to the text of the Aristotle's *Politics*:

> For just as when perfectly developed man is the foremost of creatures, so is he the worst of all if he breaks out of law and justice, for armed misdoing is the worst. Man, though, is born endowed with arms—his mental and moral capabilities—which, like no other capabilities, can be improperly used. That is why the man without any moral sense is the most wicked and the wildest creature, the vilest in sensual lust and greed. Justice, on the other hand, is the distinguishing mark of the State, for its dimension is the basis of the order existing in the State community; it depends on establishing what is just.[24]

Rousseau, too, believes that the State owes its existence only to the "sacredness of the contract," this time a free and never outdated pact, so that people can at any moment break the "social pact," for instance by a revolution.

Theories about a pact testify to the confusion between the fact of the State (its necessity), and the historical category of the structure of this State, for an analysis of the structure of the human person indicates that it is necessary for the human being to be ordered to society.

Patrimonial concepts were also known (cf. K.L. Haller's *Restauration der Staatswissenschaft* from the year 1820), according to which the State originates from its founders, that is powerful people who founded a state organization on territories they had gained control over; or else patriarchal concepts, which take up the point of view that the superior authority of the State has grown out of the authority of the head of the family. These theories, extrapolated from isolated historical cases, could hardly be accepted as being the general rule, even if those cases existed. However, the creation of a State organism by an eminent leader presupposes naturally receptive human "material."

The theory of conquest (Gumplowicz's), according to which the beginning of the emergence of the State is linked with an act of force, conquest, and the subduing of one tribe by another, presupposes the existence of a State, if the conquest was carried out in an organized way. History, though, indicates earlier organizational forms of the State before conquest came into existence.

The Marxist theory of the State is closely connected with the theory of the emergence of law, since the concepts of law and the State constitute, according to Marxism, an inseparable whole, even determining the different nature of the science of the philosophy of law. This theory is widely known, and that is why it does not require particular discussion.

The theories mentioned above as examples (and others, not taken into account here), sometimes constitute correct observations of historical facts or characteristic social features. Nevertheless, if apprehended in a one-sided and aspective manner and then extended to the whole of the problem, they give only a selective view, which is not always a fundamental interpretation, and even less an adequate one. That is why the matter is open to another solution.

If we stand in the position of realistic philosophy, we must recognize that the source of the emergence and development of State organisms in the process of historical development, is the natural inclination to social life, subjectivized in the nature of human individuals, and the expression of the dynamic structure of the person. This inclination became the natural seed in the birth of the concept of the State (among others) as the supreme organization, to which lesser social groups, which are included in it, are ordered.

In this respect, it is worth mentioning some (correct) views of Aristotle on the subject of the State:

> It appears that ... the state belongs to the creations of nature, that man is naturally created for living in a state, while the man who, in his nature, and not by accident lives beyond the state is either a villain or a super-human being. ... That man is a being created for living in a state, more than a bee or any animal living in a herd, is evident, for nature—as we say—does nothing in vain. Man alone amongst living beings is endowed with speech. The voice is a sign of joy and pain. That is why other beings also possess it (for their development has extended so far that they are capable of feeling pain and joy and also of expressing it among themselves). But speech is employed to express that which is useful or harmful as well as that which is just or unjust, for this is a property of man, distinguishing him from other living creatures, such that he alone has the ability to differentiate between good and evil, justice and injustice, and so forth; a community of such beings becomes the basis of the family and the state.[25]

The State appeared as a result of the historical experience of people forming different social groups, who perceived that the development of their personality—their "common good"—can be realized in a more perfect and a fuller way within the framework of a social organism which is larger than the tribe or the family. The tendency towards uniting into a State arose spontaneously, as the expression of the natural need of people living in specific conditions. These conditions—historical, geographical, cultural, etc.—determined, in turn, the very nature of the emerging State organization. This hypothesis is confirmed by ethnological investigations, which show that even in the life of the most primitive peoples we can observe undeveloped, but nonetheless authentic, manifestations of State formations having a superior authority, which is recognized by the inhabitants of a given territory.

That is why it is difficult to agree with Aristotle's hypothesis about the primacy of the State before the citizen. It is probably the result of the influence of Plato, according to whom that which is general comes first. His thinking is probably a definite sophism, since he conceives man as a "part," and not as a whole:

> Of its nature, the state exists before the family and each one of us, for the whole must be before the part; after the whole has disintegrated there will neither be a leg nor an arm, only the name, as when someone called a stone arm an arm, for the dead arm will be of the same nature. ...[26]

The objection made to the Stagirite's statement could, of course, be weakened, by indicating that he conceives the State as a definite whole, after which the citizen, in relation to a whole apprehended in this way, is then really merely a part.

The concept of the emergence of the State, seeking its basis and genesis in human nature, and based on a philosophical analysis of that nature, will become more comprehensible in the light of a more general theory of society, of which it constitutes a particular case, for the human being as a person is a social being, since all the functions of a person (being the manifestations of the essential "metaphysical" features previously distinguished) are realized, in the context of other persons, in that most primeval society which is the family, and then most fully in the State.

8. THE GENERAL CONCEPT OF SOCIAL BEING

Human society, in the most general sense, is a collection of mutual associations, dependencies, and the mutual activity of particular people and human groups, as well as the creations connected with them; briefly: s o c i e t y is a collection of organized inter-human relations.

Society can be viewed from different aspects—the psychological, ontological, legal aspect, and so on.

From the psychological point of view, society includes a totality of psychic occurrences, which give the agglomeration of people the specific nature of organization, and which come from a psychic feeling of order. Of course, such a psychological phenomenon presupposes, on the epistemological plane, an object towards which these experiences are directed; in a word, it presupposes a social being of some kind, and that is why we cannot accept the psychological aspect as the primary one in the analysis of social being.

From the philosophical (ontological or metaphysical) point of view, society is without doubt a certain reality, a certain being. It is not, however, a subsistent being, as is for instance a human being or another physical, living being. We can merely conceive society as a group of people connected by relations. The relations themselves, which connect people (from the philosophical point of view), are not relations constituting being in the substantial order, but are relations constituting "social be-ing"—relational being—which is "made up of" particular subjects as subsistent, rational beings.

However, what is this "social being," which is not a substantial being having an essential, immanent, unity of activity? There has not yet been a theory to advance the substantial unity of social being. Besides, such a theory would, of necessity, negate the substantial unity of particular human persons, which would be quite absurd.

If social being is an ensemble of people-persons, it can only be conceived as a u n i t y o f r e l a t i o n s between persons. In this "unity of relations," however, that is, in the still more closely undefined "relational being" (unity and being are transcendental, that is, equiponderant values) we can distinguish three moments:

a)   the basis of the existence of relational unity;

b)   the fact of existence;

c)   the nature of the relational unity that has emerged.

Ad a) The basis of relational unity, that is, of social being, are the transcendental relations of the human person to the common good as the ultimate aim, for the human person, as he or she is potentialized, cannot develop and attain good without other persons. An analysis of common good as the ultimate reason for being of society will be made below.

Ad b) The real actualization of the transcendental and necessary relations takes place through the f a c t   o f   t h e   e m e r g e n c e of categorial relations. This existential moment, that is, the very e m e r g e n c e   o f   t h e   c a t e g o r i a l   r e l a t i o n   o f   o n e   p e r s o n   to   a n o t h e r, is presupposed by the fact of the emergence of society. The emergence of categorial relations is something necessary, since otherwise transcendental relations could not be realized; they would merely be something surmised and not real. However, since the human being is real, then the relations constituting the human being are a reality of the same kind.

Ad c) The mode of existence of categorial relations, of necessity liberating themselves, is diverse, just as social creations, for example the family, tribe, class, State, Church, etc., are diverse. From the metaphysical point of view, the nature of these relations constituting a specific social being is not absolutely necessary, but only comparatively necessary. This means that being does not exhaust itself in the fact of being, say, a family, State, etc., since there exist (or there can emerge) yet other forms of social being. Moreover, from the philosophical point of view, the unity of relations, constituting a certain social being, is merely an analogical unity which leaves a big margin for making changes. These matters, however, belong to detailed analyses of problems concerning particular social creations.

From the philosophical point of view, the only important thing is the fact that the social being is a necessary "state" in its basis (of transcendental relations), and that, at the same time, t h e   a p p e a r a n c e   o f   t h e   c a t e g o r i a l   r e l a t i o n s   t h e m s e l v e s, of one human person to another, i s   n e c e s s a r y ; on the other hand, the nature itself of these relations (which form the concrete content of social being) is relatively necessary. Besides, the nature of society continually changes.

Nevertheless, the comparatively necessary relations, which constitute society, can be the object of necessary cognition, that is, the object of social philosophy. Society, therefore, is a set—a " b u n d l e " — of categorial relations connecting human persons in such a way that they can develop their potentialized personality as universally as possible, (not each individual in all aspects, but different individuals in different aspects), with the purpose of t h e   r e a l i z a t i o n   o f   c o m m o n   g o o d   f o r   e a c h   h u m a n   p e r s o n.

Of course, it would be a misunderstanding to regard society as an intentional being, if we denote the most varied cultural creations as intentional being, for every intentional being is a construction derived from human thought—and suspended on it—and not from human nature as such. Society, on the other hand, is a natural creation, necessary for the realization of "common good," and is not a being suspended on acts or products of human cognition.

The wide interpretation of intentional being is, according to St. Thomas, identified with the concept of a being which is derived from the Absolute, and that is why it cannot be useful in a philosophical analysis of society, since intentionality so widely understood includes every contingent being.

The concept of social being refers not only to the smallest social group that the family is, but also to all groups, including States, which today will probably also turn out to be a transitory reaction, a "historical category." Such a definition of society also refers to the association of the whole of humanity, whose most varied relations (most often measurable and generally perceptible in the form of the work and creation of different societies) mutually bind people (who are not necessarily of the same family, tribe, nation or State) to all smaller human organizations.

Today, we are witnesses to the fact of the formation of supra-state societies, as illustrated by the example of the United Nations and its various organs. The existence of a supra-state society becomes the necessary postulate, not only of personal development but in fact of keeping the human race alive, both in order to avoid such a war as would destroy all life, and also because of the necessity of bringing aid to starving humanity.

Against the background of the general philosophical concept of society grounded on an analysis of human rational nature, whose personal development cannot take place without the emergence of social forms of life, we can admit additional explanations, which take into account some important aspects of human nature. And precisely on the basis of additional unessential but also non-constitutive moments of human nature, there appeared, in the course of centuries, various explanations of the emergence of society. Explanations of this kind sometimes come from a very apt perception of some important society-forming factors, as for instance the theory of conflict between a specific set of individuals. This theory is still linked with the name of Heraclitus, according to whom war (battle) was the parent of all things, including also the specifically social creations. To a certain extent the theory of conflict found its expression in the concept of the class struggle of historical materialism. Gumplowicz's concept of conquest, based on Darwin's concept of natural selection, also recalls the theory of conflict. The psychological concept of society, calling on the structure of the human psyche, which requires social life, also had numerous adherents (on the basis of XIXth Century psychologism). This concept, no doubt grasping the psychic phenomenon, did not want to bring (or else could not bring) its thought to a conclusion, namely the seeking of non-contradictory factors of precisely such a psychic phenomenon of the human being. If it had posed such a question, it would have had to arrive at the solutions presented here, namely, that the structure of human personal being is potentialized and actualizes itself only in the context of other persons, within the social context. Other theories, like the famous organic theory drawn from Nicholas da Cusa, are based on strongly exaggerated analogies of society with a biological organism, which has cells, tissues and organs. Society, too, was meant to be a particular repetition of the mode of development of an organism, and to produce its cells and organs. Thus, the Emperor was to be the head of society, clerks were to be its organs, and law was to fulfill the function of the nerves of the social organism.

Theories of this kind contribute to a certain kind of explanation of society, its functioning or formation, but they do not explain the very essence of social being, they do not make clear which factor ultimately determines that society is precisely what it is, nor the nature of the factor making non-contradictable the very fact of the existence of society. And only this aspect is fundamentally of interest to the philosophy of being, since it allows us to understand the activity of the human person and shows the foundation for the emergence of legal relations. From the moment the philosophical point of view is affirmed, we can also supplement it with an extended explanation, by referring to the various aspects of human life, which became the basis for various extra-philosophical explanations of the phenomenon of human society.

9. COMMON GOOD AS THE REASON FOR SOCIETY AND LAW[27]

a) Introductory comments

At the starting-point of reflections on the fact of society (and the phenomenon of law), we can most generally distinguish two fundamental manners of approach: genetically-evolutional and causal-finalistic. Each of these approaches implies its respective objectivistic system, and so it draws in its argumentation upon extra-subjective facts.

1. In the genetically—evolutionistic approach, the very fact of the appearance of society and the historically developed human personality can be treated as a result of the necessary evolution of nature. According to this interpretation, the human being appeared in the group of "primates," and through the common work of some parts of this group, it slowly developed—by means of various indirect forms—as a historical being, reaching consciousness and self-consciousness. In this sense, life in a group was an earlier phenomenon than the appearance of human consciousness; what is more, human consciousness, sometimes leading an individual to a conflict with the group, was a work of

common labor, the common experience of the group, concerned with providing food and defense against other groups of animals. In such a sense the group was earlier than the individual who is aware of specific duties and of himself or herself.

As human consciousness increased and conditions of life became gradually more complicated, the available means serving to conserve the group had to be increased. These means, becoming more and more specialized, finally took on the form of means of production. The group of people which was first at gaining control over them completely (and the others found themselves more or less like slaves, alongside these means of production) became the ruling class. From this moment onwards, class struggle was on the agenda of human history. Concrete man and woman, everywhere, found themselves members of a human group as such, or of a specific class within the bounds of this group. A man and a woman, as members either of a group or of a specific class, always developed their consciousness within their framework, not automatically and independently of the environment. For this reason, too, class developed the personality of the human being, as its member, and either dictated its will to the remaining classes or was oppressed by other classes. The dictatorship of the ruling class—that is, the class which controlled the means of production—became the law.

In such a concept of the person and society, the common good as the basis of the binding power of law in general (and at least in a fundamental sense), does not make its appearance in a clear way. The common good, according to this concept, would fundamentally denote the good of a specific ruling class, (that is, the class controlling the means of production), and not the good of all people.

That is why, where the human being is conceived e x c l u s i v e l y as a product of nature and society, the common good does not fundamentally constitute the basis for justifying the appearance of society and the binding power of law. Of course, this is a simplified account, given in order to stress a different approach.

2. Person and society can also be approached in a different way, while still within natural categories. The human being, in spite of being a natural creation (just as the society in which he or she lives is a natural creation) does, however, essentially differ from the whole of nature through reason and ability to make a free choice; thus, the human being is conceived here as a p e r s o n, who has this aim and the means—deriving from choice—needed to realize this aim. At the same time, humans (as a potentialized personal being) cannot attain their desired aim (which is also assigned by nature) alone and without the help of others. That is why, in order to attain each aim, both the indirect one (the perfection of the activity of particular faculties), and the ultimate personal aim (the acquisition of a state of personal perfection), each human being needs other persons, and for the distribution of work, within a group of other people, he

needs society. The basis of the fact of society is deeply embedded within the potentialized person, as has already been mentioned.

In such a concept of the human being and society (already known to the Greek thinkers Plato and Aristotle), a concept which could be called f i n a l i s t i c, the problem of the c o m m o n g o o d is seen as the basis of the emergence of society, and of a binding law in it. Within the framework of this concept, the philosophical explanation of the very structure of the common good becomes necessary, for the common good, as a good, is the aim of the aspirations and activity of human persons.

b) Common good—what is it?

The response to this question, when posed in this way, becomes possible by analyzing the meanings of the two expressions appearing in the question itself: "good," and "common." In the process of carrying out analyses of these two meanings, we will have to consider the concept of human nature and the human person, with which common good is connected and, in fact, t o w h i c h common good is ordered, and of whose activity it is the object and aim.

Aristotle wrote, at the beginning of the *Nichomachean Ethics*:

> All art and all investigations, and likewise all activity and also resolution, seem to aim towards some kind of good, and that is why good has aptly been defined as the aim of all aspirations.

The concept of good accepted by Aristotle was a f i n a l i s t i c concept, that is, one that explained good as the aim, particularly of rational, but not only of rational aspirations. The Stagirite opposed here another concept of good, the e c s t a t i c one, (known to Plato, and later taken up by Plotinus), in which "good" was the name given to that which, as it is perfect in itself, "overflows" onto other beings, thereby giving them being.

The finalistic concept of good is more primordial and more general than the Platonic concept of good.

Good as the aim of all aspirations will reveal itself more clearly when we draw attention to the dynamic nature of being, for we cognize the nature of each being in the context of the activity proper to that being, and this activity in turn becomes comprehensible in the light of a commensurable object, that is, the aim. This activity, the act of existence, is the realization (proper to each being) of the inclination to a mode of existence defined by nature. The nature of being reveals and perfects itself through activity in which being, as it were, "manifests" its being. Good, the aim of activity, is proper to the nature of a given being as much as the object of the inclination known also as "desire." Aim does not differ from good in a factual way but only formally, by the fact that it includes a relation to actual desire, wherefore we speak of good as "desirable."

Consequently, good is a being, insofar as this being becomes the reason for aspiration (that is the aim of desire), for in order for activity to emerge, rather than non-activity, there must exist a commensurable reason for the emergence of this activity, thanks to which a being which did not previously exist, now is, rather than is not. This reason can, ultimately, only be being-good, which by the very fact that it becomes the reason for desire (that is, is desirable) can constitute the aim of the activity of being. Briefly: being arouses desire, because it is good; and because it is good, it becomes, for aspirations, their aim.

The good (desirability) of being will become especially understandable when we analyze the activity of rational nature—the human being. Only good can constitute the basis for explaining the existential fact of human activity, both in its objective and its subjective aspects. The fact that a human being acts with a specific aim can be explained only by the fact that the object of aspiration appeared before the individual as w o r t h y o f d e s i r e —as a good. Only for this good does the human being desire ("want") it. Considering the social aspect of human good *(resp.* human nature), we will give the name "good" to the object of human activity which can become the individual aim of e v e r y p e r s o n a l a s p i r a t i o n , and can, in this sense, be analogically common to all persons living in a society.

St. Thomas Aquinas drew special attention to this:

> A c t i v i t i e s a r e a l w a y s i n d i v i d u a l l y d e t a i l e d , but precisely such detailed activity c a n b e r e l a t e d t o c o m m o n g o o d , which is common, yet not in the way that species or genus are common, but in the way that the f i n a l c a u s e is common, and that is why we can call a c o m m o n a i m a common good.[28]

St. Thomas' text rightly indicates the only rational possibility of conceiving common good as the basis for the explanation of human activity in general—as well as law in particular—that is, strictly speaking, human activity, insofar as it is directed by law.

This matter is, of course, subject to even further explanation, which is already linked with an analysis of the very fact of law. The fact of law, however, presupposes the very liberation of human activity, that is, the "existential fact" of human activity. Human activity (that is, its existential fact), on the other hand, is explainable only by good, both for purely objective reasons and also subjective ones.

Considering purely objective reasons, the good, as really identifying itself with being (good as a being), can be constituted, in its objective content, or, to be more precise, its ontic one, by the same "element" or "moment" that constitutes being. As we know, according to a concept of philosophy justified elsewhere, the element constituting be-ing is precisely the a c t   o f   e x i s t e n c e commensurate with a concrete individual nature. Existence, on the other hand, is conceived as the most perfect ontic moment, since precisely this existence is the ultimate act of everything which is called real being, for no perfection would be real, true perfection, if it really did not exist. We cannot add anything that is more perfect to the act of existence.

The existence of being is conceived here as that which ultimately actualizes all those potentialities of being which are due to a given ontic nature. In the case of the human being, for instance, we have in mind here not only the very "naked" (hence unreal) "existence of human nature," but the kind of existence, that is, the kind of real b e i n g a human, who mobilizes all the conditions of the concrete and real person of the human being, insofar as the latter becomes ontically perfect, that is, develops in the biological and rational spheres. If we conceive being as concrete, "developed," and really existing, then good is identified with precisely such real being.

In philosophical systems, according to which being is not determined by the act of existence but by "form" (which in turn is understood in various ways, depending on whether the system is Aristotelianism, Platonism, Augustinianism, Scotism), it was usual to make a distinction between being, which is given to us (without any additions to perfect it, that is, being, constituted by undetermined "pure" form), and perfect being, which is enriched by additional ontic forms, such as, for a man or woman, "to be wise," "to be perfect," and so on. Later on, a correct distinction was made, by saying that the simplest being—still not determined—is not a good in the proper sense, *(ens simpliciter est bonum per accidens)*, whereas enriched being, developed being, is perfected, but only by a proper good, *(ens secundum quid - est bonum simpliciter)*.

Good was always conceived as a "developed" being, an analogically perfect be-ing, which causes (is the reason for) the desire for oneself, as becomes particularly evident in the human act of will, and because it is the reason for desire, becomes the basis for explaining the very fact of the activity of a being, particularly a human being. It was for the attainment of good (ontic perfection) that human beings established the sciences and all other activities which provide them with new beings (goods) which can fulfill and perfect them. By analogy (not metaphorical, but proper analogy, based on the metaphysical structure of acting being) it was understood, in the Peripatetic system, that the concept of good is at the basis of the justification of all activity, especially human activity.

Good, for the person, is the ever fuller actualization of the potentialities of human nature, different-analogical in each individual case. A man or woman strives towards a "multiplication" of his or her mode of existence, towards an enrichment of the self. He or she is moved towards acting in the direction of a personal good (that is, towards the realization of his or her "ontic status") by natural inclinations existing within a rational essence. Because of rationality, the human being can cognize them personally—he or she has the right to cognize them—and accept them, as well as make a free choice of the means that will serve for their realization. The existence of these inclinations in each individuum of a rational nature, together with the existence of the subject (the person), find their ultimate justification in the Absolute Good, towards which every being is oriented in quite a particular way, since it is conscious and free.

The ever fuller realization of one's ontic aspirations in the area of cognition, love and free auto-determination (to the extent of one's individual natural potentialities), is the "attracting force," the good; and the good is the reason for being of the activity of every human person, which, in the sense of analogical identity of aim, constitutes common good.

The good appears also as the justification of human activity from the personal-subjective point of view, for human beings, as contingent, are limited thereby; and, being only potentialized, they do not actually possess in themselves those perfections which are necessary to them for full internal and external development. And precisely the viewing, as well as the constant experience of one's contingency is, as it is a subjective expression of potentialization, at the same time a concretely-felt experience of one's ontic incompleteness. Ontic incompleteness and restriction cause a hunger for the good, which is desired but not possessed, while at the same time being perceived as a good that is in some way due to the human being. Thus, the experience of a "lack" of good, causes the sort of activity which aims at filling this lack by providing an appropriate good, through which the fulfillment of human existence takes place, in a given aspect.

And only good can become the c o m m o n p r o p e r t y of all people. The nature of this good is delineated by the human personality, for when we speak of the c o m m o n g o o d, we thereby also speak of the kind of good that concerns people as potentialized beings who have the right to personal development. In such a situation, the common good is attainable by means of human acts as personal acts; and the latter can above all be reduced to acts of the intellect and free will.

Thus, good lies where the actualization of the intellect and free will takes place, which can become the common good of all people. It is personal good in the proper sense. It is expressed by means of the most varied actualizations, which are in keeping with the tendencies and dispositions of our nature and the needs of other people, with the actual conditions and similar factors concretely determining every human activity.

The intellect and free will can actualize themselves; in fact man and woman, through the action of the intellect and the will, can actualize themselves by means of systematic acts and exercises, acquiring skills in different domains. In this way, the human personality enriches itself by the acquired skills. Along this path lie science (with its vast range of specializations, which already are here, and which are still to be), as well as enrichment through art, and finally moral and religious enrichment. And only in this order of purely personal good, attained by the intellect and will, can there be no question of any contradiction between the good of the whole society and that of particular persons as its members. What is more, only in such a concept of common good, which is the common aim of the personal activity of every human being, can we lay down the principle that the increase of the good of a particular person is, at the same time, the increase of the common good of the whole society, for personal enrichment cannot take place at anyone's expense, and it serves everyone. That is why the aim of society is to make possible the fullest realization of common good, that is, to create conditions for personal actualization to an unlimited degree.

It is evident that the very actualization of a personal good (which is at the same time common good) requires, in the normal course of events, material means such as food for the continuation of biological life (which at the same time conditions psychic life), accommodation, and technical efficiency. The latter is necessary for human life, and is measured by material energy and its consumption, to make life easier and to create the conditions for a development of specifically personal goods. Here, in the area of the distribution of material means for the realization of "common good," conflicts can occur between the individual and society as a whole. Already St. Thomas drew attention to the fact that *nemo potest superabundari, nisi alter deficiat*, for there can be—and this very often happens in practice—some proportionally unequal distribution of material goods, and that is why it is the task (aim) of social authorities, not only to distribute goods among all people proportionally, that is, justly, but at the same time to organize work in such a way as to increase material means in their effect on people, in order to make possible the realization of the essential personal good at the same time as the common good. Neither any one material good taken in isolation, nor all material goods taken together, can be accepted as the "common good" in the proper sense, which enables one to conceive of them as the reason for the existence of social order (respectively law). Material goods will always remain only a means—an important one, sometimes even an indispensable one—but still only a means to a proper end.

If a particular material good does not possess in itself the "reason" for being ultimate good,—that is, the kind that attracts by itself, as the proper, and, all the more, the ultimate limit of desire and activity—then the sum of material goods of this "reason" does not increase itself by quantitative addition, for being does not emerge from non-being and non-being does not, of itself, become being.

In the order of material goods we can perceive a certain hierarchy: there are goods of a higher or a lower order; there are more or less valuable goods. Vegetative human life is without doubt more valuable than the vegetative life of animals or plants, because it is "set into" the personal life of the human being (which is directed towards personal good), and because it is not a good b e y o n d the unity of the human person. Goods which are useful for the conservation of personal life have, for a human being, a higher value than goods which are useful for becoming more comfortably situated, and so on.

If, then, by means of an analysis of human activity and its aims, we perceive that numerous goods are desirable not on account of themselves alone, but on account of higher goods (primarily the good of desiring man or desiring woman), we can also state that in the order of nature, just as there exists a hierarchy of beings (there are "weaker" and "stronger" beings, as well as the all-justifying being of the Absolute), there also exists a hierarchy of goods, since good and being are really the same.

The highest objective good is, then, at the same time the highest being, the Absolute, which religion calls God. Good can be "attained" only through acts of being of the highest order (as indeed personal acts are), that is, through acts of the intellect and free will. Only the Supreme Good can be the objective Common Good for each person and the whole of society, and, to make it possible to attain precisely this Good is the "reason for being" of society, and thereby also the law which is binding in society. No society can rise up against its own "reason for being" and issue laws which would either make difficult or in any way attempt to make impossible the attainment of "common good," or condition the attainment of this good by means of norms-commands which are not of their nature necessarily connected with "common good." All such norms or dispositions can be acknowledged as mere pseudo-laws, which can in no way "bind from within," in his conscience, the human person who is ordered to attaining common good.

Of course, this does not mean that it is always easy to perceive and define whether, and to what extent, concrete laws issued by some such society make the attainment of common good impossible, or limit and condition this attainment by requiring other laws to be fulfilled, which are not necessarily connected with the attainment of "common good." Human acts in line with common good, that is, personal acts of cognition and love, can without interruption increase in man, and their increase not only does no harm to anyone but, on the contrary, it enriches society by contributing to a fuller connection of society with "common good." Other human acts, on the other hand—as they do not tend towards an aim but have, as their subject, material goods as such (that is, goods of the body, external goods, both in the sphere of animate and inanimate matter)—must be subordinated to social control and regulated by laws and decrees, in order to enable every human person proportionally to fulfill his of her fundamental "right," which is the real possibility of becoming positively directed towards "common good" through developing his or her personal potentialities.

St. Thomas' text cited above (and its interpretation) show the insufficiency and, in this sense, the erroneousness of other ways of conceiving "common good," which developed out of various theoretical contexts, especially since there were attempts to transplant them into St. Thomas' system. It is a question, here, of extending St. Thomas' reasoning, for instance by making his theory (of ordering components to a whole) fit the theory of ordering people by good in the same manner in which individuals are ordered by a species or genus.

According to such theories, the common good is not the personal good of the human individual, and the individual alone cannot attain the "common good"; the "common good" can be realized only by the common effort of all individuals put together, just as, for instance, the tree alone does not yet constitute a forest and a human individual does not alone constitute the complete human species.

Why are theories of this kind, which see in the "common good" a supra-human and supra-personal good (which the particular human-person cannot fulfill) unacceptable? It is because these theories negate the essential feature of personality, the "whole," that is, "completeness." According to such assumptions, the form of being of an ensemble, a Collective, or some super-human formation would be a higher form of being than a human individual. Yet there are no subsistent forms of being which are more "complete" than the human person.

Society is merely a relational creation (in spite of its necessity), and it cannot take the place of the human person. If we place a higher whole above the human-person (a whole to which the human being is completely ordered), and only this higher whole presents us with a fully valuable fullness of being, it is a "whole" which has the power to "wholly," that is, totally, make the human being happy, to fulfill all human aspirations, since it has the "knowledge" of what humans lack. Such a personification of the social creation is, then, precisely a "totalism," eliminating the nature of human personality in its basic rights. Concepts of this type, as we shall discuss later, eliminate finalistically-understood "common good" by not taking into account the essential nature of potentialized human nature.

The common good conceived finalistically on the other hand, appears before the human-person as his or her own "personal" good, capable of being grasped by the reason, hence every human person can and should understand it, and, understanding it, should at the same time adhere to it. The binding of the human person by this good is a "binding from within" and not "from without," by a command that is irrational, since it is not accepted in a conscious and free way by the human being—the person—acting through personal acts. A command imposed merely "from without"—and not understood, or accepted, or liked "from within"—is a moral force which by nature is nevertheless something immoral. In order to understand the common good, we must, therefore, d i s c e r n its essential nature, and the role of society is to give the human being the kind of education to allow one to discern and understand rational freedom by oneself "from within," and freely come to love "common good" and oneself as its participant. Any other way of connecting the human being with society, by any law whatever, is a way that eliminates human nature as free, potentialized personality.

c) Some interpretations of the realization of "common good"

Individualistic liberalism as a philosophical and social doctrine has its roots in the creative work and the formulations of J.J. Rousseau. It is derived from a particular interpretation of the saying: "every man is born free." According to the interpretation connected with Rousseau's work, this saying means that every person enjoys the state of freedom, which that person possesses from birth. It is not at all a question here of the fact that a human being has free will, which he or she can later employ in one way or another, but of the fact that the mode of human existence is such that it is independent, and that this independence is inborn in the human being. By virtue of this independence, the human being cannot give way to anyone and is obedient only to the self and to his of her own commands. Of course, though having such a mode of existence, human beings still want to live well and in comfort, and that is why they organize themselves into a society. Thus, Rousseau writes in his *Contrat Social:*

> We must find such a form of unity in which everyone, uniting with everyone, is not, however, subject to anyone and is obedient only to himself and still remains free, as he was before.[29]

This is precisely why the myth of the will of common agreement was accepted, according to which everyone, to a certain extent, renounces his or her sovereign rights and unites in a social union directed by LAW, which is not a product of the reason but a result of the will of a NUMBER of human individuals, which is why authority, appearing in the name of a NUMBER of people, can give commands to another human being.

Of course, it is from such a concept of authority, which is not fundamentally a work of a rational nature but comes exclusively from an appropriate number of people and from the will, and which is most often blind, that totalitarian authority was later derived, which arises from the will of a number of people but nevertheless leads to a complete negation of freedom.

In the concept of a society where people gather together freely, where everyone is sovereign, there takes place, in fact, a negation of authority (which is, after all, a formal element of society). Authority is in this case fundamentally a work of the reason and of rational nature for whose development social associations are indispensable in order to be able to develop more fully the individual's personal aspects, and there is also the cost of introducing social and distributive justice.

If individualistic liberalism were at the basis of people being bound to one another in a society, then of necessity the realization of "common good" would not take place, that is, no good which is both the good of the individual and of the whole of society would be done, no good whose realization would avoid contradictions between the individual (to be more precise, the human person), and the whole of society. Then, only the good of the individual would exist, without common good, and such a state of affairs could only end in anarchy, that is, in the ultimate annihilation of social being and of all law, and in that way the inter-human relations would recall the state of struggle for being described by Darwin, in which only biologically stronger individuals without moral scruples would rise above the surface of life. Social anarchy would be one consistent way out from liberalism when conceived in this way.

There is still the possibility of a second way out from the doctrine conceived in this way, namely "fascism," which was in fact the ultimate stage of the developmental process of individualistic liberalism thus conceived. Proudhon foresaw and indicated this developmental process, for the human mass is (in this hypothesis) at one and the same time the subject of sovereign authority, and also not, for it rules by means of delegates who hold forth in the name of the mass. Delegates of this kind clash in mutual conflict and weaken the government; consequently, out of the total impotence of parties and delegates there arises a need for strong dictatorial rule, that is, for an individual or a group of people to control the society over which they rule, completely and in a totalitarian way. And in this way, individualistic-liberalistic democracy really degenerated into governments made up of either one party to totally solve all difficulties, or of one race, or of one nation, or of one "providential" man—a leader, as testified by history.

Of course, this is not the only source for a system of this kind, since it already existed in antiquity in the form of tyrannical rule. It has its source in purely intellectualistic philosophical concepts (Plato, Hegel, Nietzsche), which concepts do not take account of human nature as it is, but are based on *a priori* principles, which advocate a systematized and conjectured happiness for everyone, without first asking the "people made happy" if they agreed to being made totally happy. According to these principles, the human being is evil, such as he or she is, and that is why the individual must be transformed in accordance with an *a priori* concept of the system.

We can name, after Messner,[30] the following characteristic features of the system apprehended in this way:

1. The authority of the supreme authority is absolute and the aims of authority are at the same time the aims of all organizations ordered to the supreme system, so that there can be no question of the contradiction or independence of the aims of the group or system.

2. Associated groups not carrying out the will of the supreme system do not exist.

3. There is no law against the supreme system and that is why the individual cannot enter into judicial proceedings against the supreme system.

4. The supreme system has only one official public opinion or eventually one "party."

5. The source of authority goes "from the top to the bottom" and in this direction go commands and solutions.

6. Either there is no representative of the people or a person is a decorative organ of authority and that person merely has the function of propaganda.

7. The totalitarian system is fundamentally a system of compulsion, where the individual can be completely trodden down by an external constraint.

8. In the totalitarian system, organs of control for authority do not exist.

9. In these systems there is no freedom of thinking and speech.

10. There is also no possibility of organizing legal opposition.

11. In these systems the rights of the person are not respected at all.

12. Fundamentally, the totalitarian system is the only true possessor of goods.

Summarizing all these features, we can define such a system as one in which the human person is not an aim, but merely a means realizing the aims of the system, and where it has value only as a means.

If we wanted to establish the relation of the human being to society in the light of both the trends mentioned, then, according to liberalistic individualism, the human being is not essentially and of his or her nature ordered to society, but only in some secondary aspects. The proper role of the State, and its duty, is to protect the citizen from the interference of authority. In the domain of economy, this view was expressed in the motto: *"laissez aller, laissez faire."* As a result of this, the weaker individuals and social groups or classes were deprived of the care of the State. Particularly in the XIXth Century, this led to a typical class division into the owners of capital and the proletariat, to depriving poor people of education, to misery, and so on. Such a state of affairs gave rise to quite a natural reaction, in the form of socialism.

An excessively pursued opposition to individualistic liberalism, particularly in the economic field, led of necessity to totalism, according to which the ordering of the human being to the State (society) is total, that is, complete in all aspects. The individual becomes merely a function of the State or of society. In such a case, the State (or society) has (or attempts to have) complete control over the thoughts of human beings, their technical and artistic creativity; the State establishes both the aims and the means of realizing these aims, so that human beings, as a result, become deprived of the possibility of realizing their personal aims, and by the same token, the means which could ensure for them any independence with respect to society. People and their creative initiative find their justification by way of realizing the aims of the State, and a man and woman, attempting to defend their own nonconformist aims, are regarded as enemies of society and destroyed by it. As a result, totalistic societies bring back social slavery—both State slavery, and slavery in organisms beyond the State.

The relation between the human person (who has personal aims) and the State (society) cannot, therefore, be arranged according to the extreme models presented above. Hence, in normally developing societies the relations of person to society generally take shape according to rational norms. These relations are generally reduced to the custodial function of the State in relation to subordinate social groups or people, according to the principle of assistance, that means the non-elimination of those forms of life which either the person as individual, or a natural association to do with work, is capable of developing. The State, on the other hand, restricts itself to custody of the material goods of the individual and of natural associations, to the conservation of life and cultural-moral goods. Of course, the very care of the supreme society can assume different forms: from a rather passive care to a clearly active one, which intervenes in different domains of life.

The rational model of the arrangement of relations between the human person and society is presented in the theory of p e r s o n a l i s m,[31] according to which the human being is ordered to society (the State or another society, particularly a supreme one), but not in all aspects, since in the domain of purely personal goods he and she remain free and it is not they who serve society, but society which is ordered for the human person. On the other hand, in the domain of goods—which are not objects of purely personal acts, that is, exclusively acts of the intellect and will, but which also cause other acts of human nature, essentially connected with external goods—the human being is ordered for society and the State.

Thus, the same human being is ordered and subordinated simultaneously to the State-society and, conversely, the State-society is ordered and subordinated to the person but in different respects. Since the dignity of the human person is the highest good to be encountered here on earth, the human being in his or her personality and purely personal acts is independent and free, and he or she alone, without any orders from above, can and should develop the self in his or her personal life. (Commands can be mere directives, which will become binding only insofar as man or woman, in his or her conscience, recognizes the self as bound with respect to them, on account of the necessary arrangement of being, which must, however, be personally perceived by the human being). However, where material good comes into play, even when this material good is, in an exceptional case, the human being with respect to his or her life or the good of the body (and all the more with respect to some external material good, to the use and possession of which the other person also has a right or can eventually have a right), there the human individual is ordered and subordinated to society. With respect to these goods, society has authority and somehow dominates the human being, who sometimes—in a concrete case—must agree to lose the right to an unchecked use of material goods.

It is a fact that it is, in practice, extremely difficult to establish, in a simple way, the relation of the person to society. In general, these relations in a negative form become established in the supreme law, that is, in the Constitution of the State. At present, additional assistance in the domain of State Legislation is given to States or social organizations by international organizations, for example the United Nations Organization, or Papal Encyclicals, which emphasize or even establish the never outdated rights of the human being as a person.

Personalism is merely a philosophical theory, indicating the fundamental and general basis of affirming personal rights and State laws, but it cannot become a social theory determining in a concrete way the organization of a given society, for the settlements, concerning relations between the person and society, take place within the framework of a specific cultural situation; they are to a serious degree high-lighted by the conditions in which the whole society develops; in a word: they constitute a historical category.

In any case, according to the general delimitations introduced by the philosophical theory of personalism, we cannot, in an *a priori* way, change human nature or regard human aspirations (deriving from human nature) as fundamentally erroneous, but it is only necessary to analyze the natural tendencies of rational human nature with the consent of people themselves—as the interested ones—to concretely establish in what way the structure of society should be formed for the common good to be really realized.

NOTES

THE DRAMA OF NATURE AND PERSON

[1] I have written on the subject of the human being from a philosophical point of view in a special monograph: *I—Man: An Outline of Philosophical Anthropology,* New Britain, Conn., Mariel Productions, 1983. In this work I have also presented more extensively the problem of human being. The present Chapter is an interpretation of this problem as ordered to the problems of natural law. It is, therefore, a philosophical anthropology in shortened version, showing the human person placed into a deterministically acting material nature, which nevertheless allows it to develop, in the context of other persons, that is, society.

[2] I am writing more extensively here on the subject of what is implied by structural philosophy, using papers previously published in *Znak* (The Sign) 23:1971, No. 203, pp. 561–570, and in *Zeszyty Naukowe KUL* (Scientific Journals of KUL) 12:1970, № 4, pp. 21–33, in order to draw attention to the set of problems concerning the person in relation to law.

[3] Lévi-Strauss, *The Savage Thought,* 1962.

[4] *Ibid.*

[5] *Ibid.*

[6] *Ibid.*

[7] *Ibid.*

[8] *Ibid.*

[9] *Ibid.*

[10] Particularly on this subject, cf. *S.th.,* 1a, q. 76 a. 1; *De Anima* a. 8; *Q. Disp. De Spirit. Creat.* a. 2 etc.

[11] Kant, *The Foundation of the Metaphysics of Morals.*

[12] Kant, *A Critique of Practical Reason.*

[13] Aristotle, *Politics,* Book I, Chapter 1, 1252 b. 2.

[14] Cf. on this subject: J. Messner, *Das Naturrecht,* Innsbruck 1960, pp. 467–501.

[15] These problems, taken up by Bachofen *(Das Mutterrecht)* in the XIXth Century, had numerous adherents in the XIXth as well as in the XXth Century. This theory was connected with the evolutionary concept of social organisms.

[16] Westmarck, *The history of Human Marriage,* from the end of the XIXth Century. Mainly, however, the works of W. Schmidt, that is *Die Stellung der Pygmäenvölker in der Entwicklungsgeschichte des Menschen,* Stuttgart 1910, and *Der Ursprung der*

Gottesidee Bd. 1–12, Münster 1926–1955 (this is the most important work), contributed to the consolidation of this theory.

[17] The works of Schmidt, however, arouse the highest admiration and cannot be put aside.

[18] More on this subject: J. Messner, *Das Naturrecht,* pp. 503–555.

[19] Ibid., pp. 556–572.

[20] W.I. Lenin, *Wielka inicjatywa* (The Great Initiative).

[21] Messner, p. 527.

[22] Ibid., p. 572ff.

[23] Aristotle, *Polit.* I 1252 b. 8.

[24] Ibid., 1253 a. 12.

[25] Ibid., 1253 b. 11.

[26] Ibid.

[27] J. Kondziela in *Filozofia społeczna* (Social Philosophy), Lublin 1972, wrote on the subject of various concepts of common good. Here I present the concept interpreted in the light of the theory of being in St. Thomas Aquinas, by repeating the text published in my work *I—Man,* p. 293ff., since this problem is ordered to the concept of natural law.

[28] *Operationes quidem sunt in particularibus: sed illa particularia referri possunt ad bonum commune non quidem communitate generis vel speciei, sed communitate causae finalis, secundum quod bonum commune dicitur finis communis. (S.th.,* 1a2ae, q. 90 a. 2 ad 2).

[29] Cited after A. Peretiatkowicz, *Filozofia Prawa J.J. Rousseau* (J.J. Rousseau's Philosophy of Law), Cracow, 1913, p. 133.

[30] Messner, p. 729ff.

[31] The problem of personalism, now extensively analyzed by different thinkers, was fundamentally formulated in the numerous works of J. Maritain.

Chapter IV

THE THEORY OF NATURAL LAW

1. THE EXISTENCE OF NATURAL LAW

a) Common belief

The conviction about the existence of natural law has always been very strongly rooted in human consciousness, as testified both by historical and philosophical theories from the earliest times, and by various human experiences of conflict presented in literature, particularly in drama (*vide* the classic example of Antigone), as well as by the experiences of everyone who attempts to base decisions on an objective order of things, as interpreted by reason, and who recognizes that this ontic order is good.

Our personal conviction, as well as the testimonies corresponding to it, which are contained in good literature, are an expression of the human "common-sensical" way of looking at the world, which, in the normal course of life, is sufficient as a justification for every day decisions. And in the light of "commonsense" conviction, humanity has "natural" sources of morality and "natural" criteria for the assessment of what precisely makes conduct human, both individually and socially, (although each "individual" act is simultaneously "social," since the domain of morality concerns the human being as a social entity).

These natural sources can be seen as the structure and functioning of the human being, present in the world, "immersed" in this world and subjectivized in his or her activity in existing, which, when it becomes the object and aim of activity, by the same token becomes good. Thus, the set of problems around how to interpret and justify natural law is the person in the face of good.

As we know, one of the greatest concepts in science is the concept of "nature" (*PHYSIS*) discovered by the Greeks. The knowledge of the concept of "nature" is also at the basis of the understanding of "natural law." Of course, the discovery of "nature" in philosophy could only be made on the basis of rational thought (directed by more or less reflected non-contradiction). That is why it would be futile to seek the concept of nature and natural law in, for instance, the Old Testament, since it emerged in the context of a culture that did not know the principle of non-contradiction.

In Greek culture the discovery of "nature" was preceded by a period employing other concepts, closely connected ones, as Lévi-Strauss probably aptly understands it.[1] Before the discovery of nature, the characteristic behavior of a thing was defined by the word "custom" or "mode." And, in this sense, the "custom" according to which the human being lives, would be a fundamental matter. It is true that not all members of the human group remain close to one mode (custom), but they usually go back to it, if they are reminded of it in a suitable form, for the fundamental mode is supposed to be "correct" because it is ancient: *Vetustus pro lege semper habetur.* However, not everything that is ancient is also correct. "Our" custom is good precisely because it is both "ours" and "old," that is, inherited from our forefathers (who are primary elements—like "first elements" in philosophy). But we cannot identify what is inherited, what is old, what is "ours," with what is correct, and therefore authority needed to be queried. That is why Plato indicated the necessity of questioning authority already in his *State and Laws* (which uses the form of dialogue), in order to discover the idea of natural law, for if that which has been passed down to us by our elders and "betters" is not always the truth, we ourselves must, on our own responsibility, seek the criterion of good, for people had to differentiate between a rumor (what others told them) from what they saw "with their own eyes," that is, from what they understood in the thing itself, that is nature.

From the moment of discovering and understanding nature, it could immediately be differentiated from custom or the characteristic mode of living passed down by the "elders" or "gods." Customs and modes of living have since been recognized as CONVENTIONS. If, on the other hand, the discovery of "nature" is regarded as the birth of philosophy, then from the very beginning of philosophical thought there exists a distinction between natural law and conventional law. The link between the concept of natural and conventional law is always present in philosophical thought. It merely takes on various forms and various expressions. The discovery of nature, however, and in that, above all, the discovery of human nature—that which is essentially human for the person—is a necessary condition for the appearance of the concept of natural law, which was originally hidden by convention. If primeval law is presented as identical with the law or custom in question, then the convention conceals nature itself. Moreover, conventionalism almost always puts forward its crowning argument: justice takes on various forms and changes, depending on the kind of society. If, therefore, justice as the principle of law is changeable, then natural law is impossible.

Different societies have different concepts of justice. And the variety of concepts of justice can be understood as a variety of errors, which does not eliminate, but presupposes, the existence of real systems and bases of justice. After all, where we have to deal with pure conventions, as with measures and weights, there is no dispute as to their natural values. Differences pertaining to conventional matters do not cause any major complications, while the understanding of justice, good and evil of necessity causes misunderstandings, and that is why we must refer to the very system of things and to the structure of the human being, in order to judge the matter.

Consequently, that which Aristotle wrote at the very beginning of *Nichomachean Ethics* is an indisputable truth:

> Every art and every investigation, and likewise every activity as well as resolution (decision) appear to tend towards some kind of g o o d, and that is why good has aptly been described as the aim of all aspirations.

However, what is good, for man or woman as an individual and as a social being, can only be judged by reason, which guides decision in the perspective of the other person, that is, b y that which is most human in the individual.

We can identify good, as has been done by philosophical and legal conventionalism, with what is pleasurable or useful. And that is why the critique of conventionalism went in the direction of showing that the good in itself *(bonum honestum)* was supreme over pleasure and utility.[2] Reason which shows that there are levels higher than pleasure (that is, the vegetative and animal aspect) and utility (the matter of justice), is the ultimate objective measure of what is really good for a person as a social being.

As shown in reflections about human beings as personal beings, they are by nature social beings, to the extent that they are not able to stand, be educated or live, beyond society. Lévi-Strauss aptly writes:

> Man is a social being in a more radical sense than any other social animal, since reason and speech distinguish him from other animals; speech is communication: human nature itself has a social character. Man himself directs himself towards other people, or rather he is directed towards others in each human act, whether it is a "social" or "anti-social" act. The social nature of man does not derive from relying on the pleasures which he expects to get from being in the company of others; man finds pleasure in being with others, because he is, of his nature, a social being. Love, sentiment, friendship, pity are as natural for him as caring for his own good and taking into account that which favors his own good. The natural sociability proper to man is precisely the basis of natural law in a restricted or strict sense of this word. Since man is, of his nature, a social being, the perfection of his nature embraces *par excellence* the social virtue—justice [and in it sees real good for humanity—M.K.]. Justice and law are natural.[3]

Of course, the good, when interpreted by the human reason with a view to the other "you" is beyond dispute and, at least in principle, it constitutes the concrete norm of human conduct. Thus, the drama of interpreting correct natural law takes place in human practical cognition, known as the conscience, which in the eyes of the Classical moral philosophers was always regarded as the ultimate arbiter of human moral decisions, as illustrated by St. Thomas Aquinas in question 19, parts I-II of his *Summa Theologiae*. Articles 5 and 6 of this question are particularly significant and deserve special attention. They can be reduced to the assertion that the conscience (that is, the decision of practical reason), even when erroneous (through no fault of its own), is binding. These texts correspond very well with the doctrine of St. Paul from his *Letter to the Romans,* which we quote here, precisely as a manifestation of common sense cognition:

> ... when the Pagans, who have not received the law [the law of Moses, together with its rules], naturally do what the law commands, they, who do not know the law are a law unto themselves and show that the content of the law is written in their hearts. This is also testified to by their conscience itself, by thoughts conflicting with one another, of which some accuse them and others stand in their defence.[4]

Thus, natural law, manifesting itself in the voice of conscience "DO GOOD" (that is, act—judgement—practical reason), is known to every human being in a natural way, by virtue of the fact that a man or a woman is a human being (a personal, rational being). The individual, living, as a human being, in a society, becomes aware of the fact that "doing good" is possible and necessary with respect to the other "you," open to the Transcendent "Thou." The sense of good with regard to the "you" fundamentally assumes the form of correctness and justice, of which the expression and organizer is positive law. The foundation and basis of law is always, however, the n a t u r a l s y s t e m o f b e i n g s o f t h e r e a l w o r l d, above all, the w o r l d o f p e r s o n s. This natural conviction about the basis of law in the "nature of things" can be, and is, elucidated by means of systematic philosophical thinking.

b) The Law of Human Nature*

Ever since people began to live in organized societies, they have always been guided in their conduct by laws of some kind. These laws—different for different types of society, of course—are articulated in various ways. "Laws of conduct" (precepts) are formulated differently as regards children, parents and marriage partners, in family life; differently in social organizations; differently in the State. However, we can also speak of the personal law of conduct (precept). Of course, in the general theory of the State and of law, we do not pay attention to these personally formulated precepts of conduct, nor to analogical laws, customs and precepts functioning in small social groups, that is, in the

---

* Editorial note: section b) is specially written for this English edition.

family or in different types of social organizations. This is both necessary and convenient. It is necessary, since the science of law can deal only with that which is commonly recognized as real law, and real law is precisely the law formulated and declared by the State as the supreme and sovereign society. It is convenient, as well, for in it we abandon the rather quaggy field of analogical understanding of law itself. Human life, however, has its necessary "demands," which are human rational modes of conduct, particularly towards other people. And this matter cannot ultimately be resolved by means of univocally formulated State laws, which are supposed to be the only concern of the science of law (and possibly also of the philosophy of law), for it is not true that only the State is a sovereign being, and that the human person is "not yet" a sovereign being. After all, the State is not, in its ontic structure, stronger than the individual personal being. The State as a social organization is only supreme t h r o u g h relational being, existing with an existence of human individuals, who exist independently "in themselves" as in a subject, structuralized in a necessary way. In the tradition of Classical philosophy this was called a "substantial" mode of being, as opposed to an accidental, relational one. What is more, precisely the human individual, as an "open" personal being (this will be discussed below) constitutes the focal point of human activity, and thereby the focal point of understanding the foundations of activity (that is, law) as well. Moreover, law is directed towards the concrete individual, and the concrete individual is to realize this law "in a human way," that is, in the same way as he or she carries out the precepts of parents, a marriage partner, or finally, personal resolutions.

Thus, the whole "drama" of law takes place within the human being, who alone exists (lives) independently in itself and who, living in this way, gets together with others to form a society, in order to "strengthen" and develop his or her life in various ways. Hence the set of problems regarding law in the original sense of the word is connected with the understanding of the human being and its nature, which manifests itself in characteristic "human activity." It would be futile to seek in the social (State) organization alone all the factors which would help make it possible to understand the complicated problem of law, to perceive the basis of its binding power and the very meaning of "life under the law." And conversely, when we examine all these matters on the basis of an understanding of the individual, one of the other factors resulting in an understanding of the human being and rational activity, is the consideration of social structures, and also the structure and functioning of the State and the law issued by it for people and implemented by people.

However, precisely in human activity we perceive two fundamental, yet different, ways of acting: action which is determined and submissive, and conscious and free action. This differentiation is evident and well known and is sometimes presented in the form of "something is happening in me" and "I am acting." The activity of our determined nature is normal and evident for everyone. Troubles only begin when this activity does not take its "normal" course, that is, does not take place according to the "rules" (laws) of nature. Then we have to seek medical aid, go to the doctor and take appropriate medicines, in order to help nature act normally and naturally. Sometimes, various actions of our biological nature are dependent on human will, in the sense that we ourselves can control some actions or even hinder their activity. I can begin a fast or a hunger strike by eating more (or less) of some foods. I can even sometimes control my breathing and thus change my heartbeat; I can control, or not control, my instincts, natural sexual drives, and so on. There is, then, a certain possibility of freely directing some of our natural functions, those whose use for certain ends lies within the scope of human possibilities.

The human being, nevertheless, only fulfills the self as a person in specifically personal functions, that is, in cognition and the use of reason (thinking), as also in moral conduct and diverse social and creative activity. And this is the true domain of human life. In this domain, a specifically human one, we do not encounter natural determinations towards univocally defined actions. Here we have to make a choice, concerning both the aim for, and the means to realize, our human intentions. I am not determined to take up a particular career and to do a particular job, to go to the theater or to church, to read a certain book or to watch television, to study Egyptology or philosophy, etc. In this domain the human being is o p e n . But what does it mean to be "open" and not determined? This presupposes that the human being possesses the ability to cognize reality and the possibility to choose (desire) something specific as a good. Concretely, this openness is manifested in the necessity of "auto-determination" to activity, that is, the possibility of making a d e c i s i o n . Hence, all problems of human decision, through which we determine ourselves to activity rather than non-activity, as well as to precisely such and such activity, can become the basis of understanding the very sources of law. Since human decision is the one necessary way in which the human being fulfills the self—as a free person, being the subject of law—then we must explain more fully just this decisive moment of the person's activity at its source.

It is a known fact that every human being—in living his or her life—acts. Every human activity, in order for it to be a real activity, must flow from the real source of human activity, a determined, actual source. Since nature itself has not determined us, we, being "open," must fulfill the conditions of activity by ourselves as free, self-determined sources of activity. This fulfillment by the person, can take place first of all by means of cognition. We must see reality, understand it, in order to be able to choose for ourselves the appropriate goals of activity, and then to adopt the means proportional to the end. And the understanding of reality is not universal, deep, but fairly superficial and perspectival, that is, human. Nonetheless, it is the understanding of reality as reality. This means that we understand that which is real and are able to distinguish it from what is unreal. Expressed in philosophical language, this means that we cognize being as existing, for only due to the fact that something (being) really exists in itself as in a subject, can it be recognized as real. Thus, contact with the real existence of being is something primary, which guarantees a connection with the foundation of realism. Only on the basis of the real existence of the world, the real existence of being, can we cognize its content, its nature, and recognize the very contents of cognition, drawn from really existing reality, as real. Only the human reason, in the world of living nature, has the power to discern reality as existing really in itself, and thereby reason alone has the power to "reduce everything" to a common denominator and call it "being," "reality," "good," etc. This means that every object—existing really—is a being, is real, is a good, and so forth.

Before human reason there appears, therefore, a real world, a world of really existing acting natures. Among these acting natures, the human being itself (acting as a human), appears first of all before the individual, as the object of his or her cognition. And we perceive that cognition itself (of the really existing world) is still not sufficient to produce a real act of activity, for cognition merely informs me what the world is like. In order to act, I must order the world I find to my activity: I must perceive it as precisely the m o t i v e of my activity, for, when I am not acting in one moment and then in another moment I begin to act, then there is a reason why I act rather than still not act. There is something that will "expel me from my passivity" in relation to the perceived world of things and persons. This motive, forcing me from my passivity towards activity is called a g o o d , a really existing being, which, having been cognized, arouses my d e s i r e and enkindles "love at first sight" in me, since it is, as it were, an "adaptation" of me to the perceived good (in the form of another person or thing). I can perceive various things and various "goods," which somehow arouse me to begin acting. The view of these various goods, insofar as they arouse me to act, is expressed by formulating practical judgements, like "do this now, in such and such a way," or "do not do this." There can be an enormous amount of these judgements. In reality we experience in ourselves a constantly projected "movie" of practical "judgements" as really existing, as a concrete good, as it were, in relation to the cognized world of persons and things.

Thus, in order for there to arise in me a concrete source of activity, I must determine myself to activity through a real choice of one practical judgement, among many which constantly appear to me, and which I register in myself as concrete possibilities of varied activity, for example: "eat your dinner," "do not eat your dinner," "eat only the second course, without the soup," "do not eat any cakes," "eat while standing up," "sit down to eat," and so forth. Often we do not even pay attention to this "film of practical judgements," and often we are not completely aware of the fact that the choosing of only one judgement is necessary, in order to determine oneself ultimately to activity (by means of this judgement) and to constitute oneself as a real source of activity, as the real efficient cause of one's acts. Our habits, skills and view of necessity cause an automatization of choice. Nonetheless, there exists a real c h o i c e (a spontaneous one, or else one that has either been given little or a great deal of thought) in which we ourselves with our w i l l freely choose (of our own free will) one practical judgement about a good, a judgement which will determine us to real activity. Precisely this real c h o i c e of practical judgement about a good (generally made consciously and deliberately) is our act of d e c i s i o n. Through this act of decision, I myself close my "openness" to concrete activity and determine myself to a real act of activity, constituting myself as the efficient cause of the acts which occur as a result of this decision. My practical judgement, chosen by me (though not necessarily the best or the only possible one, but one that I wanted), becomes my inner rule of activity; it becomes my n o r m of conduct; it becomes, for me, my l a w, my rule of activity.

Thus, I myself am a lawgiver for myself, in the main sense, (in the original sense), the one who constitutes the rule of my conduct, the real and primary sovereign, binding myself, by a norm of conduct chosen by myself, to real activity, for no one can force me to freely want what I do not want, in my activity. The moment of inner decision establishing the rule of my activity (through my personal choice of a practical judgement which has a determined content commanding such activity) constitutes a main reference (a main analogue) for understanding the binding nature of law as law.

The matter can be presented similarly in the case of carrying out legal precepts that are general or made by the Church or State. There, the content of the law-norm is conveyed to me through media promulgating law, for implementation. However, precisely at that moment I must cognize the content of the legal precept, I must personally take up an attitude towards this content, and I must accept it—that is, make the decision to carry out this law-precept. I can reject the law, if I decide that this law—when it commands us to do evil—is a pseudo-law, at which point I am not allowed to realize its content. Thus, the moment of personal decision, in which I myself constitute for myself a norm of conduct, explains to me in a fundamental way the functioning of law itself.

But here—for our understanding of the natural law of the human person—we must become particularly aware of the question: w h a t   f o r ? Why do I, in the act of decision, choose for myself precisely the kind of concrete practical judgement through which I determine myself to activity? The only explanation of this fact can be the structure (nature) of personal being. I choose, because being as a g o o d "arouses" me to do this, for "good" is the only motive, thanks to which I want to act rather than not act. And, concretely perceived good, proportional for me—that is, "my good"—is the reason for which I choose precisely such and such a practical judgement.

This is because the whole apparatus of my desire, my will and my feelings, is directed towards the good, which, even in an initial way, cognized and recognized as "my good," produces in me (in my will) an initial act of love, known as "first love," which forces me from passivity to action and orders me to the cognized good. In other words: good is the object of my desire, my will.

And if I desire anything, if I want it, then I want it precisely as a g o o d . If I determine myself to activity, then I discern "my good" in the content of my practical judgement, proper for me here and now. And, when choosing this judgement, I determine myself to activity, setting myself up as the real source of activity.

What does all this mean? It means that the first fundamental and chief motive of my activity is my ordering myself to g o o d ; hence, the view of this necessary ordering to good in my activity is revealed in the chief judgement of practical reason, that is, reason directing human activity—"do good" or, more generally, "o n e s h o u l d d o g o o d ." I can still ask "why," ultimately, good should be done. And this is a question directed at human nature as a contingent being. The only answer is precisely to draw attention to the fact of human ontic contingency. The human being, as contingent, is not an absolute, self-sufficient being; it is not good as such; good is for persons—something to be attained. Good should be done, for the human being to preserve the self, as a contingent being in the kind of existence it possesses. Without attaining good (without doing good), the human being will not maintain the self in be-ing. This can clearly be seen in the whole of human life. The human being must attain good in the form of food for the self, in order to preserve material life; it must choose good in the form of health, in the form of friends, in the form of truth, love for another person, for it will thereby fulfill the self in its contingent existence. Hence, contingent human nature must be ordered towards good, in order that it might act.

And precisely the interpretation of this necessary ordering towards good appears in the form of the supreme judgement at the basis of actual human activity and at the same time at the basis of the whole of morality: "d o g o o d !" The judgement formulated in precisely this way is the essential expression of human natural law, for natural law, if it is real, must really appear to every human being. What is more, it must reveal itself in a human way, that is, rationally. The highest act of the human reason is judgemental cognition, in which the human being not only distinguishes reality (in some aspects) but, actually checks, spontaneously and through accompanying reflection, its attitude to the reality it cognizes. Hence, human cognition expressed in judgement is the highest moment of human cognition. And the human being also makes itself aware of its basic attitude to reality and expresses this in judgements. The judgement "one should do good" is the interpretation of reality, which bears in itself the nature of good, capable of producing desire (want of itself). At the same time, it is the interpretation of the nature of its own personal structure as a contingent being, which, in order to exist and act must fulfill itself with the ever good, which is always missing. The supreme judgement, therefore, which is at the basis of human activity "do good," reveals both reality itself as the motive for activity and the person. It reveals the person together with his or her structure as a contingent being, which is potentialized and thereby dynamic, fulfilling itself rationally (through cognized good as "mine"), through attaining different sorts of good in human activity.

Besides the human being, the whole of contingent nature is also directed towards realizing good, through tendencies inherent in this nature, which are usually very concretely determined in a detailed way. The determination of nature is manifested by means of determined activity. In the whole of nature, given to us in everyday empiricism, only man is "open" and undetermined in his activity. An individual must determine the self in the act of decision through free choice, by the kind of practical judgement which will make the self the real source of his or her activity. The supreme motive of choice is always "good," which is—being a concrete being—at the same time and always an analogical "good." Hence, the supreme judgement of natural human law "do good" is simultaneously an analogical precept, analogically realized, for in each case the realized good cannot have in itself the kind of privations that nullify the nature of "good." Philosophers have understood this well, in the classical tradition of philosophy, when they drew attention to the fact that *"bonum ex ... defectu"* (good contains integral factors, and any lack of them is evil).

It is not possible, as we shall discuss later, to formulate the supreme law of human nature in any other way than precisely in the analogical judgement "do good." This is because all legal precepts formulated univocally, even in the form of the precept that would seem to be the supreme one—"do not kill"—were not, in the history of human culture, recognized as the supreme natural law, since they restricted its meaning by the organizing of wars (the killing of people), since sacral murders took place on a religious basis, since death penalties were carried out—and all this means that not always was this law meant to be binding. Natural human law, however, must always be binding, without any exception. That law is "one must do good," for everything and anything that a person does is directed by having to realize his or her good (which is sometimes badly interpreted and not true, but still good).

There is, in human activity and the realization of natural law "do good," one very important moment—that of deciding to use or not to use one's biological powers for other aims than those which are indicated by the determination of nature. Here it is mainly a question of man's or woman's use of progenitive forces. Using one's vegetative forces in the form of over-eating or of keeping to a starvation diet is less problematic, for these matters do not involve the human emotions to such an extent, and it is easier for that reason to judge proper limits.

Under the influence of Stoicism, natural inclinations are stressed, together with a natural biological determination: for example, the eye is for seeing, the legs for walking, the stomach for digesting and the biological, sexual forces for propagating life to future generations. On the other hand, however, emphasis is placed on the supreme role of reason, which is not directed only by determinants of nature, like an animal, but can interpret human structure and aims more deeply. On this basis, questions and doubts begin to form. Is a human being, therefore, like an animal, ordered only to preserving his or her life as an individual and the life of the species? Do human powers have to be used at all? Can they not be controlled, particularly when an individual has higher aims than those to which nature inclines? Should these powers be used only according to the determination of nature? These matters have become unusually disputable and are deeply experienced today in the face of the outburst of sexuality and homosexuality; they have been discussed on the basis of the set of problems concerning family planning and the social policy of population control, sometimes leading to a mass "slaughter" of unborn human beings.

Of course, the problem is unusually complicated and difficult to resolve in concrete circumstances. Yet certain formulations, at least negative ones, are necessary here. Above all, never and on no account can a law be formulated that bids the doing of evil, especially in important matters—and such is undoubtedly human life. Hence, a law bidding or permitting the doing of evil (especially in important matters, such as taking the life of a yet unborn human being), is a pseudo-law and cannot be binding. One should oppose it in the name of the law of human nature, which is "do good." The use of progenitive forces, ordered in their very nature to giving birth to a human being, is specific and cannot be compared to the use of other parts of the organism, for instance blood etc. This is because the human being becomes involved here in very intense psychic experiences, and in this domain it becomes comparatively easy to reach depravation. Moreover, the human sperm or ovum already contains a genetic code ordered towards the creation of a new human person. Thus, we are not concerned with some kind of "sacralization" of sexual factors: we are still concerned with the human being itself. The fertilized human ovum is already a real human being, with a complete "pulse" of information directing human development "from within," in his various stages of life in the womb. And no other explanation of the nature of the human fetus seems possible (even in the first days of life of the fertilized egg) than the statement that it is already a human being, organizing matter for itself in order to be a complete and efficient human body. The process of organizing matter for oneself, in order to be a human body, still takes place after birth, through feeding, breathing and excretion. Only a person's death puts an end to this process. It does not seem that there occur fundamentally different processes in the human being, in its life in the womb, as a fetus, and its life and "immersion" in the cosmos. Hence, laws concerning the human being, at the same time concern the person still developing as a fetus in the mother's organism.

Natural, human, law ("one should do good") concerns both the adult and the child, the white race and the yellow or black races. It concerns the human being living "in the cosmos" just as much as the one living in his or her mother's womb and organizing matter, in order to be an effectively acting human body, which allows the human spirit to be revealed and self-consciousness to be attained, and also the realization of one's human aims—"doing good."

c) Systematic justification

Because the history of philosophical thought includes a considerable number of texts and proofs concerning the existence of the conviction about natural law and its binding power, this same history testifies, at the same time, how very ambiguous the expression of this conviction is.[5] As a result of this, the justification of natural law concerns various matters, or at least various aspects of natural law.

If we take the standpoint (which has been justified in the course of these considerations) that natural law in its most primeval expression can be reduced to natural judgement of the practical reason "do good," then the justification of the existence of such a law is connected with the philosophical system employing transcendentalizing cognition, that is, with the system that has its roots in the deliberations of Aristotle, Avicenna and St. Thomas Aquinas.

All systematic philosophical justifications of the existence of natural law have the same value as the system, within whose framework we justify a given assertion. Of course, this kind of reservation does not weaken arguments but makes their meaning clearer; it connects considerations more organically with the totality of deliberations and does not exaggerate only one aspect.

In the domain of justifying natural law, we find in St. Thomas Aquinas two interesting articles in question 91 of his *S.th.*, I-II. The first article is entitled "Does there exist in us some kind of natural law?" and the next article reads "Does some kind of eternal law exist?" The course of justifying the second article presupposes the content of the first. St. Thomas, having in mind the general data from general philosophy (metaphysics) and philosophical tradition (particularly St. Augustine's Christian philosophical tradition), draws attention to the fact that law is the o r d e r i n g   o f   p r a c t i c a l   r e a s o n, insofar as the latter governs a society of some kind, usually a perfect one, that is, an autarchic one, which has a specified aim as well as all the means necessary for its realization.

When we consider the analyses made in Part I of *Summa Theologiae*, which demonstrate that the whole world (cosmos) not only emerged, came into existence and acts, from the rational will of the absolute Being, but is also g o v e r n e d by it in a way which is proper to it, we must state that the Divine intellect, known as Providence, governing the world derived from it, "directs" it and "leads" it towards its ultimate aim and destiny, the self-aware ABSOLUTE. That is why the "meaning" and "plan" of God's governing the world is in God himself as the directing Intellect, known precisely as "God's eternal law," since God's intellect is not situated in time, like the mode of duration of changeable beings, and is not subject to time but is "measured" by eternity, being the mode of divine duration. God's eternal law is Himself—God Himself—directing the world towards its eternal aim, which is known to Him alone. Generally, however, we can say that only He in Himself is the aim and ultimate destiny of the world—the world of personal rational beings.

The course of St. Thomas' reasoning, as a type of metaphysical thinking (cognition) of the ultimate kind, no longer having recourse to another, "higher," justifying cognition, is totally philosophical, though otherwise in accordance with Christian Revelation about divine Providence. Knowing that the ultimate non-contradictory reason for the existence of the world is God (in philosophical language called the Prime Being, the Absolute), the person, in the ultimate motivation of his or her conduct, calls upon God (who is at the same time Intellect and Will—the Person), who has created the world and governs it. And precisely God as Wisdom—the "governing" Intellect—can be called eternal law, insofar as law (as we understand it) is the norm directing conduct and activity.

Having outlined the point of ultimate reference, St. Thomas proceeds, in the article, to a justification of the existence of natural law. Of course, St. Thomas' understanding of natural law draws on tradition, particularly on Isodor of Seville. The latter restricted the binding nature of natural law—in the strict sense of the word—to human rational nature, correctly believing that only a rational being, who must determine the self through "law," can be the subject of law, for all other creatures are already determined by their activity.

Indicating the existence of natural law in human rational nature, St. Thomas presupposes a knowledge of human nature as analyzed in Part I of the *Summa theologiae*. The course of his reasoning runs as follows: if we can call law (in the most general sense) the specific rule and the measure of human rational conduct, then this rule or measure can be seen in two ways:

(a) as that which regulates and measures, that is, in an active sense, or

(b) as that which is regulated and measured, that is, in a passive sense.

If contingent beings that are derivative in existence, and dependent in their activity, are subject to a governing Divine Providence, then we can say that they are "governed" and measured by Eternal Divine Law. This does not really do anything other than affirm the rational meaning of the world of contingent beings. Contingent beings participate according to the measure of their being in the Eternal Divine Law, to the extent that, from the reason and will of God as the one who creates and governs, they have a particular structure, revealing itself in specific precisely these and not other inclinations towards activity as specified by nature, and towards obtaining the good proper to themselves, through activity specified by inclination.

Consequently, the human being, too, as a rational being, "participates" in Eternal Divine Law, which is expressed in a person's inclination towards a good proper to himself or herself, according to the natural indications of reason (that is, naturally acting reason). Thus, in human nature, being a rational nature, Eternal Divine Law is "reflected," is a law revealing itself in natural inclinations towards aims proper to human nature. And precisely this participation of Divine Law in human rational nature is called natural law. Consequently, natural law is nothing other than a rational inclination of human nature towards a good commensurate with the human being. The rationality of these inclinations must, of course, manifest itself in a rational way, that is, consciously, in the form of some kind of fundamental judgement made by the reason; otherwise, the rationality of the inclinations of human nature would be an empty word.

In St. Thomas' thought, the response to the second objection is particularly important.

> All activity of the reason and will is in us the consequence of something more primordial, natural, as has already been mentioned earlier in the problem of acts of the human will, since all reasoning is derived from first principles naturally given to us, and all desire, which is always a desire of means to an end, is derived from (as a result of) the natural desire for the ultimate end (happiness). For this reason too, the first direction (orientation) of our acts towards an aim takes place through natural law.

Which, of course, reveals itself in the fundamental tendency of human rational nature ordered to the fulfillment of being (good). Natural law, therefore, is conceived as the first and fundamental—of course, in some ways conscious—orientation of our human acts. This is also why natural law, apprehended in this way, is the absolute basis of our whole morality. And in each of our human acts, that is, acts deriving from rational and free human nature, natural law reveals itself as the first rule of conduct, a rule that is always present and consciously accepted. Every moral act is the realization, according to an objective measure, of natural law.

Of course, St. Thomas later draws attention, in response to the third objection, to the fact that we can also speak of natural law amongst non-rational animals, insofar as these also possess tendencies towards a good proper for their animal nature. However, here there is a difference, for human nature participates in Eternal Law in a way proper to itself, that is rationally. And law is precisely a work of the reason, that is, an act of the intellect. That is why participating in a rational way, that is, insofar as law reveals itself in the human being in the first commands of practical reason, is strictly a law of nature, whereas in animals, it is the natural instinct which is really a manifestation of the law of nature.

While animals are absolutely subject to this "law," as the objects of the law of nature (since natural inclinations totally determine their conduct), the human being acts as the subject of law, alone in the act of free decision determining itself to activity in the direction of the cognized and loved good of his nature, for only a person is a being-subject—"I"—freely subjectivizing human acts—"my" acts—in myself and for myself (but in the perspective of "you").

To become aware of the existence of the law of nature in the human being is nothing other than to become aware of one's rationality, proportional to the nature of contingent being. This means that the human being, existing contingently, is a being "through participation" in the Absolute. By participating in the Absolute he or she participates, at the same time, in its rationality and also in Eternal Law.

What does it mean, that a human being is a being "through participation"?

The theory of participation[6] *(METEXIS)* was constructed, vaguely and obscurely, by Plato. According to Plato, true reality is constituted only by ideas, which are a self-comprehensible being, while the whole changeable world, being an object of *doxal* cognition, is not real reality but participates in it, that is, it participates in ideas. Ideas are reflected in matter and multiply, without ceasing, thereby, to be ideas. The idea has the function of an exemplar and at the same time, to some extent, it has an aim.

The Platonic theory of participation was adopted by Christian thought, and, particularly through St. Thomas, it then received a fuller expression. This theory, expressed in Aristotelian language, can be reduced to the activity of three causes.

An inferior being participates in a superior being, and particularly, contingent beings participate in the Absolute, by the fact that they are:

(a) caused by the Absolute (that is God is the efficient cause).

(b) The Absolute is for them a model, that is, the ultimate exemplary cause.

(c) The Absolute is for them at the same time the final cause.

This means that the Absolute is the cause of beings participating in the sense of external causality, for every real activity is a part of three intertwined causes (factors), for the fact that activity exists, rather than does not exist, can be reduced to the function of aim. The fact that it is o r i e n t e d in a specified way and gives specified results is a f u n c t i o n o f t h e e x e m p l a r, and the fact that a p h y s i c a l m o v e m e n t o f a c t i v i t y occurred, deriving from one source, is a function of the efficient cause.

If, therefore, we affirm that natural law is the participation in Eternal Law, this means that the human being's naturally oriented inclinations come from the Absolute, in the sense of the triple causality of external causes described above. God is, then, the ultimate aim of human rational nature. He is also the exemplary cause (and this means that the fundamental orientation of the inclinations of rational nature in the direction of good does not come from our free choice but has been given to us, together with our nature): our nature is expressed and perfected in the fulfillment of our inclinations. Moreover, we ourselves, as a concrete expression of rational nature, are, in our existence, ultimately dependent on the Absolute. Life-existence is given to us, as are the whole context of life and all external factors determining our free choice, that is, all that makes our decisions—ruled by eternal law—concrete, individual-personal facts.[7]

2. THE CHARACTER OF NATURAL LAW

If, according to the understanding of Aristotle's concept of science, a definition expresses the essence of a thing, the previously given definition of natural law as the participation of eternal law existing in human rational nature, would explain and solve the matter of the nature of natural law. However, the definition cited above was directed rather towards the very f a c t o f e x i s t e n c e of natural law and not the explanation of its essence. It is true that existence and essence are two aspects of the same being, and that, to justify the existence of things, we must know what existence or the existence of what being (essence) we are justifying. That is why, of necessity, the process of justifying existence at the same time also concerns essences, in some measure. In order to indicate the existence of a not immediately cognizable "thing," we must view it in the context of the "mode" of its existence, since only a suitably delineated context—conditions, causes etc., determinations of existence—can show us the very "moment of existence," which is really, without this context, elusive.

A general indication of essence, however, when examining the fact of existence, still does not exhaust the matter. Although the sytematic definition of natural law—as the participation in Eternal Law, which takes place in human rational nature—is apt and explains a lot to someone who knows the system in its historical context, we must, nevertheless go a step further at this point, and ask: How is this natural law concretely revealed in human rational nature?

It has already been said that natural inclinations of rational nature are a manifestation of this law, and even in St. Thomas Aquinas the following saying occurs:

secundum ordinem inclinationum naturalium, datur ordo praeceptorum legis naturae[8]

(according to the order of natural tendencies, an order of commands of natural law occurs).

All these inclinations of a rational nature, however, should be revealed, in accordance with rational nature, through reason, in a full, conscious form, and should be revealed to each person, that is, in the form of a fundamental and at the same time concrete practical judgement, in which the whole contingency and at the same time rationality and telic (teleological) ordering of human rational nature is expressed.[9] This statement (inner judgement), as it is a revelation of natural law, should contain in itself the whole content of the theory of the participation of eternal law in rational human nature. All these necessary conditions are fulfilled by the statement, the general and analogical norm of natural law—"one should do good and avoid evil."[10]

Already Cicero and almost the whole of the Roman tradition were very near to the formulation *"bonum est faciendum"* and expressed it in equivalent statements. Besides, this judgement is ever present in human moral decisions and the whole of our human conduct.[11]

The judgement "one should do good" expresses:

(a) human contingency;

(b) an ordering towards common good;

(c) analogical divine exemplarism.[12]

Ad (a) My becoming aware that I should do good is above all the becoming aware and the concrete personal conviction (being the result of objective cognition) that I am not an absolute being, that I am a contingent being and as such is also not a good in myself. Good is beyond me, it is "to be acquired," or rather, "to be realized," and consequently I should strive towards this good, constantly filling myself with the "missing" good. This process of "filling oneself" with the missing good is an expression of the potentiality of the human person, deriving from the contingency of human being. If the human being were the most superior manifestation of being (as in the hypothesis of evolutional monism), he or she would at the same time be the most perfect being, to which nothing can be added, for precisely by virtue of the process of evolution itself he or she would already contain everything in himself or herself, he or she would be the "sum" of what is most perfect in the whole of nature. Yet personal insufficiency, above all in the ontic order—the "losability" of the existence of life and consequently the "losability" of other perfections—is a concrete and emphatic argument for the contingency of human existence. The human being—a contingent being—becomes convinced about his or her contingency through every act of his or her nature, which nature is rational and free and nevertheless always "lacking," and the human being experiences this nature in the context of constant need for good, which he or she lacks and which it attempts to create or attain.[13]

Ad (b) The ordering towards common good manifests itself both in the subjective and in the objective order. In the subjective order it assumes the form of a desire for happiness in every human being. The common good occurs here in the form of an undefined good in general. This experience is the result of cognizing being in general, for if the result of cognition is commensurate desire, then the result of the cognition of undefined being (to be more precise, of being—analogically conceived) is the desire for being as a good. This desire, the love of the good, is constant and necessary and reveals itself in the general disposition of mind in a human being, who desires happiness both for himself or herself and for others. The desire for happiness is the desire for some kind of common good, as the actualization and at the same time the realization of our personal potentiality, being a conscious expression of ontic contingency.

In the objective order, the ordering towards the common good takes place by virtue of the very ontic structure of being (good), for if a good is really the object of real human desire, then either this good causes someone to desire it by virtue of itself (since it is the fullness of good—the Absolute), or by virtue of participation in the absolute Good, for Good is really the same as being. And, just like being, it is a being either by itself—that is, an absolute Being, or through participation, that is, it is a being insofar as it remains in an ontic connection with the Absolute. Thus, just as the dependence of beings on the Absolute is real, so the dependence of good on the absolute Good is real, for being is really the same as good. Consequently, in every want or desire for a real, partial good, there is at the same time a real desire of the Absolute, as the ultimate reason of this good. And the kind of desire for good in which conscious and free choice is realized because of its derivation, an ontic "similarity" to the Absolute (that is, good in itself, to the extent that the desire for this good is a manifestation or partial expression of the desire for the ultimate Good), is at the same time the basis for the perfecting of human personality, for good is proportional to human desire. It is an act—*entelechia*—towards which necessary authority is directed, being a real possibility existing in the human subject ordered to the act-good. Here good is conceived in an existential-dynamic way as the peak of ontic actualization of potentiality, in accordance with the existential and dynamic concept of being, in the system of Thomistic metaphysics. Absolute Being, in this concept, is the infinity and boundlessness of act-good—"Pure Act."

Ad (c) Divine analogical exemplarism is also revealed in the principle "one should do good." As has already been said, there are no general ideas in God (for such a theory is merely a "projection" of the human mode of cognition), but concrete ideas exist; thus, every human person, being the object of divine cognition and love, is at the same time a unique, unrepeatable divine idea, insofar as God cognizes it. Consequently, every person has his or her distinct countenance and distinct way of behaving. The discovery of precisely this way of behaving, marked out as the law of nature of a concrete human person, takes place through an individual-personal understanding of what a good is for the human being, and to what extent and in what concrete way it is a good, and what is an evil. The practical cognition of good for me and evil for me is always a personal work, which cannot be carried out "in the place of" the human being by any Institution, or any general lawgiver.

General human law or institutions can merely e d u c a t e the human being to a certain extent as to the proper choice of a concrete good, a choice in accordance with the good of other people and thus also with his or her personal good, and to avoid evil; but the real choice of a personal good remains precisely the work of practical, concrete *(phronetic)* cognition, known as c o n s c i e n c e (in this case even pre-conscience, that is *s y n d e r e s i s*). And that is why, in the practical sentence made conscious to oneself: "one should do good," the concrete human being must perceive by himself or herself, by a personal effort of the mind, what is good for himself or herself, and how he or she should realize this good, etc. This type of cognition, in conditions of developed self-consciousness, is binding, and is a concrete divine exemplar and a concrete expression of "obedience" to the Absolute, being an "adjustment" and coordination with the concrete divine idea that God has about each human being as an unrepeatable, substantially distinct, rational being. There is no other way that enables a human being to realize divine exemplarism except the rationally perceived and freely recognized fulfillment of the command that "this particular" good should be done. And, what i s a good, to what e x t e n t it is a good, and h o w it is a good, are questions that the human being must personally solve and determine in a rational act of will. He or she takes personal responsibility for working out a solution and making a decision. His or her dignity, as a free person, depends on this responsibility. And even if the individual were to be objectively mistaken, that person nevertheless has the duty of following the voice of "conscience," that is, the personal perceiving of a good rather than a command, which he or she does not accept as the subject of law, even if this were to correspond to an objection against society. Human autonomy here is carried to the furthest possible limits. Nobody can free an individual from the decision to recognize good, nor can anyone take his or her place in this act of decision.

Thus, the practical judgement "One should do good" is the highest commandment for the human being, i t i s t h e r e v e l a t i o n t o m a n o r w o m a n o f n a t u r a l l a w a n d t h e b a s i s o f h u m a n m o r a l i t y. The individual extends this command of natural law to all objects of his or her conduct and, if the individual recognizes the object as good and the good is ultimately justified by a derivation from the Absolute, then he or she has a duty to fulfill them. In a "revelation" of natural law conceived in this way, the whole of human moral life and the whole of human conduct are based on natural law, since every decision is good to the extent that the individual has understood that the object is good, so that he or she should carry it out.[14]

3. THE FIRST ANALOGICAL REALIZATIONS OF NATURAL LAW[15]

An essential manifestation of law in human rational nature occurs when a person becomes aware of the judgement "one should do good." This judgement is a l w a y s rooted in us, even if someone has never formulated it clearly in his or her life and has not expressed it distinctly. The content of this judgement is contained in every practical cognition (that is, cognition, insofar as it is the source of a concrete act) as its ultimate, rational motive. The whole of our rational nature, by virtue of the fact that it is precisely a rational nature and at the same time a potentialized, contingent personality, is internally "set" and ordered to expressing such a judgement and in fact is directed by this judgement in all decisions, for even if it chooses a bad action, it chooses it because it somehow mistakenly sees its own good in this choice. When an individual consciously chooses to do a bad action—despite being aware of the command to do good—then he or she is directed by the negative statement "to choose not-good," or "not to choose good." Yet, negative statements of this kind, like all negative statements, are in fact ultimately understandable through positive sentences and draw their meaning from them.

Consequently, the command of natural law "one should do good" underlies all our moral activity, all motives of conduct, as a command which can be understood directly and of itself.

The law of nature—to the extent that it is not clearly made conscious and formulated in the form of the act-judgement "one should do good" but is merely the inner content of our being ordered towards good, that is, natural law, and to the extent that it is h a b i t u a l in us—is called "synderesis," traditionally defined as *habitus primorum principiorum,* that is, a habitual law, a permanent one deriving from the rational disposition of our nature. It is not, however, expressed in a positive form by a judgement or else a set of equivalent judgements, the first principles of our practical conduct.

The first formulation of natural law, the first commands-judgements, are an expression of becoming aware of the law of nature existing in us. In philosophical or moral literature they were called "prime" commands or commandments of the law of nature.

The chief command of natural law is formulated as follows: "one should do good." Particularizations of this judgement are revealed as a result of a subsequent examination of the basic tendencies of human rational nature. St.

Thomas Aquinas laid down the principle: *secundum inclinationem naturae datur ordo praeceptorum legis naturae* (the order of commands of the law of nature is dependent on the order of natural inclinations).[16] By following Ulpian's old legal tradition, and also by basing his considerations on the philosophical tradition (which distinguishes, as first and evident, three fundamental inclinations of human nature), he drew attention to the fact that this triple tendency is manifested in: a) conserving one's own life, b) in propagating it, and c) in the development of personality in society. The considerations made below constitute a particular type of commentary to the text quoted in endnote 16.

a) The first and fundamental manifestation of natural law is the drive to preserve one's own life, one's own existence. It is, in a way, the manifestation of natural law in a cosmic dimension, where everything, in particular an animated thing (that is, one gifted with a richer mode of existence, through which "it is" rather than "is not"), strives at the same time to "be rather than not be," to the extent of its nature. It therefore strives towards the preservation and protection of itself as an acting essence, actualizing its potentials. All activities in nature, particularly animated nature, indicate the existence of this basic law-inclination.

Analogically, this law manifests itself in human rational nature. However, to the extent that we define this inclination in nature as the "instinct of self-preservation," in the case of the human being this natural drive to preserve existence-life is manifested in a much richer way, and at the same time a more complicated way: it is not totally, nor even primarily, reduced to instinctive activity, although that activity does also occur in the human being in the form of a spontaneous self-defensive reaction.

The human person's right to live (as are all rights) is determined by motivations proportional to his or her nature (rational motivations), for the mode of existence, which the human person "has a right" to defend, is also measured by a natural tendency to "always exist," which manifests itself in human creative activity, for example, in various ways of "immortalizing oneself, fixing oneself" *(non omnis moriar)*. It is also manifest in the supra-temporal and supra-spatial nature of human culture, whose symbolism has an "eternal" significance, that is, one that refers to the intuition of "eternity" as immortality or interminable existence and so forth, irrespective of "whether" or "how" an individual "believes" in his or her own permanence, how far that person is rationally or irrationally convinced of it, and also what nature and meaning is ascribed to it.

Knowledge about the human mode of existence, although it is always extremely poor, both in individuals and in society, is nevertheless sufficient for us to be aware of at least s o m e basic consequences that come from this, the most primary natural right.

Preserving existence-life is in fact the ontic "basis" for other rights of the human being—of the person. It is, therefore, something fundamentally indubitable. The negation of this right presupposes eliminating being itself, and thus it is something contradictory in itself. Also, all activity directed against this right, all violence of which the human being is the source, as regards himself or herself and as regards another, is illegal and aimed against human nature, for no rational arguments are capable of justifying the violence that deprives people of life. Hence, motives which induce someone to commit murder, whether it is individual or mass murder, are always insufficient, since they lack a basis in natural law. That is because no human being or group of people can have the right to kill, or give such a right-command, since no human being, no human authority, possesses rights that can "correct" (or, all the more, change) nature and its manifestations (that is, natural law and—consequently—human nature itself). No human being can possess rights greater than those which derive from his nature. What is more, he or she cannot make laws against the basic, ontic inclinations of his or her nature, since precisely this nature is a measure of what is good for the person. Equally, the aim of human activity c a n only be "good."

In the light of these assumptions, neither any justification of the death penalty applied in human societies, nor theories forged in medieval times about *bellum iustum* (just war) stand up to criticism. Only the Being who is the ultimate efficient and final cause of human existence has the right to make decisions about a man's or woman's life-existence. Even the fact of "natural death" is aimed at the basic inclination of human nature and can find an explanation only with reference to an absolute Being, towards whom this inclination is ultimately directed, even in the light of the "existence" of evil as an ontic privation, a flaw, a deficiency of nature (but not in the sense of natural limitation, that is, the limitation of potentiality). The fact of evil as the fact that human nature is entangled in insurmountable difficulties encountered when trying to realize the natural potentialities, and the objective inability of realizing its natural potentialities (the objective inability to attain the aims of life, that is, the fullness of existence and the happiness connected with it, in the dimensions of human finite existence)—cannot, however, be an explanation for activity whose aim is evil, for then evil (non-being) would be explained by non-being, which is absurd. Conversely, evil-privation is "visible" only because it is a p r i v a t i o n o f g o o d, which exists. Privation can be explained only as a privation (or lack) of something of which it is a lack; evil (non-being) can be explained only in the light of being (good). Human activity, aiming towards the removal of this lack and towards "overcoming" evil, can also be explained only in the light of good as the aim of activity. In this sense, that is, on account of ultimate good (absolute Good), certain human acts, which are defined as "giving" or "offering" life—and also (in certain conditions) the duty of sacrificing one's life for some kind of good—can be justified, when rationally motivated.

Such situations and activities occur and are correct only in the context of the "permanence" of human life, that is, in the light of the fact that it "rises" above life or "outgrows" "temporal" dimensions, for such a perspective justifies acts of free human decision, at the sources of which lie acts of cognition and love which, in turn, justify loss of one's life by a person's own free will. Only in such a context is death-evil the lesser good, being the object of decision. What is more, this good (aim) is, then, an "overcoming" of the greatest evil for a person—his or her own death. The motivations concerning acts with which a "sacrifice of life" is connected, and also the explanation of the fact of death, are considered most properly in the context of religion.

b) The second natural inclination, which St. Thomas considers, appears in his writings in the traditional formulation drawn from *Iustinian's Code,* and deriving from Ulpian:

> *Dicentur ea de legem naturali, quae natura omnia animalia docuit ut est coniunctio maris et feminae et educatio liberorum et similia.*[17]

In this text, the author also draws attention to the co–occurrence of this inclination in the world of nature and humans. Both the living non-rational beings and rational human beings strive towards the propagation of biological life through sexual relations and the bearing and education of their issue, for the natural property of the human being, and likewise of an animal, is to be an individual of a specific sex—male or female.

This "community" of human beings with animals in the realization of the second inclination of natural law, was treated, in some traditional interpretations, particularly theological-mystical ones, so liberally and univocally that the marital state and the sexual functions connected with it were regarded as a degradation (eclipse) of human "rationality" *(iactura rationis).* The risk of this "decline of the reason" could be overcome and "ennobled" only by the fact of giving birth to a child. Hence, the primary, and in fact the justified, aim of sexual relations could only be parenthood, while human experiences connected with sex which are not aimed directly and univocally towards this end were believed to be immoral. The marital state, in which the sexual drive is tolerated only on account of the fact of giving birth to a new human being, and as an institution ordered to the biological progenitivity of the "human genus," was of necessity obliged, in the hierarchy of human good, to have a much lower position than the state of virginity, in which "uncontaminated rationality" enjoys the greatest freedom, though at the price of giving up one of its most primordial rights—that is, natural tendencies.

However, in such a restricted way of understanding this natural inclination of human beings, that is, in reducing this right e x c l u s i v e l y to the function of biological reproduction, and reducing these functions, in turn, to non-personal functions, even anti-rational ones (univocally common with the functions of animals), it is not certain if it can still be recognized as an e s s e n t i a l manifestation of natural law in the human being, since the "non-exploitation" of this inclination, and especially an opposition to it, an eradication of it from the sphere of personal life, does not only not injure human nature, but even raises it up and ennobles it.

St. Thomas—referring to Ulpian's statement "That which nature itself taught all animals belongs to the law of nature, namely, the union of man and woman and the rearing of children, and other similar functions"—does not identify the "union of man and woman" with exclusively reproductive functions, and the conjunction "and" used by him in that expression can be conceived in the sense of an enumeration of successive activities concerning the second of the natural inclinations mentioned by him.

"The right to procreate life" was, nevertheless, traditionally conceived in too restricted a sense. The life of a man or woman as a person is not exhausted by the psychic-biological sphere, which in any case is a more suitable object for investigation by the natural sciences, together with experimental psychology, rather than by philosophical anthropology or the philosophy of law. Although it is true that this "procreation of life," in the most "literal" and experimentally apprehensible way, is manifested in the tendency to give physical life to children, nevertheless, at the basis of this tendency there lies a general attitude of the human being towards fully personal action in relation with other persons, that is, one that is not reduced exclusively to matters of sex but towards having an influence on their lives, towards procreating not only biological life but also varied intellectual and experiential contents, of which the "inner world" of the human individual is composed. Taking into account such an understanding of that inclination, a decision to live in celibacy—as in the case of losing one's own life and free will—though it undoubtedly causes an essential privation and does harm to nature, is nevertheless not devoid of a rational justification in the form of thereby attaining a greater personal good.

The perfect natural "model" for mutual action—in the framework of which the human being "lives for" another person, giving of himself or herself what the other needs, at the time, and to which the other has a right, educating others and being educated by them—is precisely the family. The common good of the family is the good of each person or member thereof, who equally has a right to certain benefits from other members of the family for his or her personal development. Sharing one's own life and conveying one's experience to others is also a right. The life of the human person begins and develops in the family. The person's manifold "procreation" takes place there, first and foremost. It is the second of the phenomena mentioned above, an essential manifestation of natural law. That is why it is often said of social groups, which fulfill their tasks with regard to other people well, that a "family atmosphere" prevails in them. This expression lies close to the basic model, which is based on the fact that other communities are formed precisely "on the model" of the family, so that in them too the inclination to "propagate life" might be realized, in spite of the fact that, among the direct purposes of their activities there is no propagation of biological life. Marital and parental love generally remain the natural "model" for people living together in community or in other social groupings, the model for analogical "parenthood" or "procreation of life" realized beyond the "community of blood ties" yet preserving the most essential personal values, which are the characteristic properties of living together in a family. We can list here, by way of example, various forms of such "family-like' communities: religious Orders, associations for social care, work associations and even organized amusement, youth clubs, various circles around common interests and common action, and finally communities of such types as the Church, the State or else—humanity.

Although the missing realization of this natural tendency, this lack of a full-blown relationship between human beings, which can only be realized in marriage and the family, is an essential and real lack (evil) for human nature, nevertheless, the "procreation of life" in the wide sense of the word can also be realized in celibacy, without physical relations between the sexes and without physical parenthood. It cannot, however, be realized in conditions of isolation from other people, that is, without the need for, and the obligation of, giving of one's own, personal "fund of life" in various forms, for example care and concern for others, help, cooperation, and also the co-experiencing of various human values.

The "procreation of life," like all those natural inclinations that are a manifestation of natural law in humans, has a personal aim. It too is realized because of the good of the person as a unique and free individual-subject, and it cannot be realized independently of the person, to serve other objective goods. That is why both the purpose and the common good of marriage cannot be merely the "bearing of children," but is the education of a human being—the children and both the parents to an equal extent. Likewise, the purpose of the State cannot be territorial and military power, nor material riches, but is the development of the personal abilities of every citizen, as well as the mutual exchange of cultural and civilizational good, serving the personal development of people. In like manner, too, the purpose of religious communities should be nothing other than the educating of their members in cognition of, and love for, the ultimate Good. Elsewhere, too, natural law, having its natural and cosmic counterparts, is generally realized analogically, as in the case of human beings, and not univocally, as in the world of non-rational beings.

c) The third inclination of human rational nature is an expression of its social and dynamic character. The right to personal development in society was formulated briefly by St. Thomas:

ut homo ignorantiam vitet; ut alios non offendat cum quibus debet conversari.

(that man might avoid ignorance and not offend others, with whom he should associate).

Some authors express themselves in a different way: *ut pacifice in societate vivet* (that he might live in peace in society).

Both formulations place the emphasis on the social determination of human life. The individual must live in a social group, in order to develop that person's personality, that is, in order that he or she might cognize personal aims and individual abilities (that he or she might avoid ignorance); that he or she might cognize needs and the needs of those living with him or her (that he or she might not offend others); and finally, that he or she might be able to satisfy those needs, that is, to realize the potentialities of his or her nature in relation to other persons, who are indebted to him or her, and for whose good he or she has a duty to act. It must be a social group organized in such a way that mutual contact, co-operation and exchange of goods can develop, as far as possible without interference with, or detriment to, the common good. It is clear that normal human life—individual and social—can be realized in this way only in conditions of peace and without resorting to violence in any form whatever, with full respect for the rights of each person as an individual.

The problem of positive co-existence of people, in societies of various kinds, is a very extensive and complicated problem, and so it is often the subject of investigation by many scientific disciplines. From the point of view of philosophy of law, we can merely note that the third fundamental tendency of human nature draws attention to the fact that individual good and the good of society are two aspects of the same object—the good—inasmuch as it is the aim of activity of every human individual. The human person will not attain his or her own good by living in isolation from society (if that were possible in the first place), without at the same time acting, in suitable proportion, for the good of other persons, nor will he or she attain his or her own good by acting to harm them.

The human being can attain a considerable degree of personal maturity in both the intellectual-volitive and the experiential-emotional spheres, but this will not reveal itself on the outside, in the form of individual and properly human creativity, if person-to-person relations (expressed in acts of mutual cognition and love, as well as co-operation), are impeded or become seriously warped. That is why every activity that does not have as its direct aim the good of human nature above all else, is an activity against natural law, in certain ways. This does not, of course, mean that, as the so-called physiocrats believed, a detailed and univocal codification of natural law might be possible, or a detailed list of what, when, how and why something should be done, or what should be avoided within the framework of particular social groups, in order that natural law might always be respected. Natural inclinations, being the first "exteriorization" of rational human nature, can be compared to signposts, thanks to which the human being recognizes its personal aims and knows, in the most general way, what constitutes its own good: in a word, he or she becomes aware of the practical judgement "one should do good." The way to realize this good, that is, the concrete actualization of truth, is individual work, proportional to each individual nature. In fact, an individual character is forged by human decision—the inner co-ordination of individual and personal activity with its object and the taking of personal responsibility[18] for the realization of good, ultimately with respect to the Absolute. The way in which personal good is realized is always unique and unrepeatable. Consequently it cannot be circumscribed by any positive (univocal) command. Likewise the matter of positive (legal) settlements, the degree to which different codes of constituted law are binding in conscience, cannot be solved generally and once and for all in a binding way. What i s possible, is this: to establish in a negative way the fact that constituted law, insofar as it forces a human being to act against the basic inclinations of his or her nature, is merely a pseudo-truth, or rather, an abuse of authority in the name of a pseudo-truth, and a command which cannot bind the individual "from within"—in conscience—although sometimes a man or woman is forced to appear to listen to such a command (for example to preserve his or her own life or that of others). Violence, both physical and moral, can never be exercised "by rights," and neither can the thoughtless and submissive ceding to violence. An apparent obedience to pseudo-truth can be justified only when it is undertaken for the purpose of safeguarding essential human good, which could suffer in the case of open opposition towards an unjustified command; it can never, however, be "by rights" transformed into passive submission to lawlessness and violence.

In practice, however, in many "crucial situations," the decision as to when and to what extent, and also on what account, or why, an apparent obedience to pseudo-truth can be justified is extremely difficult. Likewise, it is difficult to establish, to what degree, in what circumstances and how, we can sometimes apply coercion towards individuals who manifest "ill will" and who are evidently acting to the detriment of the common good.

An extreme case of passive submission to pseudo-truth can be found, for instance, in the facts of genocide during the last war, when attempts were made to justify mass murders by obedience to authority. These facts, however, not only revealed an improper understanding of authority and law, but, above all, a flagrant depravation of human nature, a depravation of consciences that were incapable of indicating essential good and assuming personal responsibility for action. It is a fact that, in different systems of slavery, the domain of activity of free human decision is reduced to the minimum, and the vindication of natural human rights often demands heroism. An increasingly better and deeper awareness of what is a person's true good, or what is harmful for him or her, and also to what extent the three most essential tendencies of human nature are respected by positive law in human societies, is the basis for the process of vindication of natural law as the source of the binding nature of all norms and commands given by authority, as well as the basis for establishing how various social groups should be constituted, in order to enable their co-existence in a manner which is proper to human nature.

4 . THE PROPERTIES OF NATURAL LAW[19]

Speaking in a general way of the existence, nature and first manifestations of natural law we have, of necessity, said a great deal about its characteristic features. Be that as it may, the following characteristic features are mentioned in the traditional presentation of the theory of natural law:

a) morality;

b) immutability;

c) universality together with promulgation.

Ad a) In order to explain the first feature, namely the c o n n e c t i o n between the m o r a l and l e g a l order (in the order of the law of nature), we must above all become aware, in a general way, of what the moral order itself is.

In the tradition of realistic ethics, the term "morality" was given to the relation between the conformity (or non-conformity) of the human act with the rules of practical conduct. The relation is regarded as a transcendental, that is, a necessary relation, which is inseparable from the human act. This means that every time a human act comes into existence, that is, a conscious and free act (that has already taken place in the person's interior self in the form of a practical-practical judgement, which has been made by the individual's will), then, by the same token, such an act is already a moral act, in the positive or negative sense. The rule of morality, on the one hand, with which an act can be in conformance or not in conformance, is primarily the human conscience (practical reason), dictating in an indubitable way, *hic et nunc,* that one must act in precisely such and such a way in a specific case. The ultimate rule of human conduct, on the other hand, is the Absolute (Eternal Law), which, having created human nature, is the ultimate guarantee of the correctness of its natural, rational tendencies.[20]

Of course, between God, as the ultimate rule of moral conduct, and concrete human practical cognition, revealing itself "externally" in the form of a dictate of practical reason (that is, conscience), there still lies a series of "mediating instances" in the form of society: different groups of people connected by a mutual co-activity, who can indicate to one another some general norms of conduct in concrete life circumstances, and can thereby educate one another in the moral order through a common solution to the problem of what values and what norms should be taken into consideration in a decision which is specified by circumstances at that moment, on account of the fact that the object of this decision lies in conforming either with human social nature or with the will of God, who intervenes through the Revelation in the history of mankind.

The natural intervention of human society in establishing moral conduct is not, however, the most essential for activity to be moral. The sphere of morality extends only to the person's interior self and is precisely the necessary relation contained in every human act, that is, in every human decision, which is not able to be anything but a decision made under the influence of reason, and which cannot be indifferent to the good realized by the will. Human decision, insofar as it is directed by the reason with a view to good, is the essence of morality, whereas all "education" and "direction" is something external and heteronomous in relation to autonomous human decision.

Bearing in mind the fact that every human act (precisely as human act) is directed by the reason towards a good to be realized by the will, that is, that every conscious and free human act cannot be indifferent in relation to good, for it is a realization of the good which the human being, as a contingent being, lacks, we perceive that every human act (decision) is at the same time the realization of natural law. When we become aware of natural law in the form of the practical judgement "one should do good," then every act is the realization of the good perceived. By this token, natural law is internally connected with morality, for there is no act which is not the realization of a personal good, that is, an act carried out precisely under the influence of natural law.

When this good is merely apparent, that is, not grounded on natural law, that is another matter. If, when cognizing such a good and assessing it precisely as merely apparent, we decide to realize it in spite of this, we then go against natural law; although we do find ourselves within the moral order, it is a moral order in the negative sense of carrying out a morally evil act—an act that does not connect us with the common good, but objectively removes us from the common good.

Keeping in mind that every act, every decision, is the realization of good, that is, that it is carried out under the influence of natural law and cannot be indifferent in relation to judgement (which judgement is a manifestation of natural law), we can say that all realization of natural law is at the same time a realization of morality itself (the moral order), and that there is no such thing as an act which could both be carried out under the influence of the dictates of natural law as put forth by the conscience (natural law here being understood in its fundamental sense) and also be a morally indifferent act.

This does not mean, however, that the scope of morality is coextensive with the domain of natural law conceived in the restricted sense,[21] a sense connected with justice. The scope of moral order is more extensive, since it can embrace a person's supernatural motives as well as horizons of his or her conduct which are not, in the strict sense, a realization of natural law (since they posit supra-natural criteria "beyond" the assessments of practical reason, as they have recourse to a higher, supernatural, that is, Divine influence, which directs human actions). A decision for such acts is based above all on motives coming from faith and not on purely rational, practical cognition. In spite of this, however, even the acceptance of a set of supernatural motivations, that is, a decision to "take as one's own" (a personal acceptation of) a system of values in the supernatural order, is based on natural law, for it is based on the personal assessment of the supernatural order as "something good for me"; as a result, it also turns out to be, for the practical reason, a form of realization of natural law without having to negate the set of supernatural motives.

However, the very process of making decisions on the basis of this order, or else on the basis of specific commands of authority (in whose competence man believes), is not the realization of natural law in the restricted sense. Only that which is revealed to the person as a real possibility for fulfilling some good, which is proportional to his or her rational nature, is a realization of the natural law; in particular, natural law appears as the basis of justice and, through justice, of the whole order governed by positive law.

In the history of natural law, the first advocates of separating it from the domain of morality were Samuel Pufendorf (1632–1694) and Christian Thomasius (1655–1738). They were followed by Kant, Fichte and Hegel. Their point of view was justified to a great extent by theories of natural law, different from the one analyzed here, deriving from an analysis of human social nature, and also of morality, as either an absolutely free domain of practical life or the science of virtues (aretiology). Hence, the reflections of Thomasius, Kant or Hegel do not concern the problem considered by us, while the authors,[22] attempting a discussion from their point of view, are committing the fallacy of *ignoratio elenchi,* that is, they do not understand what is in question.

Another matter is, that even if one did accept this concept of natural law and morality, there still appear tendencies, in some interpretations of the moralists to treat human acts as acts coming from positive or negative moral values because they are either the realization of certain virtues or the manifestation of specific intentions, or else the fulfillment of rules or of law. In such interpretations a person's rational-volitive acts (inner acts) are morally good, not because they realize a good objectively cognized and assessed by him or her and directed towards another person, but because they are in some sense "virtuous," "finalistic" (telic) or "obedient." The object of assessment is not, in this case, an objective good in itself, which a human being is urged to fulfill by the command of natural law—the judgement of practical reason, "one should do good," but "virtue," that is, the "perfecting value" of the act itself, or another value. Here, however, there occurs a transposition of the sequence between reason and consequence: the good of an act results from the fact that it is directed towards the good of a personal being as an aim, but not vice versa. The objective good of the object—in the most important case, the person—influences the positive moral assessment of the human act, which, as a result of being ordered towards this good, perfects the subject (the human person), becomes a virtuous act and actualizes the moral potentialities of the person. In reality we are directed in the choice of an act, not just by the fact that it is virtuous or that it fulfills another value, but also that it realizes something that appears to us to be a good; otherwise, the moral assessment would not speak of a "good" act, but of a "virtuous" one.

Ad b) The problem of unchangeableness of natural law[23] was posed on the ground of the "essential" concept of natural law occurring in St. Augustine, Duns Scotus, Suarez and also in some formulations of St. Thomas. According to this concept, concrete reality and, within this, the human being also—as a stratification of forms (to be more precise, forms univocally marking out understood natures)—forms the most detailed individual nature through gradually more general natures, which natures are conceived of as species and genera, to the most extensive "layer" of being. However, each of the natures stratifying concrete being can, while being precisely determined in itself and unchangeable, accept secondary, accidental modifications. For this reason, too, it was accepted, together with the domination of this "essential" concept of being, that "natural law," since it is "imprinted" on the particular "natures" or "forms" which form the layers of concrete being, is as unchangeable as these forms, and that it would accept a non-essential modification only in a secondary way, for accidental reasons. Thus, natural law would be immutable, in an essential sense. Yet this immutability concerns only the most important rules of natural law, in relation to which, precisely the derivative, secondary rules and commands are mutable; they change, depending on concrete objective-subjective situations.

If, however, we recognize the judgement of practical reason that "one should do good," as the essential manifestation of natural law, then a command of this kind cannot be "mutable," for it is always absolutely binding, although the very way this command is realized may undergo individual modifications. It is not a "material" law (if we may use Kant's terminology, even if improperly), a law that is univocally laid down, but a "formal" law, as it were. This means that, although the very command (of doing good) as such cannot change, the concrete content of this command, its actualization, that is, the concrete "matter" of good, is different and unrepeatable in every conscious and free human act, since each realization of good is the realization of analogical good. This does not mean, however, that Kant's systematic interpretation is correct, for, what has been called here, in Kant's terminology, a "formal" command, as it were, is, in fact, not the "form" but precisely the content, the a n a l o g y of the good itself, and thereby the analogy of cognition itself, as apprehended in the norm of the judgement: "one should do good." Thus, the key to understanding the content of the norm of natural law is the analogy of good and the analogy of our judgemental cognitive interpretations.

Having in mind, therefore, the basic inclinations of rational human nature mentioned above, that is, the right to preserve life and the right to peaceful personal development, and the fact that all these inclinations are an exteriorization of rational human nature, we can take on the traditional standpoint—that natural law, apprehended in its essence, that is, commanding us to do good, is, particularly in its first manifestations, which affirm the good of the life of the individual, species and person—fundamentally immutable. A basic right of a human being is to be considered as behaving rationally when choosing a good. Thus, rational conduct (in affirming a good, on all three paths marked out by natural inclinations) is something essential to the life and development of the human being, in the set of problems concerning natural law.

However, directing oneself by one's reason differs in the purely theoretical as opposed to the practical order, for in the purely theoretical order, we can manage to attain a greater independence from emotions, a greater objectivism of assessment, while in the order of practical conduct we have to deal with a greater instability in the domain of rational order and the use of reason. This is also why in many cases, concerning detailed problems of human conduct, it is extremely difficult to establish the direction to be taken by specific solutions, and even more difficult to establish concrete laws, which would be a kind of "specification" of natural law.

The traditional solution to the problem went in the direction of differentiating the first principle of natural law from the further, already deduced norms of conduct. It was claimed that the first principles of natural law are immutable, whereas the further practical deductions of natural law are mutable.

This kind of solution, proceeding from St. Thomas,[24] is connected with his special concept of the developmental dialectic of natural law, which is discussed below: a) *per modum conclusionis,* and b) *per modum determinationis.* In the development *per modum conclusionis* it was possible to take into account the conclusions which are more connected with the first principles of natural law, and precisely such conclusions were regarded as immutable, whereas conclusions from further down the line were regarded as mutable.

Yet, apart from the general formulation "one should do good," there are basically no first principles of natural law, formulated in a detailed and positive way, that might more specifically define "good." There merely exist certain "signposts," that is, general directions of activity of human rational nature through "primordial inclinations," but they are not detailed definitions of natural law. It is a well-known fact that the human being has the right to live and that one cannot directly deprive a human of life; that a human has the right to get married and to pass on life; that humans have the right to personal development in a society. These are, however, merely the analogical g e n e r a l w a y s, on grounds of which some detailed legislation can and should arise. The law of nature itself does not define c o n c r e t e l y "h o w" these fundamental natural tendencies are to be realized in society. Only on the basis of natural inclinations can a concrete law be formed, which regulates—in societies of a specific type—all those matters that constitute the content of natural inclinations. We only know that positive (constituted) laws opposed (contrary) to natural inclinations are not laws in the proper sense but merely pseudo-laws. It does not normally happen, however, that an organization constitutes laws which are directly and manifestly contrary to natural inclinations.

Consequently, it is difficult to maintain that there exist any primary formulations of natural law which bind people always and everywhere. We can, at the most, say, as has been indicated above, that there exist only the most general primordial indications deriving from natural tendencies. And precisely these natural inclinations, as the first manifestations of natural law in the human being (though not exactly defined, but nevertheless recognized as signposts of a person's life and development), can be regarded as the "first" or "primary" commands of natural law, which are immutable. We must nevertheless stress that even these primary manifestations of natural law in the form of natural inclinations, are only an a r e a in which we will be able to establish positive laws, in a detailed and concrete way, fulfilling, in specific conditions, postulates which are concealed in natural human inclinations.

The greatest difficulty, when considering the immutability of natural law, was the fact (universally known to theoreticians) that there have always been (and there are still) the most various misunderstandings as to how "good" may be realized. Acts were often incorrectly evaluated, that is, an act was regarded as being natural, while in reality it struck a blow at the very basis of natural law. Such examples as ritual cannibalism among primitive peoples, which according to their customs, was recognized as an act which undoubtedly realized some kind of "good"; or else the banditry of the Germanic tribes quoted by St. Thomas after Caesar, which was also not regarded by them as something evil—

> *propter hoc quod aliqui habent depravatam rationem ex passione, seu ex mala consuetudine, seu ex mala habitudine naturae, sicut apud Germanos olim latrocinium non reputabatur iniquum, cum tamen sit expresse contra legem naturae, ut refert Julius Caesar in libro D e b e l l o G a l l i c o.*

(The Gallic War, I 6 c. 23)[25] —could be proof of some kind of legal and moral relativism. In connection with this, St. Thomas asks himself the question: Can natural law be eradicated from human nature to such an extent that we might no longer be able to speak of any natural foundations of the binding nature of constituted law?

Both these questions, closely connected with one another, are solved by St. Thomas in the following way: distinguishing among the commands of natural law—the commands commonly known to everyone ("primary") ones), and commands that on account of the object have a secondary value and are not always universally known—he argues that only the primary commands of law are not prescribed and cannot be eradicated from human nature: *quantum ergo ad illa principia communia, lex naturalis nullo modo potest a cordibus hominum deleri in universali,* for they derive from the fundamental inclinations of this nature; the secondary commands of law, on the other hand, which are derived from the primary ones, can be and are often warped and deformed in particular cases, and can even be almost completely destroyed, for a certain time among certain groups of people.[26] Thus, primary commands are an immutable and never obsolete "base" for the binding nature of law, to which we can and should always return, every time when—in the practical aspect of human behavior—there arise erroneous tendencies and deformations of law, under the influence of emotions or other factors which deform and deprave the activity of rational human nature.

St. Thomas' considerations are fundamentally in accordance with what we previously said about the necessary immutability of natural law in its basic manifestations, in the form of natural inclinations. The fact that human nature is entangled in evil, which in turn causes a depravation of a person's activities resulting from incorrect assumptions and assessments of the reason as well as erroneous and bad habits, does in fact complicate, in practice, the application of the commands of natural law and the realization of good in concrete conditions of human existence. These errors, however, merely indicate the difficulties connected with the practical realization of the indications of reason, and the instability of human judgements due to emotions and selectivity in cognition, but in no case do they prove that human nature itself and its fundamental inclinations (laws) are something fundamentally relative, and that natural law as such does not exist objectively at all. On the contrary, the fact that errors do occur proves that the natural law is a norm which enables us to differentiate error from truth. The negation of those natural norms which have been discovered by reason would lead to the negation of the very existence of the human being. The person alone, among the whole of nature, which acts towards definite ends, telically, would turn out to be a contradictory being, what is more, a consciously contradictory one. That would, of course, be absurd, for as the human being would be undetermined "from within" and "from without," it could not determine itself and act as a human being.

Thus, in spite of "depravations" and "deformations," self-reflection is always possible and law must be revindicated by returning to the basic inclinations of human nature, which inclinations assign the direction for correct conduct as well as showing the source of the binding nature of constituted laws. We can, and must, become aware once again of "one should do good" and educate the human conscience to correctly recognize what is good and what is bad for rational human nature, and develop the human "legal psyche" in the direction of a proper understanding of fundamental inclinations and the realization of them in concrete, specific situations.

Ad c) The set of problems concerning the p r o m u l g a t i o n of natural law is fundamentally simple, for, if natural law is the participation of eternal law and we become concretely aware of it in the judgement "one should do good," then the promulgation of law conceived in this way is dependent on human nature itself and its rational activity. Every human being, as a rational being, is capable of employing reason; and precisely the first sign that one is employing reason in the practical order, is that he or she becomes aware and formulates for the self the judgement "one should do good," since it is an expression of a person's ontic "state"—of the fact of human ontic contingency. Thus, the promulgation of natural law is at the same time coextensive with the possibility of employing reason in the most fully human order—the practical order—which involves all the powers of the person.

An essential manifestation of humanity, that is, of human personality, is the ability to make d e c i s i o n s . The human being, as a subsistent being, stands in relation to the whole of nature and to other people as a subject not determined to activity in any one specific way, that is, the human being is completely different from all other creatures of nature. The person is not determined from the outside but from within. The person determines himself or herself by concrete practical cognition and through the decisive moment of free choice, when a practical judgement defines purposeful activity—free to a human extent, proportional to the act of cognition. This critical moment of self-determination, which happens by necessity, for the individual— undetermined in the face of nature and other people, would not be capable of doing anything: *ab indeterminatio nil sequitur*—is nothing other than the critical moment of decision-making. The making of a decision, that is, the ordering of oneself to activity with a definite aim, is a specifically human moment from which a man or woman can never on any account "free" himself or herself. The person is not freed from personal responsible decision by any vows of obedience, which in fact merely modify but do not abolish the personal decision to act in "such and such a way" in the direction of "such and such" a good, for a person's resignation from the right to self-determination is impossible, since it would be resignation from humanity itself. It is true that in self-determination there are at work whole series of factors which predetermine a man or woman to go in a particular direction or to act in such and such a way, but despite this, the essential moment of making a decision is always and above all dependent on the rational will of the person, choosing for the self the kind of practical judgement through which a person determines himself or herself, and that is why every moment of self-determination is a moment distinguishing the human being from the whole of nature.

The essential factor and basis for self-determination or decision-making (the choice of practical judgement) is a human being's general determination (through its contingent nature itself) in the direction of a good which it does not possess. Rational determination in the direction of good is nothing other than merely becoming aware of the statement "one should do good," that is, it is becoming aware of the essence of natural law. Consequently, natural law and our awareness of it (at least virtual awareness of it) which takes place in each moment of decision-making, exists in every human being when releasing activity from within the self. By this same token we can speak of the u n i v e r s a l p r o m u l g a t i o n of natural law among all people. Nobody can make the excuse that he or she does not know this law, since it is revealed to every human being in the form of an inclination towards good, an inclination which is expressed in a reflected way by the judgement "one should do good."

Thus, at the very basis of every human decision lies an affirmation of natural law. It is precisely here that the essential convergence between God's Eternal law and natural law occurs; here every human being discovers, not in a theoretical way, but in a thoroughly practical way, his or her personal aim in life and his or her unique mode of natural activity. Speaking in religious terms, a person chooses God in the moment of decision-making and in the light of the reflected principle of natural law that "one should do good," whenever he or she chooses a concrete good, since he or she thereby affirms God's eternal law which leads every human being along an individually distinct (and only analogically common) road.

5. THE DEVELOPMENTAL DIALECTIC OF NATURAL LAW

After establishing the existence of natural law, its essential manifestations, nature and properties in general, we must, towards the end of our considerations on the set of problems concerning natural law, pose one more very important question: What is the relation of natural law to positive law or—vice versa—of positive law to natural law?

This question is rather extensive, and that is why we shall obtain a fuller answer by first considering: a) the problem of whether there is any possible "transition" or some kind of developmental dialectic from natural law to positive law (that is, when analyzing the problem of an eventual c o n t a c t between positive law with natural law), and then, b) taking a closer look at the problem of the binding power of positive law. Of course, these two problems complement one another and the answer to the first will become, to a great extent, the basis for giving an answer to the second question: How, and to what extent, do positive laws bind man and woman?

The first problem, which discusses the developmental dialectic of natural law, found its historical solution already in St. Thomas Aquinas' response to the question: "Does any law made by a human being derive from natural law?"[27] St. Thomas takes the view that any positive law, insofar as it is really a law, that is, insofar as it fulfills the previously analyzed definition of law: *ordinatio rationis ad bonum commune ab eo, qui curam communitatis habet, promulgata,* is derived from natural law, for if it were not in agreement with natural law, it would merely be a pseudo-law, a deformation or an abuse of law.

In order to justify this hypothesis, St. Thomas draws attention to two kinds of derivation (that is, logical "deduction") of some sentences from others. The first kind occurs in the model of conclusions, as reached in really conclusive syllogisms, and the second is similar to determinations introduced by an artisan or artist into his or her material, which is, of itself, undetermined towards one shape or another.

In the case of a deduction in the manner of a necessary conclusion from a syllogism, St. Thomas claims that there really are human laws, constituted ones (as for instance the law of Moses "do not kill"), which are, according to him, the direct conclusion drawn from natural law, namely from the command that one should not do evil to anyone (since to kill is in fact to do someone an evil, and as a consequence one should not kill).

An example of the second mode of derivation of constituted law (positive law) is the infliction of a penalty by a Court of Law, although, as St. Thomas claims, while a punishment should be inflicted by virtue of natural law on the offender for a crime, this punishment is not strictly determined by natural law, so that one ends up with specific, concrete determinations on the part of a judge.

The presentation by St. Thomas of the process of derivation of positive law from natural law appears to be too closely connected with the Aristotelian concept of scientific cognition, and it is also not really in accordance with real legislative practice, for in legislative practice there do not exist any kind of established universal principles of natural law which would be recognized and binding in all societies, nor do any of the world's Parliaments or any legislative authorities appeal to established principles of natural law when making concrete laws. Equally, St. Thomas' solution is too abstract and has never been confirmed in the history of legislation (and if it has, the concept of natural law would still be found to be erroneous).

On the other hand, according to the Aristotelian concept of science (which concept had just found or was just beginning to find acceptance in Western culture in St. Thomas' time), a very coherent model of scientific cognition could be constructed, for any type of scientific cognition needed to be cognition of a necessary, unchangeable and general kind. Such a type of cognition was delineated by axioms, that is, the most important sentences accepted in any science through *EPAGOGE,* namely heuristic induction, from which derivative assertions could be deduced. These were also elaborated in metaphysics, as indeed each of the chief sciences had its own distinct axioms elaborated for itself. The first sentences (axioms) were not in fact deduced, since they were supposed to be self-evident. Thus, for instance, mathematics had its self-evident axioms, which were then also used by dependent, subordinate sciences, for example music.

The axioms of the main sciences were formed by means of directed abstraction, that is, Aristotelian induction, known as *EPAGOGE*. Acquired in such specifically conceived induction, these chief principles (axioms) formed the basis of knowledge. They could be further developed by means of syllogistic deduction *EPAGOGE,* and the conclusions obtained were also recognized as indubitable, if they were deduced with the aid of one of the modes of syllogism established by Aristotle. Besides, if the axiom constituting the major premise of the syllogism was a definition of the thing, that is, if it grasped (according to Aristotle's theory of definition), the formal cause, then syllogistic deduction was conceived as a type of strictly demonstrative cognition *DIA TI—propter quid*—for it passed from showing the essential cause to showing its properties, or from the cause in the direction of a result. If, on the other hand, the major premise of the syllogism was not a definition of form but a cognitive apprehension of a fact, usually a change, then the syllogistic deduction indicated, in a general way, the cause of the fact that had come into existence, and this was called *HOTI—quia*—thinking.

In short, syllogistic deduction became an inspiration for St. Thomas Aquinas' concept of the dialectic of natural law. However, the reception of Aristotle's thought in medieval times took place too stormily, and as a result the scientists did not investigate to what extent the Stagirite himself applied his own theory of science in practice. Today we have found out that, although Aristotle formed a theory of science, he himself did not apply it, either in the area of metaphysics or in the area of the natural sciences, or in his ethical writings. Quite simply, this theory of science constructed upon the model of the fundamental concepts of mathematical cognition, did not quite "fit" real sciences, and that is why it could not find any application in the area of metaphysics. It is true that Scholasticism attempted to coordinate the actual method of deduction in the area of metaphysics with the theory of science outlined by Aristotle, but the method of deduction did not turn out to be successful and resulted in the famous scholastic verbalism and pseudo-solutions to problems.

Bearing all this in mind, we must, therefore, take a different approach to the problem of the development of natural law. First of all, we cannot speak of the development of natural law and its "passage" into positive law, in the fundamental sense. This would be possible only if we could create some kind of "code" of natural law. Attempts at creating such a code had already been made by the philosophers and lawyers of the school of natural law, but they turned out to be deceptive, and sometimes even humorous, when "social codes," "officers' codes" or even "professional codes" of natural law were formed for some professions on the basis of the law of nature.

As we can conclude from previous considerations, natural law appears in our consciousness only in the form of the practical judgement "one should do good—one should avoid evil," and all other (derivative) manifestations of natural law do not possess a content defined in a positive and detailed way. These other manifestations of natural law, derivative in relation to the chief principle, appear to us as directions which are not closely defined, that is as ways of conduct marked out by objective human natural inclinations. We only know, therefore, that a person has an incontestable, natural right to preserve his or her life, to procreate this life (particularly by a right to marriage and to educating of children), and to personal development in a peacefully organized society. Such inclinations, however, are too general to be grasped positively in some collection of commands, being indisputably a code of natural law.

As in all kinds of philosophy, so too in the philosophy of natural law, we encounter negative as opposed to positive cognition. This means that we can justify negatively rather than positively the necessity of the existence of something, and the necessity of the connection between a certain fact with a defined nature; that we can grasp this nature and existence directly through cognition and "deduce" some properties or else some further specifications from this nature. A positive description of some states of things given for philosophical investigation constitutes an introductory and auxiliary cognitive operation in relation to metaphysical explanation in the strict sense.

In applying this to natural law we can state that, beyond one analogically general sentence ("one should do good"), we have no principles of natural law that are univocally and generally binding, and that we cannot possess them, since natural law is the participation in Eternal Law, and since there are no such univocally and generally binding principles. In connection with this, we cannot univocally deduce, by means of syllogistic thinking, any necessary conclusions which could be regarded as necessarily binding norms of positive law. The example given by St. Thomas, of the derivation, by means of syllogistic conclusion, of the positive command "do not kill" from natural law is not, in fact, just any kind of conclusion but a directly evident statement, a negative formulation of the fundamental manifestation of natural law: "one should do good—and avoid evil." No syllogistic thinking is needed in order to perceive the binding power of the command "do not kill," since this command is a negative apprehension of man's natural tendency to preserve life. If we can speak of any kind of syllogism here, it would merely be of an "explanatory" syllogism, which does not introduce anything new in relation to the premise, making it difficult to recognize this as a type of syllogistic deduction. The example given by St. Thomas is, therefore, correct in the sense that the command "do not kill" is really connected with natural law, but it is difficult to recognize it as an example of syllogistic deduction of constituted law from natural law.

We must, therefore, pose our question in a different way. The deduction of positive (that is, constituted) law from natural law is not possible. The reason for this impossibility is the "inability to formulate" natural law in univocal terms: it is formulated in exclusively analogical terms. Analogical formulations, on the other hand, do not provide a basis for syllogistic deduction *sensu stricto*—for precisely the content expressed in analogical speech, in each concrete case, is fundamentally different and the same only in a certain way; besides, this "certain way" is realized differently in every case. Thus, from such an undetermined content we cannot "deduce" any univocal legal rules. Let us use an example to illustrate this. When I claim that "one should do good," there are no two acts (two actions), in which the content "good" is the same, even with reference to apparently "the same" object, for there have emerged other conditions of activity—both personal and objective—and no general cognition can concretely indicate to man or woman what is good and what is bad in any particular circumstances. This can only be done by a special type of practical cognition, known commonly as the "conscience," in which we discern a concrete content, a concrete act and a concrete way of carrying out this act. General indications would not be of much use here, since a very detailed cognition, of its nature different from both general and theoretical cognition, is needed.

Speaking in the most general terms, all deduction in the strict sense is a certain logical operation on the extension of terms, and that is why deduction, when understood in this way, is fundamentally impossible in the area of philosophy, since here we are not using "extensive" cognition but "intensive," analogical cognition, proportionally apprehending concrete, individually existing contents.

As a consequence, we should not pose the question of the evolution of natural law in the direction of constituted, positive, law at all; rather, we should show the necessary connection of constituted law with natural law and then apply an auxiliary "method," namely that of elucidating natural law with the help of particular formulations of positive law.

If we cannot, as a result of the specific nature of natural law, show the process of deduction from natural law in the direction of constituted law, we can at least show the connections between constituted law and natural law. A similar situation obtains in the whole of philosophy. We do not first establish an absolute principle, for example, the fact of the Absolute, and then "deduce" concrete ontic facts from the Absolute, for such a procedure is not really possible; but rather, we establish particular ontic facts and then seek the only non-contradictory factors which can explain the existence of concrete ontic facts. One of these factors, in the order of "external causes," is the existence of the Absolute, making non-contradictory the existence of the world. Likewise, in the area of positive law and natural law, we depart from the interpretation of different constituted laws and seek a necessary connection between constituted laws, positive laws and natural law.

If, in analyzing positive law and seeking the ultimate reasons for its binding nature, we perceive that the rejection of a positive law (that is, the elimination of its content and binding power) is of equal importance to the elimination of the judgement "one should do good," then we thereby perceive that positive law has a necessary basis in natural law and the rejection of such a positive law is at the same time a rejection of natural law, as expressed in the judgement "one should do good," in some particular aspect. It follows that such a connection between positive law and natural law is a necessary connection and, employing St. Thomas Aquinas' terminology, it could be called the "derivation" of positive law from natural law *per modum conclusionis.*

If, on the other hand, we perceive that some concrete positive law can be put into practice in various ways, or else we perceive that the failure to put a certain law into practice is not the same as the elimination of the content of the judgement "one should do good," then this connection of positive law with natural law is not a necessary connection. It is true that law determines man's conduct in some specific domain and thereby guarantees social order, but this social order can be determined in various ways, not only by the content of the law laid down by the legislative authority. The breaking of such a law is not simultaneously a breaking of natural law, since it does not come into conflict with the chief manifestation of natural law, that is "one should do good."

Undoubtedly, on account of the social order established and guaranteed by such a law, the individual should not break the established law. However, a person is not bound "from within" by this law in a necessary way, and every time there are positive reasons, proportionally important ones, a person can, and sometimes even should, not heed such a positive law, whose aim (which is social order) can be realized better in another way than through the material keeping of this law. It is difficult, at this point, to establish some concrete casuistic rules in this matter, but a general indication of the nature of positive law and its non-necessary connection with natural law (revealing itself when the breaking of law is not an elimination of the personally perceived principle: "one should do good") should be sufficient for understanding the second type of connection of positive (constituted) law with natural law. This is a connection which St. Thomas called the derivation of constituted law from natural law *per modum determinationis,* employing the example of the function of "art," thanks to which the artist introduces into material that is of itself undetermined to a particular form of art (like marble in relation to the form of Hercules, Diana, a dog, a horse), a concrete form, for example, Hercules, determining the marble to precisely such a shape of being.

We must, however, draw attention to the fact that it can, and does, happen that a positive law, introduced in order to keep social order, but not of itself connected in a necessary way with natural law—can, in certain circumstances, take on the characteristics of a law binding itself in a necessary way to natural law; and then, not keeping such a law would be the equivalent to turning against natural law and not heeding the command that "one should do good."

The problem raised here can be illustrated by an example. Driving on the right on the Continent of Europe and driving on the left in England assumes, on account of the possibility of causing a fatal accident or becoming crippled, the nature of a necessary connection between positive law and natural law, for although the direction of driving is of itself indifferent and in an evident way does not of itself have a necessary connection with natural law, yet on account of the heavy traffic on the roads and the real possibility of causing an accident, one is not allowed to use the road in any other way than has been determined by law, since one would otherwise be rejecting the principle of "one should do good." The above example illustrates even more clearly, moreover, how very much the "deduction" (as St. Thomas calls it) of positive law from natural law is not "deduction" conceived in the sense of scientific deduction, and that in the practical order these connections must retain the essential moments of the very "practical order" of human conduct, the moments of consciousness and free will, and that they cannot do without them. We cannot, in the area of practical domains proceed in the same way as in the area of purely theoretical sciences, where the connections between sentences can be shown in a purely objective way. In the practical order we can never abstract from the human person and his or her essential personal life, that is, his conscience and free choice. Thanks to this, positive laws made by human beings can sometimes have necessary connections and bind in an absolute way, and sometimes they may not have these necessary connections and are not binding in an absolute way. Moreover, it can happen that the implementation of such laws can even become a crime and a violation of natural law, as for instance in the often quoted example of giving a knife to a madman. According to natural law, one should give back to the man those objects which are useful to him personally and indispensable for life, and on the other hand, precisely the fulfilling of this command could sometimes be the cause of evil, because the madman could misuse the knife and harm himself or someone else. The role of the reason is something essential, here, for assessing how one should act.

6. THE PROBLEM OF "BINDING IN CONSCIENCE" OF POSITIVE LAW

The problem of whether (or when) positive law,[28] both Church and State law, would be "binding in conscience" has a very long and equally stormy history. Let us merely draw attention to some moments in history when a revolt took place against law, particularly Church law, and to the reactions of the Church towards attitudes of this kind.

In the history of the Church, there is a constant flow of theories against Church law and Church jurisdiction. The desire to get away from being under the influence of law was justified in various ways: a) an accusation was levelled directly at the morality of the legislative authority—and the accusers maintained that authority, if and when it is in a state of sin, is not capable of issuing any precept that is binding in conscience—and it appears that J. Wyclif and J. Hus taught this (according to the testimony of the Council of Constance, which condemned a statement of this kind); b) or it was claimed, (for example by the

Cathars and Waldensians), that true and just Christians are no longer subordinate to law, and the words of the Apostle were quoted: *lex iusto non est posita* (the law is not for the just); c) or finally, as in the times of Febronianism, it was claimed that legislative authority in the Church rests in the hands of the whole Church community, and not only in the hands of Popes and Bishops.

Here are some extracts from writings,[29] illustrating the Church's reaction to theories of this kind: from the Council of Constance, the article relating to John Hus:

> Obedience to the Church is an obedience thought up by the priests of the Church, and is not in accordance with the evident authority of the Bible;[30] ... Nobody can exercise the curacy of Christ or Peter if he has not been initiated in the customs;[31] ... The Pope is not the real and professed successor of Peter, the prince of the Apostles, if he is at cross purposes with Peter.[32]

These statements are condemned. Wyclif's statement is also condemned:
> Nobody is lay ruler, nobody is Superior, nobody is Bishop, when he finds himself in the state of mortal sin.[33]

Leo X condemned Luther's statements:

> Christ's words to Peter, "whatever you bind on earth," and so forth, concern only that which Peter himself bound,[34] ... [and], it is certain that it does not lie within the power of the Church or the Pope to establish articles of the faith or even laws of morality, that is, the doing of good deeds.[35]

The following pronouncements were made at the Council of Trent:

> Nobody, even though he may be most perfect, can regard himself as free from keeping the commandments;[36] ... Whoever claims that a just man, even the most perfect man, is not obliged to keep the commandments of God and the Church, but is only obliged to believe, may he be damned![37]

In the *Syllabus* of Pope Pius IX, the following statements are condemned:

> Authority is merely the sum of numbers (of voters) and of material forces. ... It is permissible and legitimate to disobey authority, and even to combat it.[38]

Alexander VI condemned the statement:

> The people do not sin if, even without any reason, they refuse to accept a law promulgated by authority.[39]

There are a great number of similar Church decrees. According to these decrees, just law issued by a legitimate authority binds man in conscience to keep it. This matter is particularly emphasized in the area of Canon Law, which itself defines how and to what extent it is binding.

In the article entitled "Does human law necessarily bind in conscience?"[40] — St. Thomas differentiates between just and unjust law. If a law is just, then it binds in conscience, since it obtains its binding power from Eternal Law, from which it derives. According to St. Thomas, laws are just when:

1° their aim is just, that is, ordered to the common good;

2° their legislator is just, that is, when the law made does not go beyond the competence of the legislator;

3° their form is just, that is, when it refers to the "subjects" proportionally in the same way, proportionally distributing the burdens of common obligation in relation to the whole.

Unjust, on the other hand, are all those laws which are not in accordance with human good, whether on account of the e n d (when laws that do not contribute to the common good are established), or on account of the l e g i s l a t o r himself (when he makes laws, the making of which does not lie within his power, and which go beyond his legislative competence), or finally, on account of the f o r m (when the burden of social obligations is unjustly distributed). Laws of this kind cannot bind in conscience, but sometimes they can be binding for reasons of prudence in order to avoid a greater evil.

The solution given by St. Thomas is fundamentally convincing but seems to be incomplete, since it does not take into account two important factors, namely the subject of law, that is, the real human person (who is to be bound by law), and also the legislator's intention.

It can, and does, happen, that there exist laws in an organization in which the legislator himself does not wish to bind in conscience those for whom he establishes the law. Such is the case in the Dominican Order, where the Constitutions do not bind in conscience to any responsibility by virtue of the Constitutions themselves, but only entail a punishment for those who break them. This is the famous *"lex mere poenalis"*—law punishable only externally. This law is binding for the purpose of keeping order, but the breaking of the regulations of such a law, merely because it is a law, is not connected with any inner sanction—any "sin"—due to not keeping the law as a law. It can happen, that that which is a precept of law is also, at the same time, good in itself, for reasons of one kind or another, and then, when viewed as a good, binds a choice in conscience, by virtue of the very fact that it is a good. This is, however, quite a different matter in relation to the binding by law as law, for the legislator, who wants to make human life easier and not more difficult, establishes that the law constituted by him is not binding in conscience under pain of sin, but only under external punishment. The fact that the legislator wants to make life easier for man is stressed, for instance, in the Dominican Constitutions n. 32 par. 1:

> *Ut igitur unitati totius Ordinis provideamus, volumus et declaramus ut Regula nostra et Constitutiones nostrae ac Ordinationes Capitulorum et Praelatorum non obligent nos ad culpam, seu ad peccatum, sed tantum-modo ad poenam pro transgressionibus in ipsis Constitutionibus taxatam, vel a praelatis.*[41]

It appears that in modern legislation, as a result of the theories of the school of natural law, which separates the legal order from the moral order, as well as a similar theory advocated by Kant, it has become the general conviction, both of the legislator and of all citizens, that state laws do not have the sanctions of sin as a result of the breaking of law, but, as it was first put in the Dominican Constitutions, they are binding only under the sanction of punishment for breaking them, if this is judicially proven. This does not mean, however, that a person breaking such a law does not sin, when he or she perceives that by breaking the law he or she is doing evil; for one can never do evil, since that is a breaking of natural law, which is always binding in conscience. The doing of an evil action, irrespective of whether this act is forbidden by law or permitted, is always a sin and carries inner sanctions. The breaking itself of a law as such, does not become a sin if it is not connected with some kind of "matter." "The matter of sin," that is, evil, which is measurable in the categories of an injury (that which lies ultimately in the categories of natural law), determines whether a given breaking of the law burdens the human conscience and becomes a "sin." According to St. Thomas' theory, on the other hand, already the breaking of a law became something evil, and that is why it was inwardly not allowed. A theory of this kind can, however, be contrary to the intention of the legislator, who may not wish, formally, clearly, or virtually, as a result of a commonly accepted theory, that a human law should bind a person "from within," and that the transgression of a law, precisely because it is a transgression and breaking of a law, should be for the individual something evil in itself. The fact that a transgression of law is always punishable is another matter. This theory is commonly accepted today with reference to state laws. Thus, as in the Dominican Constitutions, state laws are not binding in conscience by virtue of the fact that they are laws, since the legislator does not want them to be binding in such a way.

The second matter, which was overlooked by St. Thomas[42] in the theory of law, is the matter of the acceptance of law by the human person. All laws, just as all precepts, must be cognized by the subordinate, that is, by the human person, and they must be cognized in a practical way, that is, cognized as binding. No law can bind a person in conscience if it does not bind through cognition. In the act of practical cognition there must occur a becoming aware of the fact that positive law personally and really binds "me." If a person either does not make the self aware that a given law is binding, or else reaches a justified and insurmountable conviction that a law is not binding in conscience, then such a law, while binding externally, nevertheless does not have the power of binding in conscience. It is internally contradictory for something to bind in conscience if it has not been recognized as binding by conscience itself, for binding in conscience is only possible when conscience itself (that is, concrete, phronetic practical cognition) perceives something as a personal "good" which "should be done." If a person, on the other hand, really perceives, in his or her practical cognition, that something that the law commands is evil, then he or she must not do it, even if the law were to strongly command it and to threaten with the greatest punishments for not carrying out the command. The most supreme law is natural law, revealing itself to the person in the form of the command "one should do good."

Thus, every legal positive command cannot but pass through the "filter" of the human conscience, which always personally relates the person to the legal command. Otherwise, a person would not act as a person who is free and responsible for actions which he or she undertakes in the face of the law, but would act like a machine which is univocally directed "from the outside." For this reason too, the role of the conscience or, in a wider sense, the role of the human person seeking his or her own personal mode of procedure and directing the self—in the choice of methods—only by good, is something fundamental in the question of the binding nature of law, from which there cannot be and there is no "release." Personal decision, the agreement (or disagreement) of the human person with constituted law (positive law), the acceptance of this law as a personal norm of conduct—these cannot be replaced by any external factor, since this would amount to an elimination of one's humanity. There is not, and there cannot be, any higher instance directing a person's conduct than his or her own conscience. This does not mean, however, that this conscience always acts without error, "without conflict," that is, that it always chooses the proper good, and that a human being cannot be educated to make right decisions. That is the aim of ethics, the science of morality and the science of law, as well as other practical disciplines.[43] All education aims at a fuller preparation for conscious and free decision-making, and not at putting pressure on the conscience. This also applies to persons who have made vows of obedience. These vows do not free an individual from "being a person," neither do they free him or her from the necessity of making personal a decision, nor from the responsibility for choice and activity. Only one supplementary element needs to be added here, as it will determine a decision: the will of the superior, his or her command, which a person taking a vow of obedience freely promises to take into consideration when entering into any activity.[44]

Thus, the question of inner acceptance of a legal rule is essential to the fact that positive constituted law is binding, both with reference to State law and Church law, for everywhere law is related to the free human individual—the person, who has the right to activity determined by his reason and free will. Considering precisely these two decisive moments which define the way in which the person is bound by law, we must furthermore take into account three factors essential for law mentioned by St. Thomas,[45] namely the problem of aim and the proportionality of law to the aim; the problem of the competence of the legislator, and the problem of the very form of law: is a law just and proportional, binding all members of a given society in the same way?

These factors, analyzed by St. Thomas, derive from the very nature of positive law. All of them, however, converge as in a focal point in the concrete human conscience, that is, in the concrete, practical cognition of a person, who must therefore perceive for the self and, seeing, recognize and make a personal decision to observe the law. This decision is the ultimate human expression of obedience to law, and then, when a person decides to observe the law (to which only an objective cognition can oblige him or her) the person accepts this law as "his or her property," and at this moment law, binding "from within," becomes his or her personal law; at this moment, opposition between the heteronomy of law and the autonomy of the person disappears, since through auto-determination heteronomy becomes autonomy.

Here we must also emphasize the situations in life in which an individual perceives that he or she is not bound by law as a result of some objective lacunae in law or its collision with perceived natural law, and when, in spite of this, sometimes for reasons of prudence, that person yields to law externally in order to avoid a greater evil, whether personal evil or evil done to others, for example scandal. An apparent submission to such a pseudo-law cannot, however, be taken as the doing of evil, for this would be equivalent to eliminating natural law, which binds in conscience in a necessary and absolute way.

7. THE PROBLEM OF CHANGE IN POSITIVE LAW AND DISPENSATIONS FROM POSITIVE LAW[46]

In old legal terminology, concepts such as the following occur: *mutare legem, abrogare, irritare, interpretare,* and *dispensare.* All these terms refer fundamentally to positive law, not to natural law.

The most radical case is the e x c h a n g e of one law (or a bill) for another. When law loses its binding power, we call this the "abrogation" of the law or the bill *(abrogare legem).*

A bill does not yet have binding power until it has been ratified by a competent higher legislative body, and this is called *irritare legem.*

The interpretation of a bill (or legal rule) can be reduced to the following functions:

a) declaring whether the law is binding in particular cases or not;

b) establishing a main meaning where there is ambiguity in the expression of a legal rule;

c) introducing a new meaning; or finally

d) establishing a vague or general meaning.

A dispensation from law, on the other hand, is the releasing of a person or group of persons from the obligation of keeping the law which nevertheless retains its general binding power.

Having made general terminological distinctions in the domain of the binding power of law, we will deal with two particular cases, in which a legal rule obtaining hitherto loses its binding power, in general or in concrete cases.

The most frequent case, in which a bill hitherto in force loses its binding power in relation to all persons, is the exchange of one law for another. Of course, there occurs *ipso facto* an abrogation of the binding power of the bill at the moment of exchange of one law for another (which regulates given factors in a different way).

In the set of problems surrounding the exchanges of positive law we can distinguish two important aspects (among others): a) the very fact of the exchange of certain legal rules for others, and b) the meaning of such a fact.

When we consider the actual fact that certain legal rules get exchanged for others, this takes place incomparably more often today than it did in earlier periods. Particularly in States run by People's Democracies, bills passed by Parliament are replaced by decrees issued by superior legislative bodies.

According to St. Thomas Aquinas, there is (or there can be) a twofold cause for the eventual change of rules of positive law. One is the formulation of a more perfect, more rational law; for our reason and our cognition are subject to evolution and proceed from imperfect states to perfect states, and that is why reason can always improve on how a legal rule is expressed. Besides, this fact is confirmed by history, for not only do the purely theoretical sciences develop, but also the form of social life, and through these the bills and legal rules develop and become perfected.

Another reason for the exchange of legal rules can be a change in the conditions of individual life and of forms and systems of social life, for some laws that are good in certain circumstances turn out to be of no use in changed circumstances. A glaring example of this was, in the course of history, the change in constituted law from that of enslaved societies to that of democratic societies.

The two reasons mentioned for changes in law are only manifestations of some general factors which have not been specified in detail. This does not mean, however, that every time one perceives the possibility of a better formulation of a bill, the legal rule should in fact be changed. All changes of legal rules are connected with a great social shock, especially in social organisms such as the Church, where law binds in conscience and where a change in legal rules is connected with a deep moral experience of many people, amongst whom it can be transformed (and is generally transformed) into contempt of law.

For this reason too, St. Thomas draws attention to the fact[47] that one cannot freely change legal rules, but only when a new law will contribute more to social good than the social harm that can be caused by a change in the law, for legal custom and the custom of respecting laws that have been made play a large part in the domain of law. Horace's remark *quid leges sine moribus? - inanes proficiunt* has a very correct psychological application, for legal custom is that which is the direct purpose of law itself. Law aims at making people become accustomed to be directed by reason in life, in specific situations, and that is why too frequent changes of legal rules cause not only disrespect for the law, but something more: a disregard for the rational element as a factor directing human life. For most people, law, together with harmful consequences when it is broken, is merely an effective factor preventing not only social anarchy, but also the non-education of people, for already the ancients (and also St. Paul) remarked that law is made not for good people, who are directed by rational factors, but for bad people, who are directed in life by passions. And the effective buffer for such a state of affairs is precisely law, the consequences of which, when it is not kept, frighten those who would favor a life of crime, harming other people in a specific society, and discouraging them from doing evil.

Precisely these goods which endure when law remains unchanged could disappear if changes in law occurred too often. Then there would be no hope of gaining à greater good, a good which might only have been gained under a previous law. What is more, even if the legal rule were to turn out not to be very effective by itself, then, on the basis of certain legal rules, certain legal customs develop, which, as a direct result of the legal rule, can sometimes be either a direct interpretation of law, or they can change in a practical way the meaning of the law made and finally become a law themselves and take on legal force. That is also why permanent social organisms, such as England, for instance, or the Church, have such a great respect for legal custom. Custom, however, is not a good in itself, and if it is not rational, law should remove it.

The second problem raised here concerns the question of dispensation.[48] We can approach this problem from a twofold aspect: we can perceive in the dispensation a *vulnus legis* and we can also perceive a better application of general law to concrete human cases. Among lawyers of different schools there is a generally widespread opinion that a dispensation is an "injury" done to law. An opinion of this kind is based on the conviction that law formulated in a general way expresses (in some aspects) essential social needs, and that this is why any departure from "common good" represented by a generally formulated legal rule is in some sense an evasion of law and thereby an injury to law itself.

St. Thomas Aquinas here represents a different view, namely, that a dispensation not only is not an injury to law but, on the contrary, is a better, and in concrete cases a more perfect, way of keeping the law in a certain environment. He draws attention to the fact that a dispensation in the proper sense aims at a better adaptation of the general content of a legal rule to concrete cases: *dispensatio est commensuratio alicuius communis ad singula* (a dispensation is the adaptation of something general to that which is individual). The person who is responsible for the common material good of a social group is called a *dispensator* in Latin, that is, the one who, from a common treasury, gives to concrete individuals the kind of good that a given individual needs in given circumstances. In the natural course of affairs, the father or mother of a family is to be precisely such a *dispensator* in the smallest community.

That is why, in every community, a person who directs that community is needed, someone who may be better able to apply general rules of law to the needs of particular individuals. These rules of law, being general, are thereby made imperfect, since life always goes on in individual and concrete conditions. It does happen that a general rule of law does not suit the individual for justifiable reasons, and then it is the responsibility of the superior or the leader of the community to exempt this individual from the general rule of law, in order for the person who is exempted from the general rule of law to fulfill better the fundamental aim of the community.

Thus, in order to obtain a dispensation, the person to whom the dispensation is given must have a reason for demanding it. This reason, however, cannot be of the kind that might dispense someone from keeping the law, since in such a case the legal rule is not binding anyway, by virtue of *epikeia,* or a higher justice. The granting of a dispensation for no reason, however, that is, without a very important need of the person to whom the dispensation is given, would be just that which is called *vulnus legis;* it would be something imprudent, harming society and making it difficult to acquire the good to which the legal rule is ordered.

Of course, natural law is not subject to any dispensations, since we cannot free a person from doing good. As far as "Divine" law is concerned, the rules of procedure as to such a law are already contained in the nature of the accepted revelation.

.

As it has already been mentioned, dispensation differs from correctness—*epikeia* and its application in concrete cases. St. Thomas Aquinas, after Aristotle and others, calls *epikeia*—correctness[49] —a more superior rule of human conduct, for if human acts are to a great extent defined by legal rules or custom, then it is not possible anyway for law or a rational custom to foresee all the individual circumstances of the life of particular persons. It can, and does, happen that precisely the keeping of the letter of the law, custom or propriety is something evil and infringes on unwritten but essential justice. And then the individual is not allowed to follow an indication of the letter of the law, since it would be an infringement of natural law, but he or she should do that which in practical cognition appears as correct, as in accordance with common good, with the essential good of the human being itself. The perception of what is in accordance and what is not in accordance with positive law is called correctness—*epikeia*. Thus, where correctness appears, man or woman is released from carrying out the letter of the law, since the person is bound by a higher law, a natural one, which he or she would have to break in order to carry out the legal rule to the letter.

In the case of *epikeia,* therefore, we must not seek to obtain a dispensation from law, for a dispensation takes place where a fundamentally correct law is binding and achieves its essential aim, and where the keeping of particular norms of law is sometimes more difficult and more senseless than not keeping a given norm of law on account of the fact that the person to whom the dispensation is given fulfills other important functions, contributing to common good. Then, a dispensation from positive law is an even better keeping of the very meaning and task of law than an absolute submission of being directed by law, and is not an exception to this rule. Thanks to dispensation, society can better achieve its aim, and is a living and flexible society, adapting to life's conditions.

NOTES

The Theory of Natural Law

1. The Existence of Natural Law

[1] Lévi-Strauss, The Savage Thought, p. 79ff.

[2] Ibid., p. 119.

[3] Ibid., p. 121.

[4] St. Paul, *Letter to the Romans,* 2, 14–16 *(HOI TINES ENDEIKNENTAI TO ERGON TOU NOMOU GRAPTON EN TAIS KARDIAIS AUTON).*

[5] Cf. below, footnote 10. The systematic, Thomistic justification, both of the existence and the nature of natural law interpreted by St. Thomas, is presented by A. Bednarski *(La deduzione delle norme morali generali della legge naturale,* Rome, 1969). The author, employing some logical forms, analyzes the following questions in successive chapters: whether it is at all possible to deduce moral norms from natural law; whether natural law exists; what aims-tasks are imposed by natural law; what is the object of this law; the question of human acts; the question of moral norms on the basis of natural law, as well as relations between duty and law. As I understand it, the matters analyzed in the quoted work are fundamentally evident and do not require any intervention from contemporary formalized logic. Also on this subject is St. Thomas' treatise on law from the *S.th.* 1a2ae, cf. Cz. Martyniak, *Obiektywna podstawa prawa według św. Tomasza z Akwinu* (An Objective Basis of Law according to St. Thomas Aquinas), Lublin, 1949. The series of considerations made here coincides with Martyniak's course of analyses and commentaries; the basis for the justifications is different, however, on account of a differently interpreted concept of being and the emphasized mode of transcendentalizing cognition.

[6] A monograph on this subject has been written by Z. Zdybicka: *Partycypacja bytu* (The Participation of Being), showing both the historical and the epistemic and ontic basis of the theory of participation. Kalinowski mentioned the subject of participation incidentally, but in a penetrating way in his *Le problème de la vérité en morale et en droit* (The problem of Truth in Ethics and Law), pp. 190–195. He compares the concept of natural law to the famous triple state of the universal: *universale ante rem*—this would correspond to "divine eternal law"; *universale in re*—natural law, insofar as it is rooted in man's nature, which is a rational nature, capable of "interpreting" good and being itself; *universale post rem*—that is, natural law in the proper sense, insofar as it expresses the content of the command, in our case "do good." The triple differentiation of *"universale"* is convenient for conveying the very nature of natural law, its relation to eternal law, to the human being's personal nature—but we must nevertheless always have in mind the theory of ideas elaborated by St. Thomas and already mentioned here earlier, for there is no general "ideal state" *ad instar universale* in the Divine intellect.

[7] This is, of course, an "ultimate" explanation, no longer having recourse to another type of cognition which would supplement this type of knowledge; it is an interpretation of the metaphysical kind, characterized by an operation on being and its negation.

[8] S.th., 1a2ae q. 94 a. 2.

[9] Ibid., ad. 1. In this sense, too, St. Thomas speaks of one natural law: *Omnia ista praecepta legis naturae inquantum referentur ad unum primum praeceptum, habent rationem unius legis.*

[10] Cf. on this subject ibid., q. 94 a. 2. We shall quote this article literally here, on account of its importance: *Praecepta legis naturae hoc modo se habent ad rationem practicam, sicut principia prima demonstrationem se habent ad rationem speculativam: utraque enim sunt quaedam principia per se nota. Dicitur autem aliquid per se notum dupliciter: uno modo, secundum se; alio modo, quoad nos. Secundum se quidem quaelibet propositio dicitur per se nota, cuius praedicatum est de ratione subiecti: contingit tamen quod ignoranti definitionem subiecti, talis propositio non erit per se nota. Sicut ista propositio, homo est rationale, est per se nota secundum sui naturam, quia qui dicit hominem, dicit rationale: et tamen ignoranti quid sit homo, haec propositio non est per se nota. Et inde est quod, sicut dicit Boetius, in libro de Hebdomad, quaedam sunt dignitates vel propositiones per se notae communiter omnibus: et huius modi sunt illae propositiones quarum termini sunt omnibus noti, ut, Omne totum est maius sua parte, et, Quae uni eidem sunt aequalia, sibi invicem sunt aequalia. Quaedam vero propositiones sunt per se notae solis sapientibus, qui terminos propositionum intelligunt quid significent: sicut intelligentii quod angelus non est corpus, per se notum est quod non est circumscriptive in loco, quod non est manifestum rudibus, qui hoc non capiunt.*

In his autem quae in apprehensione omnium cadunt, quidam ordo invenitur. Nam illud quod primo cadit in apprehensione, est ens, cuius intellectus includitur in omnibus quaecumque quis apprehendit. Et ideo primum principium indemonstrabile est quod non est simul affirmare et negare, quod fundatur supra rationem entis et non entis: et super hoc principio omnia alia fundantur, ut dicitur in IV Metaphys. Sicut autem ens est primum quod cadit in apprehensione simpliciter, ita bonum est primum quod cadit in apprehensione practicae rationis, quae ordinatur ad opus: omne enim agens agit propter finem, qui habet rationem boni. Et ideo primum principium in ratione practica est quodefundar supra rationem boni, quae est, Bonum est quod omnia appetunt. Hoc est ergo primum praeceptum legis, quod bonum est faciendum et prosequendum, et malum vitandum. Et super hoc fundantur omnia alia praecepta legis naturae: ut scilicet omnia illa facienda vel vitanda pertineant ad praecepta legis naturae, quae ratio practica naturaliter apprehendit esse bona humana.

[11] When we draw attention to the various propositions of understanding natural law, which occur in the history of human philosophical thought, we will perceive without difficulty that they were either equivalent to the statement "do good," or a specification thereof.

[12] Precisely these three meanings, when distinguished, constitute the content of the philosophical concept of participation. This is also why St. Thomas' proposition of understanding natural law as, ultimately, the participation of eternal law, becomes comprehensible.

[13] The ontic contingency discussed at this point, which manifests itself in the lack of fullness of good in itself, is equivalent to ontic derivation. The lack of good is a sign of the lack of identity of essence and existence, that is, it constitutes the essence of contingency.

[14] The considerations made here constitute a fundamental response to the problem posed in this work. It requires the consideration of further difficulties derived from those mentioned: the developmental dialectic of natural law, as well as its relation to all positive, constituted laws.

[15] How natural law is to be conceived, and its developmental dialectic, involve different concepts of law itself. The concept, analyzed below, of triple tendency, is fundamentally a heritage of Stoic thought, wherein law was conceived as a natural inclination. The concept of law itself as an act of practical reason ("do good") is connected with man's rational structure, grasped in the state of actualization, which draws on St. Paul's concept from his *Letter to the Romans*. Paul himself is a witness, here, of the rational Socratic Greek tradition, drawing on an inner demon who commands rightful conduct. Human rational structure, when grasped as in an habitual state ordered towards moral actualization, is in the understanding of the Augustinian line of thought *(signatum est super nos lumen vultus Tui, Domine),* particularly of St. Bonaventure (in II *Sent.* d. 39 a. 2), the essence of moral law. This habitual ordering, however, as St. Thomas interprets it, is s y n d e r e s i s as a *habitus primorum principiorum.* Law, on the other hand, is essentially an act of human rational nature—in the understanding—as has already been analyzed. The act *par excellence* is j u d g m e n t (cf. *S.th.,* 1a2ae q. 94 a. 1). Thus, different ways of understanding law are integrated in St. Thomas, forming an analogical unity, in which the main analogue of understanding natural law is the act of judgment of practical reason: "do good"; some lesser analogues are the concept of law as an habitual state of rational nature (s y n d e r e s i s) or rational nature itself, revealing itself in its fundamental (natural) inclinations.

[16] Cf. *S.th.,* 1a2ae q. 94 a. 2. On account of the essential role of the article, the second part of it must be quoted in the original version (for the first part, see endnote 10 in this chapter): *Quia vero bonum habet rationem finis, malum autem rationem contrarii, inde est quod omnia illa ad quae homo habet naturalem inclinationem, ratio naturaliter apprehendit ut bona, et per consequens ut opere prosequenda, et contraria eorum ut mala et vitanda. Secundum igitur ordinem inclinationum naturalium, est ordo praeceptorum legis naturae. Inest enim primo inclinatio homini ad bonum secundum naturam in qua communicat cum omnibus substantiis: prout scilicet quaelibet substantia appetit conservationem sui esse secundum suam naturam. Et secundum hanc inclinationem, pertinent ad legem naturalem ea per quae vita hominis conservatur, et contrarium impeditur. – Secundo inest homini inclinatio ad aliqua magis specialia, secundam naturam in qua communicat cum ceteris animalibus. Et secundum hoc, dicuntur ea esse de lege naturali quae natura omnia animalia docuit, ut est coniunctio maris et feminae, et educatio liberorum, et similia. – Tertio modo inest homini inclinatio ad bonum secundum naturam rationis, quae est sibi propria: sicut homo habet naturalem inclinationem ad hoc quod veritatem cognoscat de Deo, et ad hoc quod in societate vivat. Et secundum hoc, ad legem naturalem pertinent ea quae ad huius modi inclinationem*

spectant: utpote quod homo ignorantiam vitet, quod alios non offendat cum quibus debet conversari, et cetera huiusmodi quae adspectant.

[17] *S.th.,* 1a2ae q. 94 a. 2.

[18] We should differentiate "responsibility for" and "responsibility towards." On the one hand, responsibility "for" presupposes the freedom of the person who, by his or her free activity, changes the arrangement of things and "thing" relations or personal relations. Changed relations are a result brought about by the freely acting person, who, making new situations is, in relation to them, in a new relation to a freely acting cause. And this relation is called "responsibility for." Responsibility "towards," on the other hand, is built up on the basis of a personal dependence on a freely acting cause, one that causes new situations t o w a r d s a person, taking care of the order of personal activity. Therefore, while "responsibility for" focuses on responsibility for the changed situation, "responsibility towards" focuses on responsibility for the person taking care of established order.

[19] *S.th.,* 1a2ae q. 94 a. 3–6.

[20] A statement of this kind makes sense only in the classical (pluralistic) stream of philosophy, as shown by chapter II, the understanding and acceptance of which is a necessary condition for accepting the statements formulated here.

[21] Natural law in the restricted sense draws on the Aristotelian concept of natural law connected with equity and justice. Of course, equity and justice among people is a good. However, not everything that is a good is exhausted by equity and justice.

[22] For example G. Manser. *Das Naturrecht in thomistischer Beleuchtung* (Natural Law in the Light of Thomistic Thought), Freiburg, 1944, pp. 32–40.

[23] Ibid., s. 50–61.

[24] Cf. *S.th.,* 1a2ae q. 94. a. 4.

[25] Ibid., a. 5. I am quoting this text in the original on account of its importance for culture, ever present in European awareness.

[26] Ibid., a. 6.

[27] Ibid., q. 95. a. 2.

[28] This problem was considered by St. Thomas in *S.th.,* q. 96, a. 4.

[29] They are collected in H. Denziger, *Enchiridion symbolorum...,* Edit. 33, Barcinone, 1965, and also in the commentary to the *S.th.,* 1a2ae q. 96 a. 4. Ed. Marietti, Turin, 1948, p. 448ff.

[30] *Oboedientia ecclesiastica est oboedientia secundum adinventionem sacerdotum Ecclesiae praeter expressam auctoritatem Scripturae.* Denziger 641 (1215).

[31] *Nemo gerit vicem Christi vel Petri, nisi sequatur eum in moribus; cum nulla alia sequela sit pertinentior, nec aliter recipiat a Deo procuratoriam potestatem; quia ad illud officium vicariatus requiritur et morum conformitas et instituentis auctoritas.* Denziger, 638 (1212).

[32] *Papa non est verus et manifestus successor Apostolorum principis Petri, si vivit moribus contrariis Petro.* Denziger, 639 (1212).

[33] *Nullus est dominus civilis, nullus est praelatus, nullus est episcopus, dun est in peccato mortali.* Denziger, 595.

[34] *Verbum Christi ad Petrum, Quodcumque solveris super terram etc. (Mt. 16) extenditur dumtaxat ad ligata ab ipso Petro.* Denziger, 766 (1476).

[35] *Certum est, in mnau Ecclesiae aut Papae prorsus non esse statuere articulos fidei, immo nec leges morum seu bonorum operum.* Denziger, 767 (1477).

[36] *Nemo autem, quantumvis justificatus, liberum se esse ab observatione mandatorum putare debet.* Denziger, 804 (1536).

[37] *Si quis hominem justificatum et quantumlibet perfectum dixerit non teneri ad observantiam mandatorum Dei et Ecclesiae, sed tantum ad credendum, quasi vero Evangelium sit nuda et absoluta promissio vitae aeternae, sine condicione observationis mandatorum, anathema sit.* Denziger, 830 (1570).

[38] *Legitimis principibus oboedientiam detractare, immo et rebellare licit.* Denziger, 1763 (2963) and *Auctoritas nihil aliud est, nisi numeri et materialium virium summa.* Denziger, 1760.

[39] Denziger, 690. The reader is referred to Denziger, 1235: *Quilibet tyrannus potest et debet licite et meritorie occidi per quemcumque vasallum suum vel sudditum, etiam per clanculares insidias, et subtiles blanditias et adulationes, non ostante quocumque praestito iuramento seu confoederatione factis cum eo, non expectata sententia vel mandato judicis cuiuscumque ... erroneam esse in fide et in moribus, ipsamque tamquam haereticam, scandalosam, et ad fraudes, deceptiones, mendacia, proditiones, periuria viam dantem reprobat et condemnat. Declarat insuper, decernit et diffinit, quod pertinaciter doctrinam hanc perniciosissimam asserentes sunt haeretici.*

[40] *S.th.,* 1a2ae q. 96 a. 4.

[43] Above all, the education of the human being has a very important influence here. And that is why Horace had it in mind when he said: *Quid leges sine moribus? Inanes proficiunt!*

[44] This does not mean that the subordinate person, in listening to his superior and carrying out his instructions, is by the fact of obedience not responsible for his act.

[45] *S.th.,* 1a2ae q. 96 a. 4–6.

[46] Ibid., q. 97.

[47] Ibid., a. 1 and 2.

[48] Ibid., a. 4.

[49] Ibid., 2a2ae q. 120.

CONCLUSION

NATURAL LAW AND THE RIGHTS OF THE PERSON

Bearing in mind the reflections and analyses made so far on the problem of natural law, we can perceive that two great tendencies appeared in the understanding of the law of nature: a) the tendency to s p e c i f y this law, its formation and c o n c r e t e expression, by forming supreme legal rules; b) the tendency to understand natural law i n g e n e r a l, which took on a twofold appearance:

1° a f o r m a l one in Kant, already outlined in some German theorists of the school of natural law, and

2° a contentual-analogical one, in the form of the superior judgement of practical reason "do good—do not do evil," while at the same time the understanding of good and evil oscillates between a personal view and a social grasp of good and evil.

The latter was preponderant in recognizing the accepted good and it was probably the expression of a rather universal, commonsense cognition and commonsense morality than individual views of the human being. However, at the same time, in the ultimate case (for example, of a dispute between individual and social opinion), the individual decides, for as the source of decision and only he or she—as a person—is the carrier of morality.

The general state of affairs outlined here is the consequence of a particular polarization of the understanding of the human being, as a determined nature, and a free human person. And this is also connected with polarizing human cognition, which is universalizing on the one hand and transcendentalizing on the other. In emphasizing the human being as a specific nature, having a fundamentally determined activity, there simultaneously appears a trend, coupled to this, of the articulation of basic human laws and obligations. Unfortunately, all real principles (not only formal ones, as in Kant and some of his predecessors, like Thomasius) turned out to be to a great extent illusory in the history of human thought, for in this history of culture there was no concrete formulation of natural law which would not at the same time be disputed in the name of some ideals or values, even religious ones. If we were to take into account even such a radical formulation as the Fifth Commandment of the Decalogue, "do not kill," this too, in different cultural eras and schools of thought, was in particular cases disputed or by-passed with the help of theories, for example, the "just war" or sacral murders, as in the culture of the Incas or some ancient religions of the land of Canaan. In the name of religious-sacred reasons, exceptions were also admitted from other basic human natural inclinations which otherwise constitute the object of precepts of natural law.

The general analogical formulation of natural law in the form of the judgement "do good" is connected more with the concept of transcendentalizing cognition and the conceiving of the human being as a free person, capable, through reason, of an objective interpretation of the content of being and good, and at the same time capable of taking responsibility for the interpretation of these contents and for the decision liberating moral conduct. Of course, this morality is already fundamentally and formally contained in the act of decision. However, a person is not merely an intellectual person, a person who has completed a process of gaining perfection; he or she is a potentialized, dynamic person—that is, a person entangled in matter and expressing the self through matter; briefly, he or she is an inner tension and, as it were, the "drama" both of nature (that which is determined, made uniform) and of the person, that is, of free decisive moments, becoming self-determined through the intellect and free will. And if the supreme formulation of natural law cannot be other than merely this analogical "do good," being the expression of transcendentalizing cognition, we can, nevertheless, and should support it through concrete formulations (in universalizing cognition) of the supreme "natural" rules of human conduct. These rules of moral conduct generally correctly express the analogical content of the natural law "do good," but they cannot be recognized formally as natural law itself, since by the nature of things it appears in the human act of moral, personal judgement, being the ultimate foundation of human decision. Such a formulation can occur only in a personal view. Society, formulating precepts and prohibitions helps the human person to correctly interpret good, but it does not replace and does not eliminate personal interpretation and a personal decision, as well as personal responsibility.

The formulation of precepts, prohibitions or natural laws in the history of human culture appeared many times; often they attracted religious or social sanctions and that is why they constituted a very valuable vehicle for the moral development of humanity; however, the whole of their content and power derived from the natural law "do good" which is contained in them, and also from the objective value of good. The formulations of concrete precepts, although they cannot formally be recognized as natural law itself (for the reasons mentioned above), have the following "advantage" over analogical natural law itself: they can be the foundation of logical-judicial claims, whereas natural law itself cannot become the basis for such claims, for what is seen as good or evil is always a personal view of man and woman. The supremacy, however, of analogical natural law, manifesting itself in the judgement "do good" (in all its derivative formulations, in all articulation of it), relies on the fact that it constitutes for the person the basis of the whole of morality, the basis of a defense against the interference of any authority that could command the human being to do evil. A person recognizing that a precept is a precept to do evil must not listen to the voice of authority, for it would be precisely contrary to natural law, an inner betrayal of good, and thereby of being, in a fundamental expression of being—a personal one, both of the human being and, ultimately, God himself.

1.   UNIVERSAL DECLARATION OF HUMAN RIGHTS

The concrete formulations of human laws and responsibilities, however, educate society and the individual towards an objective interpretation of good and are an inestimable aid in an objective contact with the real environment. That is why there always appeared tendencies to formulate supreme rights of the human being. After the cataclysm of the last World War, and after the genocidal murders which humanity experienced, the General Assembly of the United Nations, at its session on December 10th 1948 in the Palais de Chaillot in Paris, voted in the Universal Declaration of Human Rights, which we include here by way of illustrating the articulation of the "natural law" which is manifested in the judgement "do good." A careful study of this Declaration of Rights will immediately show its essential content—the realization of good.

Here is the final authorized text of the Declaration:[*]

UNIVERSAL DECLARATION OF HUMAN RIGHTS

Whereas recognition of the inherent dignity and of the equal and inalienable rights of all members of the human family is the foundation of freedom, justice and peace in the world,

Whereas disregard and contempt for human rights have resulted in barbarous acts which have outraged the conscience of mankind, and the advent of a world in which human beings shall enjoy freedom of speech and belief and freedom from fear and want has been proclaimed as the highest aspiration of the common people,

Whereas it is essential, if man is not to be compelled to have recourse, as a last resort, to rebellion against tyranny and oppression, that human rights should be protected by the rule of law,

---

[*] Published by United Nations Office of Public Information.

Whereas it is essential to promote the development of friendly relations between nations,

Whereas the peoples of the United Nations have in the Charter reaffirmed their faith in fundamental human rights, in the dignity and worth of the human person and in the equal rights of men and women and have determined to promote social progress and better standards of life in larger freedom,

Now, Therefore,

THE GENERAL ASSEMBLY

proclaims

THIS UNIVERSAL DECLARATION OF HUMAN RIGHTS as a common standard of achievement for all peoples and all nations, to the end that every individual and every organ of society, keeping this Declaration constantly in mind, shall strive by teaching and education to promote respect for these rights and freedoms and by progressive measures, national and international, to secure their universal and effective recognition and observance, both among the peoples of Members States themselves and among the peoples of territories under their jurisdiction.

Article 1. All human beings are born free and equal in dignity and rights. They are endowed with reason and conscience and should

Whereas Member States have pledged themselves to achieve, in co-operation with the United Nations, the promotion of universal respect for and observance of human rights and fundamental freedoms,

Whereas a common understanding of these rights and freedoms is of the greatest importance for the full realization of this pledge,

act towards one another in a spirit of brotherhood.

Article 2. Everyone is entitled to all the rights and freedoms set forth in this Declaration, without distinction of any kind, such as
race, color, sex, language,
religion, political or other opinion,
national or social origin, property,
birth or other status.
Furthermore, no distinction shall be made on the basis of the political, jurisdictional or interational status of the country or territory to which a person belongs or under any other limitation of sovereignty.

Article 3. Everyone has the right to life, liberty and security of person.

Article 4. No one shall be held in slavery or servitude; slavery and the slave trade shall be prohibited in all their forms.

Article 5. No one shall be subjected to torture or to cruel, inhuman or degrading treatment or punishment.

Article 6. Everyone has the right to recognition everywhere as a person before the law.

Article 7. All are equal before the law and are entitled without any discrimination to equal protection of the law. All are entitled to equal protection against any discrimination in violation of this Declaration and against any incitement to such discrimination.

Article 8. Everyone has the right to an effective remedy by the competent national tribunals for acts violating the fundamental rights granted him by the constitution or by law.

Article 9. No one shall be subjected to arbitrary arrest, detention or exile.

Article 10. Everyone is entitled in full equality to a fair and public hearing by an independent and impartial tribunal, in the determination of his rights and obligations and of any criminal charge against him.

Art. 11. (1) Everyone charged with a penal offence has the right to be presumed innocent until proved guilty according to law in a public trial at which he has had all the guarantees necessary for his defence.

(2) No one shall be held guilty of any penal offence on account of any act or omission which did not constitute a penal offence, under national or international law, at the time when it was committed. Nor shall a heavier penalty be imposed than the one that was applicable at the time the penal offence was committed.

Article 12. No one shall be subjected to arbitrary interference with his privacy, family, home or correspondence, nor to attacks upon his honor and reputation. Everyone has the right to the protection of the law against such interference or attacks.

Article 13. (1) Everyone has the right to freedom of movement and residence within the borders of each state.

(2) Everyone has the right to leave any country, including his own, and to return to his country.

Article 14. (1) Everyone has the right to seek and to enjoy in other countries asylum from persecution.

(2) This right may not be invoked in the case of prosecutions genuinely arising from non-political crimes or from acts contrary to the purposes and principles of the United Nations.

Article 15. (1) Everyone has the right to a nationality.

(2) No one shall be arbitrarily deprived of his nationality nor denied the right to change his nationality.

Article 16. (1) Men and women of full age, without any limitation due to race, nationality or religion, have the right to marry and to found a family. They are entitled to equal rights as to marriage, during marriage and at its dissolution.

(2) Marriage shall be entered into only with the free and full consent of the intending spouses.

(3) The family is the natural and fundamental group unit of society and is entitled to protection by society and the state.

Article 17. (1) Everyone has the right to own property alone as well as in association with others.

(2) No one shall be arbitrarily deprived of his property.

Article 18. Everyone has the right to freedom of thought, conscience and religion; the right includes freedom to change his religion or belief, and freedom, either alone or in community with others and in public or private, to manifest his religion or belief in teaching, practice, worship and observance.

Article 19. Everyone has the right to freedom of opinion and expression; this right includes freedom to hold opinions without interference and to seek, receive and impart information and ideas through any media and regardless of frontiers.

Article 20. (1) Everyone has the right to freedom of peaceful assembly and association.

(2) No one may be compelled to belong to an association.

Article 21. (1) Everyone has the right to take part in the government of his country, directly or through freely chosen representatives.

(2) Everyone has the right of equal access to public service in his country.

(3) The will of the people shall be the basis of the authority of the government; this will shall be expressed in periodic and genuine elections which shall be by universal and equal suffrage and shall be held by secret vote or by equivalent free voting procedures.

Article 22. Everyone, as a member of society, has the right to social security and is entitled to realization, through national effort and international co-operation and in accordance with the organization and resources of each State, of the economic, social and cultural rights indispensable for his dignity and the free development of his personality.

Article 23. (1) Everyone has the right to work, to free choice of employment, to just and favorable conditions of work and to protection against unemployment.

(2) Everyone, without any discrimination, has the right to equal pay for equal work.

(3) Everyone who works has the right to just and favorable remuneration ensuring for himself and his family an existence worthy of human dignity, and supplemented, if necessary, by other means of social protection.

(4) Everyone has the right to form and join trade unions for the protection of his interests.

Article 24. Everyone has the right to rest and leisure, including reasonable limitation of working hours and periodic holidays with pay.

Article 25. (1) Everyone has the right to a standard of living adequate for the health and well-being of himself and of his family, including food, clothing, housing and medical care and necessary social services, and the right to security in the event of unemployment, sickness, disability, widowhood, old age or other lack of livelihood in circumstances beyond his control.

(2) Motherhood and childhood are entitled to special care and assistance. All children, whether born in or out of wedlock, shall enjoy the same social protection.

Article 26. (1) Everyone has the right to education. Education shall be free, at least in the elementary and fundamental stages. Elementary education shall be compulsory. Technical and professional education shall be made generally available and higher education shall be equally accessible to all on the basis of merit.

(2) Education shall be directed to the full development of the human personality and to the strengthening of respect for human rights and fundamental freedoms. It shall promote understanding, tolerance and friendship among all nations, racial or religious groups, and shall further the activities of the United Nations for the maintenance of peace.

(3) Parents have a prior right to choose the kind of education that shall be given to their children.

Article 27. (1) Everyone has the right freely to participate in the cultural life of the community, to enjoy the arts and to share in scientific advancement and its benefits.

(2) Everyone has the right to the protection of the moral and material interests resulting from any scientific, literary or artistic production of which he is the author.

Article 28. Everyone is entitled to a social and international order in which the rights and freedoms set forth in this Declaration can be fully realized.

Article 29. (1) Everyone has duties to the community in which alone the free and full development of his personality is possible.

(2) In the exercise of his rights and freedoms, everyone shall be subject only to such limitations as are determined by law solely for the purposes of securing due recognition and respect for the rights and freedoms of others and of meeting the just requirements of morality, public order and the general welfare in a democratic society.

(3) These rights and freedoms may in no case be exercised contrary to the purposes and principles of the United Nations.

Article 30. Nothing in this Declaration may be interpreted as implying for any State, group or person any right to engage in any activity or to perform any act aimed at the destruction of any of the rights and freedoms set forth herein.

2. *PACEM IN TERRIS*

Likewise the Church, through Pope John XXIII's Encyclical *Pacem in terris,* has declared human rights and obligations, so that they objectively help the individual to make good human decisions. Here are the essential formulations of the Encyclical in this domain:

> Any human society, if it is to be well ordered and productive, must lay down as a foundation this principle: that every human being is a person; his nature is endowed with intelligence and free will. By virtue of this, he has rights and duties of his own, flowing directly and simultaneously from his very nature, which are therefore universal, inviolable, and inalienable. If we look upon the dignity of the human person in the light of divinely revealed truth, we cannot help but to esteem it far more highly; for men are redeemed by the blood of Jesus Christ, they are by grace the children and friends of God and heirs of eternal glory.
>
> Beginning our discussion of the rights of man, we see that every man has the right to life, to bodily integrity, and to the means which are necessary and suitable for the proper development of life; these are primarily food, clothing, shelter, rest, medical care, and finally the necessary social services. Therefore, a human being also has the right to security in cases of sickness, inability to work, widowhood, old age, unemployment, or in any other case in which he is deprived of the means of subsistence through no fault of his own.

By the natural law every human being has the right to respect for his person, to his good reputation; the right to freedom in searching for truth and in expressing and communicating his opinions and in pursuit of art, within the limits laid down by the moral order and the common good, and he has the right to be informed truthfully about public events.

The natural law also gives man the right to share in the benefits of culture, and therefore the right to a basic education and to technical and professional training in keeping with the stage of educational development in the country to which he belongs. Every effort should be made to ensure that persons be enabled, on the basis of merit, to go on to higher studies, so that, as far as possible, they may occupy posts and take responsibilities in accordance with their natural gifts and the skills they have acquired.

Every human being has the right to honor God according to the dictates of an upright conscience, and therefore the right to worship God privately and publicly. ...

Human beings have the right to choose freely the state of life which they prefer, and therefore the right to establish a family, with equal rights and duties for man and woman, and also the right to follow a vocation to the priesthood or the religious life.

The family, grounded on marriage freely contracted, monogamous and indissoluble, should be regarded as the first and natural cell of human society. To it should be given every consideration of an economic, social, cultural, and moral nature which will strengthen its stability and facilitate the fulfillment of its specific mission.

Parents, however, have the prior right in the support and education of their children. ...

Human beings have the natural right to free initiative in the economic field, and the right to work.

Indissolubly linked with those rights is the right to working conditions in which physical health is not endangered, morals are safeguarded, and young people's moral development is not impaired. Women have the right to working conditions in accordance with their duties as wives and mothers.

From the dignity of the human person, there also arises the right to carry on economic activities to the degree of responsibility of which one is capable. Furthermore—and this must be specially emphasized—there is the right to a proper wage, determined according to the criteria of justice, and sufficient, therefore, in proportion to the available resources to provide for the worker and his family a manner of living in keeping with the dignity of the human person. In this regard, Our Predecessor Pius XII said: "To the personal duty to work imposed by nature, there corresponds and follows the natural right of each individual to make of his work the means to provide for his own life and the lives of his children, so profoundly is the empire of nature ordained for the preservation of man."

The right to private property, even of productive goods, also derives from the nature of man. This right, as we have elsewhere declared, is an effective aid in safeguarding the dignity of the human person and the free exercise of responsibility in all fields of endeavor.

Finally, it strengthens the stability and tranquillity of family life, thus contributing to the peace and prosperity of the commonwealth.

However, it is opportune to point out that there is a social duty essentially inherent in the right of private property.

From the fact that human beings are by nature social, there arises the right of assembly and association. They also have the right to give the societies of which they are the members the form they consider most suitable for the aim they have in view, and to act within such societies on their own initiative and on their own responsibility in order to achieve their desired objectives. ...

Every human being has the right to freedom of movement and a residence within the confines of his own country; and, when there are just reasons for it, the right to emigrate to other countries and to take up residence there. ...

The dignity of the human person involves the right to take an active part in public affairs and contribute one's part to the common good of the citizens. ...

The human person is also entitled to a juridical protection of his rights, a protection that should be efficacious, impartial, and inspired by the true norms of justice. ...

The natural laws with which we have been dealing here are, however, inseparably connected, in the very person who is their subject, with just as many respective duties; and rights as well as duties find their source, their sustenance, and their inviolability in the natural law which grants or enjoins them.

For example, the right of every man to life is correlative with the duty to preserve it; his right to a decent manner of living with the duty of living it becomingly; and his right to investigate the truth freely with the duty of seeking it and of possessing it ever more completely and profoundly. Once this is admitted, it is also clear that, in human society, to one man's right there corresponds a duty in all other persons: the duty, namely, of acknowledging and respecting the right in question, for every fundamental right draws its indestructible moral force from the natural law, which in granting it imposes a corresponding obligation. Those, therefore, who claim their own rights, yet altogether forget or neglect to carry out their respective duties, are people who build with one hand and destroy with the other.

The formulations of the Encyclical show ways of realizing human good in the normal course of events and that is why they can be regarded as the concrete social interpretation of natural law—the ultimate Court of Appeal and the essential foundation of human, personal morality.

BIBLIOGRAPHY

Ambrosetti, Giovanni. *Diritto naturale cristiano. Profili di detodo, di storia e di teoria.* Rome: Editrice Studium, 1970.

Aristotle. *Nicomachean Ethics. Politics.* Cambridge, MA: Loeb Classical Library 1935-1965.

Augustine, St. *The City of God (De Civitate Dei).* London: D. Appleton— Century Company, 1945.

Battaglia, Anthony. *Toward a Reformulation of Natural Law.* New York: Seaburry Press, 1981.

Battaglia, Felice. *La crisi del diritto naturale.* Venice: Le Nuova Italia, 1927.

Bednarski, Feliks. *La deduzione delle norme morali generali della legge naturale.* Rome: Institutto degli studi ecclesiastici, 1969.

Begin, Raymond Francis. *Natural Law and Positive Law.* Washington: Catholic University of America Press, 1959.

Bender, Ludovicus. *Philosophia Juris.* Rome: Officium Libri Catholici, 1947.

Benson, Peter. "Grotius' Contribution to the Natural Law of Contract." *Canadian Journal of Netherlandic Studies (Canada).* 6/2 (1985), pp. 1–27.

Bloch, Ernest. *Natural Law and Human Dignity.* Cambridge: MIT Press, 1986.

Bobbio, Norberto. *Il diritto naturale nel sec. XVIII.* Turin: G. Giappichelli, 1947.

Bourke, Vernon J. "Is Thomas Aquinas a Natural Law Ethicist?" *Monist,* 58 (January 1974), pp. 52–66.

————. "Two Approaches to Natural Law." *Natural Law Forum,* 1 (1956), pp. 92–96.

Boyle, Joseph. *Free Choice: A Self Referential Argument.* Notre Dame: University of Notre Dame Press, 1976.

————. "Natural Law, Ownership and the World's Natural Resources." *Journal of Value Inquiry,* 23 (Summer 1989), pp. 191–207.

Burns, J.H. "St. Germain, Gerson, Aquinas, and Ulpian." *History of Political Thought,* 4 (1983), pp. 44-50.

Brunner, Emil. *Gerechtigkeit.* Zurich, Europaverlag, 1943.

Carl, Maria Teresa. "The first Principles of Natural Law: A Study of the Moral Theories of Aristotle and Saint Thomas Aquinas." Ph.D. Dissertation, Marquette University, 1989.

Carmichael, D.J.C. "The Right of Nature in Leviathan." *Canadian Journal of Philosophy,* 18 (June 1988), pp. 257–270.

Cathrein, Victor. *Recht, Naturrecht und positives Recht.* Freiburg: Herder, 1909.

Chroust, Anton Hermann. "Hugo Grotius and the Scholastic Natural Law Tradition." *New Scholasticism,* 17 (April 1943), pp. 101–133.

_____. *The Philosophy of Law from St. Augustine to St. Thomas Aquinas.* Notre Dame, Ind.: University of Notre Dame Press, 1946.

_____. "The Philosophy of Law from St. Augustine to St. Thomas Aquinas." *New Scholasticism.* 20 (January 1946), pp. 26–71.

Coing, Helmut. *Die obersten Grundsätze des Rechts.* Heidelberg: L. Schneider, 1947.

Composta, D. *Natura e ragione. Studio sulle inclinazioni naturali in rapporto alla diritto naturale.* Zurich, 1971.

Crowe, Michael Bertram. *The Changing Profile of Natural Law.* The Hague: Nijhoff, 1977.

_____."The Irreplaceable Natural Law." *Studies,* (Dublin) 51 (1962).

_____. "The Pursuit of Natural Law.: *Irish Theological Quarterly,* 44 (1977).

Cunningham, Stanley B. "Albertus Magnus on Natural Law." *Journal of the History of Ideas,* 28 (October—December 1967), pp. 479–502.

Cvek, Peter P. "Francisco Suarez on Natural Law." *Vera Lex,* 9 (1989), pp. 2–7.

Degan, Daniel A. Jr., Daniel A. "Two Models of Positive Law in Aquinas: A Study of the Relationship of Positive Law and Natural Law." *Thomist,* 46 (January 1982), pp. 1-32.

Delhaye, Philippe. *Permanence du Droit naturel.* Louvain: Editions Nauwelaerts, 1964.

Del Prado, N. *De fundamentali veritate philosophiae christianae.* Freiburg, 1911.

Denziger, Heinrich. *Enchiridion symbolofum...* 33rd edition. Barcinone: Herder, 1965.

Dolan, Joseph V. *Natural Law and Modern Jurisprudence.* Quebec: Presses Universitaires Laval, 1960.

Dworkin, R.M. "'Natural' Law Revisited." *University of Florida Law Review,* 34 (1982), pp. 165–88.

_____, ed. *The Philosophy of Law.* London: Oxford University Press, 1977.

_____. *Taking Rights Seriously.* Cambridge: Harvard University Press, 1977.

Farrell, Patrick Maria, O.P. *Sources of St. Thomas' Concept of Natural Law.* Melbourne, 1957.

_____. "Sources of St. Thomas' Concept of Natural Law." *Thomist,* 20 (July 1957), pp. 237–294.

Farrel, W. *The Natural Moral Law According to St. Thomas and Suarez.* Freiburg: St. Dominic's Press, 1930.

Finnis, John. "The Basic Principles of Natural Law: A Reply to Ralph McInerny." *American Journal of Jurisprudence,* 26 (1981), pp. 21–31.

_____. *Fundamentals of Ethics.* Washington D.C.: Georgetown University Press, 1983.

_____. *Natural Law and Natural Rights.* Oxford: Clarendon Press, 1980.

_____. "Natural Law and the 'Is'—'Ought' question: an Invitation to Professor Veatch." *Catholic Lawyer,* 26/4 (Autumn 1981), pp. 266–277.

_____. "Natural Law and Unnatural Acts." *Heythrop Journal,* 11 (October 1970), pp. 365–87.

_____. "The Natural Law Tradition." *Journal of Legal Education,* 36 (1986), pp. 492–504.

Fluckiger, Felix. *Geschichte des Naturrechts.* Zollikon—Zurich: Evangelischer Verlag, 1954.

Friedrick, Carl J. *The Philosophy of Law in Historical Perspective.* Chicago: University of chicago Press, 1958.

Fuchs, Joseph. *Lex naturae. Zur Theologie des Naturrechts.* Dusseldorf: Patmos Verlag, 1955.

Galiano, J. *Derecho natural.* Madrid, 1972.

Garcia, Joaquin F. "The Natural Law." *Proceedings of the Catholic Philosophi cal Association,* 22 (1947), pp. 1–17.

Gautierrez, G.J. *Ius naturae.* Valladolid, 1954.

Gelinas, E.T. "*Ius* and *Lex* in Thomas Aquinas. *The American Journal of Jurisprudence,* 15 (1970), pp. 154–170.

Gilson, E. *Elements of Christian Philosophy.* Garden City, N.Y.: Doubleday, Catholic Texstbook Division, 1978.

_____. *L'être et l'essence.* Paris: J. Vrin, 1948.

_____. *The Spirit of Medieval Philosophy.* New York: C. Scribner's Sons, 1936.

_____. *A History of Christian Philosophy in the Middle Ages.* New York: Random Hause, 1955.

Godling, Martin P. "Aquinas and Some Contemporary Natural Law Theories." *Proceedings of the Catholic Philosophical Association,* 48 (1974), pp. 238–247.

Goerner, E.A. "On Thomistic Natural Law: The Bad Man's View of Thomistic Natural Right." *Political Theory,* 7 (Fall 1979), pp. 101–122.

_____. "On Thomistic Natural Right: The Good Man's View of Thomistic Natural Law." *Political Theory,* 11 (1983), pp. 393–394.

Graneris, G. *Contributi tomistici alla filosofia del diritto.* Turin, 1949.

Graney, Maurice Richard, Jr. "Natural Law as a Ground for the Common Good in Jacques Maritain." Ph.D. Dissertation, St. Louis University, 1975.

Grisez, Germain Gabriel. *Contraception and Natural Law.* Milwaukee: Bruce Publishing, Co., 1964.

_____; Boyle, J., and Finnis, J. "Practical Principles, Moral Truth, and Ultimate Ends." *American Journal of Jurisprudence,* 32 (1987), pp. 99–151.

Grotius, Hugo. *De iure belli ac pacis libri tres.* Batavorum: E.J. Brill, 1919.

Hall, Richard B. "The Alterability of Natural Law." *New Scholasticism,* 55 (Autumn 1981), pp. 474–483.

Harris, E. "Natural Law and Naturalism." *International Philosophical Quarterly,* 23 (1983), pp. 115–124.

Hart, Charles A. "Metaphysical Foundations of the Natural Law." *Proceedings of the Catholic Philosophical Association,* 24 (1950), pp. 18–27.

Hervada, Xavier. *Natural Right and Natural Law: A Critical Introduction.* Pamplona: University of Navarra, 1990.

Hittinger, Russell. "After MacIntyre: Natural Law Theory, Virtue Ethics, and Eudaimonia." *International Philosophical Quarterly,* 29 (December 1989) pp. 449–461.

Ingarden, R. *Spór o istnienie świata.* Vol. I, Państwowe Wydawnictwo Naukowe, Warsaw, 1961.

Jaeger, Werner Wilhelm, *Die Theologie der frühen griechischen Denker.* Stuttgart: W. Kohlhammer, 1953.

_____. *Paideia, The Idea of Greek Culture.* New York: University Press, 1965.

James, Theodore. "Some Historical Aspects of St. Thomas' Treatment of the Natural Law." *Proceedings of the Catholic Philosophical Association,* 24 (1950), pp. 147–55.

Jarra, E. *Historia filozofii prawa.* Warsaw: Gebethner i Wolf, 1923.

_____. *Ogólna teoria prawa.* Warsaw: Gebethner i Wolf, 1922.

John XXIII, Pope. *Pacem in terris.* Vatican, Vatican Press, 1963.

Kalinowski, J. *Le Problème de la vérité en morale et en droit.* Lyon: E. Vitte, 1967.

_____. "Querelle de la science normative." *Librairie generale de droit et de jurisprudence,* Paris, 1969.

_____. *Teoria poznania praktycznego.* Lublin: Katolicki Uniwersytet Lubelski, 1960.

_____. *Teoria reguły społecznej i reguły prawnej Leona Duguit.* Lublin: Katolicki Uniwersytet Lubelski, 1949.

Kamiński, S. and Krąpiec, M.A. *Z teorii i metodologii metafizyki,* Lublin: Katolicki Uniwersytet Lubelski, 1962.

Kant, Immanuel. *Foundations of the Metaphysics of Morals.* New York: Boobs—Merrill Educational, 1959.

_____. *Critique of Practical Reason.* Chicago: Encyclopaedia Britannica, 1952.

Kennington, Richard. "Strauss' Natural Right and History." *Review of Metaphysics,* 35 (Summer 1981), pp. 57–86.

Kesler, Charles Reeder. "Cicero and the Natural Law." Ph.D. Dissertation, Harvard University, 1985.

Klubertanz, George P. "The Empiricism of ThomisticEthics." *Proceedings of the American Catholic Philosophical Association,* 31 (1957).

Knight, Frank H. "'The Rights of Man and Natural Law' by Jacques aritain." *Ethics,* 54 (January 1944), pp. 124–145.

Kondziela, J. *Filozofia społeczna.* Lublin: Katolicki Uniwersytet Lubelski, 1972.

Krąpiec, M.A. *Arystotelesowska koncepcja substancji.* Lublin: Katolicki Uniwersytet Lubelski, 1966.

_____. "Filozofia i Bóg." In *O Bogu i człowieku.* Edited by Bishop B. Bejze. Vol. 1, Warsaw: Loretanki, 1968.

_____. *Ja—człowiek. Zarys antropologii filozoficznej.* Lublin: Katolicki Uniwersytet Lubelski, 1974.

_____. *I—Man: An Introduction to Philosophical Anthropology.* New Britain, Ct: Mariel, 1983.

_____. "Intencjonalny charakter kultury." In *Logos i Ethos,* Cracow: Polskie Towarzystwo Teologiczne, 1971.

_____. *Metafizyka. Zarys teorii bytu.* Lublin: Katolicki Uniwersytet Lubelski, 1978.

_____. *Metaphysics: A History of Being.* New York: Peter Lang, 1991.

_____. *Teoria analogii bytu.* Lublin: Katolicki Uniwersytet Lubelski, 1959.

_____. *Z teorii i metodologii metafizyki.* Lublin, Katolicki Uniwersytet Lubelski, 1962.

Krokiewicz, A. *Zarys filozofii greckiej (od Talesa do Platona).* Warsaw: PAX, 1971.

Krzymuski, E. *Historia filozofii prawa.* Cracow: Gebethner i Wolf, 1923.

Lachance, L. *Le concept de droit selon Aristot et St. Thomas.* Montreal: A. Levesque, 1933.

Lande, J. *Historia filozofii prawa.* Cracow: Gebethner i Wolf, 1931.

Leclercq, Jacques. *Lecons de droit naturel.* Vols. 1—4. Namur: Wesmael Charlier, 1947—50.

_____. "Natural Law, the Unknown." *Natural Law Forum,* 7 (1962).

Lex et Libertas. Studi Tomistici 30. Città del Vaticano, 1987.

Lottin, Odon. *Le droit naturel chez S. Thomas et ses predecesseurs.* Bruges, 1926.

_____. "Natural Law, Natural Right and Natural Reason." *Philosophy Today,* 3 (Spring 1959), pp. 10—18.

Luijpen, Wilhelmus A. *Phenomenology of Natural Law.* Pittsburg: Duquesne University Press, 1967.

Manser, G. *Das Naturrecht in thomistischer Beleuchtung.* Freiburg: Verlag der Paulusdruckerei, 1944.

Martyniak, C. *Filozofia prawa.* Lublin: Katolicki Uniwersytet Lubelski, 1939.

_____. *Moc obowiązują prawa a teoria Kelsena.* Lublin: Katolicki Uniwersytet Lubelski, 1938.

_____. *Obiektywna podstawa prawa według św. Tomasza Akwinu.* Lublin: Katolicki Uniwersytet Lubelski, 1949.

Maritain, J. *Les droits de l'homme et la loi naturelle.* Paris: Hartman, 1947.

_____. "On Knowledge Through Conaturality." *Review of Metaphysics,* 4 (June 1951), pp. 473—482.

_____. *Man and the State.* Chicago: Uniwersity of Chicago Press, 1951.

_____. *The Person and the Common Good.* Notre Dame, Ind.: University of Notre Dame Press, 1966.

McDonnell, Kevin. "Does William of Ockham have a Theory of Natural Law?" *Fran. Stud.,* 34 (1974), pp. 383—392.

McInerny, Ralph. *Ethica Thomistica: The Moral Philosophy of St. Thomas Aquinas.* Washington D.C.: Catholic University of America, 1982.

_____. "Naturalism and Thomistic Ethics." *The Thomist,* 40 (1976), pp. 222-242.

_____. "Truth in Ethics: Historicity and Natural Law." *Proceedings of the American Catholic Philosophical Association,* 43 (1964), pp. 71—82.

McNabb, Vincent. *St. Thomas and Law,* London: Blackfriars, 1955.

May, William E. "Natural Law, Conscience, and Developmental Psychology." *Communio (US),* 2 (Spring 1975), pp. 3—31.

Messner, Johannes. *Das Naturrecht.* Innsbruck: Tyrolia Verlag, 1960.

Moore, Michael S. "A Natural Law Theory of Interpretation." *Southern California Law Review,* 58/2 (January 1985), pp. 277—398.

Niethe, Terry L. "Natural Law, the Synderesis Rule, and St. Augustine." *Augustin Stud.,* 11 (1980), pp. 91—97.

Noonan, John Thomas. *The Scholastic Notion of Usury.* Cambridge: Harvard University Press, 1957.

Novak, Michael. "Bernard Lonergan, A New Approach to Natural Law." *Proceedings of the Catholic Philosophical Association,* 41 (1967), pp. 246—249.

O'Connor, Daniel John. *Aquinas and Natural Law.* London: Mcmillan, 1967.

Offler, H.S. "The Three Modes of Natural Law in Ockham: A Revision of the Text." *Fran. Stud.,* 37 (1977), pp. 207—218.

Olafson, Frederick A. "Thomas Hobbes and the Modern Theory of Natural Law." *Journal of the History of Philosophy,* 4 (January 1966), pp. 13—30.

Opałek, K. *Prawo natury u polskich fizjokratów.* Warsaw: Państwowe Wydawnictwo Naukowe, 1953.

Opałek, K. and Wróblewski, J. *Współczesna teoria i socjologia prawa w Stanach Zjednoczonych Ameryki Północnej.* Warsaw: Państwowe Wydawnictwo Naukowe, 1963.

Passerin d'Entreves, A. *Natural Law. An introduction to Legal Philosophy.* London, Hutchinson University Library, 1967.

Periatkowicz, A. *Filozofia Prawa J.J. Rouseau.* Cracow: Gebethner i Wolf, 1913.

Perry, Michael J. *Morality, Politics, and Law.* New York: Oxford University Press, 1988.

Petrażycki, L. *Wstęp do nauki prawa i moralmości.* Warsaw: Państwowe Wydawnictwo Naukowe, 1959.

Plato. *Laws.* London: Dent, 1960.

_____. *The Republic.* London: W. Heineman, 1906.

Prado, Norberto del. *De fundamentali veritate philosophiae christianiae.* Freiburg: Paukusverlag, 1911.

Radbruch, Gustaw. *Rechtsphilosophie.* Stuttgart: Koehler, 1956.

Reilly, James P. *St. Thomas on Law.* Toronto, 1990.

Robilant, Enrico di. *Significato del diritto naturale nell'ordinamento canonico.* Turin: G. Giappichelli, 1954.

Rommen, Heinrich. *Die ewige Wiederkahr des Naturrechts.* Munich: J. Koesel, 1947.

_____. *The Natural Law.* London: B. Herder Book, Co., 1948.

Ross, James F. "Justice is Reasonableness: Aquinas on Human Law and Morality." *Monist,* 58 (January 1974), pp. 86—103.

_____. "Two Approaches to Natural Law." *Natural Law Forum,* 1 (1956).

Russell, John L. "The Concept of Natural Law." *Heythrop Journal,* 6 (October 1965), pp. 434—446.

Ryffel, H. *Das Naturrecht.* Bern: H. Lang & Cie., 1944.

Sauter, Johann. *Die philosophische Grundlagen des Naturrechts.* Vienna: J. Springer, 1932.

Sertillanges, A.D. *Dociekania nad prawem natury czyli o potrzebach człowieka.* Warsaw: PAX, 1972.

Schmidt, Walter. *Die Stellung der Pygmäenvölker in der Entwicklungsgeschichte des Menschen.* Stuttgart: Schwabe, 1910.

_____. *Der Ursprung der Gottesidee.* Vols. 1—12. Münster, 1926—1955.

Simon, Yves R. *The Tradition of Natural Law: A Philosopher's Reflections.* New York: Fordham University Press, 1965.

Sokolowski, Robert. "Knowing Natural Law." *Tijdschr. Filosof.,* 43 (D1981) pp. 625—641.

Solmsen, F. *Aristotle's System of the Physical World.* Ithaca: Cornell University Press, 1960.

Starr, William C. "Dworkin and Natural Law." *Proceedings of the Catholic Philosophical Association,* 59 (1985), pp. 250-257.

Strauss, L. *Natural Right and History*. Chicago: University of chicago Press, 1953.

Striker, Gisela. "Origins of the Concept of Natural Law." *Proceedings of the Boston Colloquum of Ancient Philosophy*, 2 (1986), pp. 79—94.

Szyszkowsha, M. *Dociekania nad prawem natury, czyli o potrzebach człowieka.* Warsaw: PAX, 1972.

_____. *Neokantyzm. Filozofia społeczna wraz z filozofią prawa natury o zmiennej treści.* Warsaw: PAX, 1970.

_____. *U źródeł współczesnej filozofii prawa i filozofii człowieka.* Warsaw: PAX, 1972.

Thomas Aquinas, St. *Summa theologica I—II. Opera omnia Sancti Thomae Aquinatis.* Turin—Rome: Marietti, 1948-1967.

Tonneay, Jean. "The Teaching of the Thomist on Law." *Thomist*, 34 (1970), pp. 13-83.

Ueberweg, Friedrich. *Grundriss der Geschichte der Philosophie.* Basel: Benno Schwabe & Co., 1957.

United Nations. *Common Declaration of the Rights of Man.* Paris, 1948.

Utz, Arthur. *Éthique sociale.* St. Paul, Switzerland: Editions Universitaires Freibourg, 1961.

Vander-Waerdt, Paul A. "The Stoic Theory of Natural Law." Ph.D. Dissertation, Princeton University, 1989.

Veatch, Henry B. *Human Rights: Fact or Fancy*. Baton Rouge: Louisiana State University Press, 1985.

_____. "Natural Law: Dead or Alive?" *Literature of Liberty*, 1/4 (1978) pp. 7-31.

_____. "Natural Law and the 'Is'—'Ought' Question. *Catholic Lawyer*, 26/4 (Autumn 1981), pp. 251–265.

Vecchio, Giorgio del. *Il concetto della natura e il principio del diritto.* Bologna: N. Zanichelli, 1922.

Verdross, Alfred. *Statisches und dynamisches Naturrecht.* Freiburg: Rombach, 1971.

Vidley, Alexander R. and Whitehouse, W.A. *Natural Law: A Christian reconsideration.* London: S.C.M. Press, Ltd., 1946.

Waddicor, Mark H. *Montesquieu and the Philosophy of Natural Law.* The Hague: Nijhoff, 1970.

Weinreb, Lloyd. "The Complete Idea of Justice." *University of Chicago Law Review*, 51/3 (Summer 1984), pp. 762–809.

_____. *Natural Law and Justice.* Cambridge: Harvard University Press, 1987.

_____. "The Natural Law Tradition: Comments on Finnis." *Journal of Legal Education*, 36/4 (December 1986), pp 501–504.

Welzel, Hans. *Naturrecht und materiale Gerechtigkeit.* Göttingen: Vandenhoeck & Ruprecht, 1962.

Wild, John D. *Plato's Modern Enemies and the Theory of Natural Law.* Chicago: University of Chicago Press, 1953.

Wilenius, Reijo. *The Social and Political Theory of Francisco Suarez.* Helsinki: Societas Philosophica Fennica, 1963.

Wojtyła, Karol. *Osoba i czyn.* Cracow: Polskie Towarzystwo Teologiczne, 1969.

————. *The Acting Person.* Dordrecht/Boston/London: Reidel, 1979.

Wright, Benjamin F. *American Interpretations of Natural law.* Cambridge: Harvard University Press, 1931.

Wu, John C.H. *Fountain of Justice: A Study in the Natural Law.* New York: Sheed and Ward, 1955.

Zdybicka, Z. *Partycypacja bytu.* Lublin: Katolicki Universytet Lubelski 1972.

INDEX OF PHILOSOPHERS

INDEX OF CONCEPTS